Free Range Education

How home education works

Edited by
Terri Dowty

Hawthorn Press

Published by Hawthorn Press, Hawthorn House, 1 Lansdown Lane, Stroud, Gloucestershire, GL5 1BJ, UK
Tel: (01453) 757040 Fax: (01453) 751138
E-mail: info@hawthornpress.com
www.hawthornpress.com

Cover images by Viv Quillin
Cartoons by Sarah Guthrie
Typesetting and cover design by Hawthorn Press, Stroud, Gloucestershire
Printed in the UK by The Bath Press, Bath
Reprinted 2003

Printed on environmentally friendly chlorine-free paper manufactured from renewable forest stock.

British Library Cataloguing in Publication Data applied for

ISBN 1 903458 07 2

Contents

FAQs

Foreword

Dr Alan Thomas, FBPsS

The number of children being educated at home has increased steadily during the last twenty years. Home education is no longer the rarity it once was and features regularly in the press, radio and on TV. Parents who take up the option come from a wide variety of social and educational backgrounds, as indeed do those who contribute to this book. Their reasons for choosing to home educate are varied and many, from those who decide before their children are born, to those who would never have considered the option had not their children experienced insurmountable problems in school – learning difficulties, bullying and so on.

For those who withdraw their children from school, the thought of how to go about educating a child at home can be quite daunting. However, as parents gradually gain in confidence, the great majority find the experience worthwhile and enriching, not least because they are actively involved in their children's education and have the privilege of watching their progress at first hand. Parents also learn a great deal that is new about education. This is because education at home leads many parents to view learning and child rearing in a very different light, as the contributors to this book explain.

Of course home education has its pitfalls, frustrations and day-to-day difficulties. It also requires a great deal of commitment. But as parents see their children developing, academically competent and socially assured, they realise they have a lot to tell the world, not least teachers and other professional educators. That is what the contributors to this book do, engagingly, with humour and with a humility born of the knowledge that they have actually discovered what has eluded educational research for the past 100 years: ways in which the quality of education for all children can be significantly improved. Not that there is a single best practice. Far from it. The main attraction of home education is that parents are able to work out, with their children, what is the kind of learning that suits them best.

Let's get out of the way what the book is not. It is not anti-school, it does not push for one approach to home education, it is not ideological. It is what it says it is – free range! Each of the accounts of educating at home is fascinating in its own particular way as parents adapt what they do to suit their children's approach to learning, in some cases different approaches within the same family. Perhaps, because of this, the book is real, vital, in the way a book about classroom-based education can never be. At the end of the book you feel you know these people personally and can empathise with their difficulties and frustrations as well as their joys and successes.

The book is liberally supplemented by FAQs about home education, educational quotes which have influenced the parents, contributions from the children, and from a legal expert.

A word of warning! By the time you've finished this book your views on how to educate children may be irreversibly changed.

Dr Alan Thomas FBPsS
Visiting Fellow
Learning and Development in Education Group
Institute of Education, University of London

Acknowledgments

There are so many people I would like to thank for their part in making this book happen. I only have room to single out a few for specific mention and I hope that anyone who feels that they have been missed out will forgive me.

It all started with Malcolm Muckle's inspirational Home Education 2000 Conference, which lit the fire that brought this particular pot to the boil. Thanks, Malcolm, for that and for everything else that you have done for home education.

Next, I must thank all the contributors, not only because without you there would have been no book, but for your generous advice, your creative writing and also your bravery in opening your family life to the world.

Thank you, too, Anya, Alison and Charlotte for uncomplainingly suffering the many drafts and for your sigh-less encouragement.

I must also mention my debt to fellow members of the UK-HE List and the HE Special List, who provide ongoing support, encouragement and food for thought.

Last but not least, thanks to Ian for burning the midnight oil with me, for constructive criticism, dreadful puns and many cups of tea. And thank you Biggs and Ollie, my wonderful children, who have made home education such fun. Without you this book would have been impossible!

Terri Dowty
September 2000

Dedication

Just two months after the first edition of *Free Range Education* was published, our celebrations ended abruptly: Louise Verran, one of our contributors, died suddenly on 14th February 2001.

We grieved for her husband and her three sons, whom she loved so deeply, and for our own loss of a friend and champion of home education. Louise was a generous and spirited person whose warmth supported many families as they began the journey into home education, and we will never forget her.

Introduction

Terri Dowty

The objective of getting all school-aged children to school and keeping them there until they attain the minimum defined in compulsory education is routinely used in the sector of education, but this objective does not necessarily conform to human rights requirements. In a country where all school-aged children are in school, free of charge, for the full duration of compulsory education, the right to education may be denied or violated.

The core human rights standards for education include respect of freedom. The respect of parents' freedom to educate their children according to their vision of what education should be has been part of international human rights standards since their very emergence.

United Nations Commission on Human Rights,
Statement by Special Rapporteur on the Right to Education
8/4/99

One morning, I was listening to a radio discussion about home education while I ironed my sons' cricket kit. The boys themselves were busy elsewhere in the house, one of them copying out a piece for his harp ensemble, the other learning his lines for a drama club production of 'Alice in Wonderland'. Suddenly, this unusually idyllic scene was interrupted by a voice of unmistakable authority wafting across the airwaves: 'But these home-educated children will never know the joy of the school play, the sports team, of playing in an orchestra!' Astonished, I stopped in mid-iron stroke, torn between hurling abuse at the radio and roaring with laughter at the extraordinary synchronicity of this statement.

There are so many misconceptions, myths and downright untruths about home education that it is small wonder if parents considering it as a possible option are daunted by the whole business. For this reason, a group of us decided to write a book; a collection of stories from established home educators – adult and child – about how they reached their decision to home educate, how it works for each family, and the thrills and spills which they have encountered along the way. *Free Range Education* is the result. It is not a 'how-to' guide because that would go against the whole spirit of home education: the purpose of the exercise is to find the particular path which suits your particular family. As you will read, no two families go about it in the same way, or for the same reasons. Some parents choose to home educate from the outset, others come to home education after becoming disillusioned with the school system. Some families travel, or live abroad. A small but growing number feel able to use school as one of several potential learning resources and succeed in arranging flexi-time schooling. One parent who has done this, Kate Oliver, explains how it can work in practice.

Perhaps you will find reassurance in the variety of experiences, or feel drawn to one or two accounts which suggest a place to begin. It may be that some stories will crystallise what you do not want, at least for now – including home education itself. Nobody is claiming that it is the One Right Way, and most would dearly love to see real diversity of choice in education.

Home education is an option for all families and, contrary to some irritating stereotypes, crosses all arbitrary boundaries of race, class, creed, income, academic achievement or ideology. It is by no means a soft option, but it can be a very satisfying way of life, requiring no special skills beyond those possessed by any ordinary, loving parent. John Holt puts it succinctly in *Teach Your Own:*

> *We can sum up very quickly what people need to teach their own children. First of all, they have to like them, enjoy their company, their physical presence, their energy, foolishness and passion. They have to enjoy all their talk and questions, and enjoy equally trying to answer those questions. They have to think of their children as friends, indeed very close friends, have to feel happier when they are near and miss them when they are away. They have to trust them as people, respect their fragile dignity, treat them with courtesy, take them seriously. They have to feel in their own hearts some of their children's wonder, curiosity and excitement about the world. And*

they have to have enough confidence in themselves, scepticism about experts and willingness to be different from most people, to take on themselves the responsibility for their children's learning. But that is about all the parents need.

'Home education' is a blanket term for any education which is based around a child's family and community and is not a definition of any particular method. In fact there is a whole spectrum of ideas on how best to go about it, ranging from an 'autonomous' approach (discussed in Jan Fortune-Wood's book: *Doing It Their Way)* which relies on a parent's ability to facilitate a child's current interests, to the daily study of particular subjects, using set texts and workbooks according to a timetable – often described as 'school-at-home'. Nobody is right or wrong in choosing a particular point on that spectrum, unless they opt for something which causes stress and unhappiness; parents are uniquely well-placed to understand what is best for their own family. Individual children within the same family may need very different things and, as long-term home educators have observed, children's changing needs can dictate gradual shifts of style and emphasis over the years. If we are able to respond flexibly to each of our children and listen to them as equal partners in their education, rather than relying on predetermined academic theories about children in general, we can trust them to make us into the educators they need.

To those who grew up in the culture of school, it can seem rather radical to assert that there are many other ways of gaining an education, and bordering on the subversive to claim that children are, to a large extent, capable of masterminding the process for themselves. Yet nobody would deny that children learn a fantastic amount before any kind of school figures in the equation. Their knowledge is gained partly by watching and copying more experienced humans, and also by constantly asking questions.

A classroom can offer only one example of an adult at work, and simply could not function if pupils kept up the stream of questions which they normally ask at home.

A study of thirty four-year-olds entering school revealed:

The girls asked their mothers on average twenty-six questions an hour, but they only asked two questions an hour of their teachers... Of those questions that were asked at school, a much smaller proportion were 'curiosity' questions and 'Why?' questions, and a

much larger proportion were 'business' questions, of the 'Where is the glue?' type, than was the case at home. 'Challenges' were very rare at school, and 'passages of intellectual search' were entirely absent.
Tizard & Hughes: *Young Children Learning*

When a child is home-educated, the questions never dry up, and a style of learning develops which Alan Thomas has described as 'Conversational Learning':

> *If there is one aspect of the informal 'curriculum' which, above all others, contributes to learning, it is conversation. We have already seen how important dialogue is in more structured learning, allowing parents to strike while the iron's hot and deal with any problems immediately they arise. But informal conversation was also stressed by parents, whatever their approach.*
> Alan Thomas: *Educating Children at Home*

Quite apart from the obvious benefit of sharing information, conversation demonstrates immediately to a parent where something needs further exploration. It removes the need for repeated testing or 'writing down' because it is patently obvious when an explanation has made sense. The structures which a school imposes in order to check that learning has occurred do not need to apply to home educators, freeing them to follow a line of enquiry until the *child* expresses satisfaction. Moreover, the absence of school bells means that a dialogue can last for as long as necessary, whether that be ten minutes, several hours, or intermittently over many weeks.

Whilst 'home' and 'family' are cornerstones of home education, this is not to imply that families spend their time closeted in claustrophobic isolation. As the stories in this book will demonstrate, home educators are often busy people, leading active lives both within their local community and further afield. The educationalist Roland Meighan mentions having experienced the following difficulty when he was researching home education:

> *When I was collecting information from home-schooling families in the late 1970s and 1980s, I found that I had to do most of my visits on Sundays. This was because whenever I telephoned to fix appointments, I would find that the learners were learning out-and-about in various libraries, museums, exhibitions, gatherings*

*such as auctions, expeditions, sports centres, meetings with adults
who had offered some learning opportunity, and the like. They had
already taken on the idea of the community as a source of learning
sites.*

Roland Meighan: *The Next Learning System*

The benefits to children are immense: in addition to having a tailor-made education, they can taste independence relatively early because they have the protection of being known in their neighbourhood by virtue of their constant presence. Moreover, because they are not excluded from adult life, they learn how to cope in public, on transport or in shops from a young age, and they also gain experience in handling the dilemmas and crises of real life. The mature confidence displayed by many home-educated children is a far cry from any stereotyped idea of them as coddled innocents, tied to parental apron strings.

This book also includes a chapter about the legal position of home educators, written by Ian Dowty, my husband and fellow home educator of our sons. He is a solicitor with considerable knowledge of the law relating to home education – a helpful combination of personal and professional experience which enables him to bring a great deal of insight to the whole area.

Successive Education Acts have always recognised home education; more than that, they state that it is the responsibility of *parents* to ensure that their children are educated ...*according to age, ability and aptitude, and any special needs he may have, either by regular attendance at school or otherwise.* In other words, regardless of where it takes place, if a child's education is a disaster the buck stops with his or her parents and nobody else.

Schools are institutions to which many parents may choose to delegate their responsibility, but they also have the power to choose *not* to do so. Children are born to families, not to the State. Parents are far more than nannies to the nation's children and decisions about what constitutes a proper education or upbringing rest with them. The role of the public servants whom we elect, or who are appointed in our name, is to assist us in our task of representing and protecting our own children's best interests and human rights until they are old enough to maintain for themselves the balance between being an individual and a member of society.

The role of the family in protecting children's rights is an important one, enshrined in human rights legislation. It is all too easy for a child's vulnerable individuality to be subsumed into the greater generality of society's needs, inevitably the primary concern of government. During her review of the British school system in October 1999, the UN Special Rapporteur on the Right to Education, Dr Katerina Tomasevski, expressed concern about: '…the inherited legal status of the child as the object of a legally recognized relationship between the school and the child's parents rather than the subject of the right to education and of human rights in education.' Dr Tomasevski views the provision of education by the State in England and Wales as reflecting the position which pertained before the development of the present concepts of human rights, and expresses the hope that these concepts will '…gradually influence English educational policy, law and practice'. Home education provides a real opportunity to ensure that children have an effective say in their own education and that their right to be full partners in the learning process is respected.

During the 1950s, a few ordinary people decided that they did not want to hand over responsibility for their children's education to schools. Gradually, others followed their example and in 1977 the first of the home education organisations, Education Otherwise, was born. It was a mutual support group for those involved in an epic struggle: some home educators were hounded into leading a nomadic lifestyle in order to avoid harassment, prosecution and care orders. Others did not manage to evade the full weight of the establishment's disapproval.

Home education was often automatically regarded as a 'welfare' issue, replete with suspicions that abuse, forced labour and neglect were a likely consequence of leaving families to chart their own course. Regrettably, we are currently seeing something of a resurgence of this view in some quarters; to borrow words from the Scottish Consumer Council's disturbing report, published in May 2000, on the treatment of home educators by Scottish education authorities:

> *The confusion over the continuing role of local authorities in home education can leave families vulnerable to poor practice by those who simply do not agree with the concept of home education. Worse, there appears to be a growing trend towards a blurring of the distinctions between education and social welfare issues by local authorities, leading to parents facing the terrifying prospects of legal action and social work intervention – all because of a decision they have legitimately made about their children's education.*
> Graeme S.Millar, Chairman Scottish Consumer Council,
> Home Works

Whereas the well-to-do had traditionally been unhindered in choosing home education, the pioneering home educators of the 50s, 60s and 70s were not of that ilk and thus lacked the tacit immunity from State intervention enjoyed by their 'betters'. They frequently paid a high price for their assertion that they could find better ways of nurturing their own children's potential. One can only admire their courage, whilst gasping and stretching one's eyes at the depths to which the establishment was prepared to sink in order to preserve the status quo.

> *The 'educational heretics' who met in the farmhouse near Swindon in 1977 did not know how things would develop. They saw their task as something like 'bringing happiness to a few children' rather than blazing a trail to the next learning system. Events have been on their side, however, since it has become obvious to more and more people that mass compulsory schooling is obsolete. People who begin to find that they can learn more in hours on their home computers than they can in days in school, are bound to start to question what all the public money spent on mass schooling is achieving.*
>
> Roland Meighan: *The Next Learning System*

Although the debate about whether mass schooling was born out of benevolence or the State's need for control is beyond the scope of this rather more pragmatic book, there is plenty of evidence that the first National Curriculum was developed with an end product in mind: the provision of a compliant workforce with just the right level of skills to meet the demands of an industrialised society, and with the unquestioning sense of national identity essential to an expanding empire. It is worth noting that, in 1911, the disillusionment of the newly-retired Chief Inspector for Schools led him to publish a book entitled *What Is and What Might Be*, denouncing the direction education had taken:

> *The Chief Inspector for Schools, Edmond Holmes, declared in 1911 that thirty years of trying to make the first National Curriculum work had shown him that the result was 'The Tragedy of Education'.*
>
> Editorial Comment: *Education Now*, Winter 99/00

Despite all the efforts to halt its progress, home education has gathered momentum as growing numbers of parents question whether 'school' is in fact synonymous with 'education' or whether there might be other ways of meeting their children's needs.

It is now widely accepted as a valid educational option and some Local Education Authorities show an exemplary grasp of the law combined with considerable respect for the diversity within home education. As a result, the home educators within their boundaries can enjoy a cordial and supportive relationship. However, it would be misleading to suggest that dealings with LEAs are always straight-forward, and so long as some continue to misrepresent their lawful powers, whether unintentionally or otherwise, it is important that we do not become complacent. Knowledge of the law and an ability to assert it confidently are certainly helpful to a home educator, but should never become home education's entrance requirements. The fact that some people are intimidated by apparent authority does not mean that they are any less capable of home educating effectively than those to whom assertiveness comes more easily. We still need strong networks to help each other, and to safeguard our own freedom to make choices about how we each home educate. Like footpaths, legal rights can gradually vanish for lack of use.

Some questions about home education crop up with such regularity that it seemed most helpful to answer them directly, although the answers can also be gleaned from individual stories. There was no difficulty in deciding which concerns qualified as 'Frequently Asked Questions', and all prospective home educators could do worse than have their own answers ready for the day when they meet these inevitable enquiries. Addresses and contact information for all the organisations mentioned in the 'FAQs' can be found in the back of the book.

There are many quotes scattered throughout the book. Some are pithy one-liners, others are longer excerpts from books, some of which may tempt you to read the whole thing. Details can be found in the book list, together with some other ideas for further reading.

As I was putting all the different elements of *Free Range Education* together, it suddenly occurred to me that both this book and the process of creating it are a dynamic parallel of home education itself. Certainly there is a serious purpose here, but there is also room for humour, illustration and a wide range of voices. I have been able to call on the expertise, generosity and wisdom of many other people. At times the process has felt impossibly chaotic, but gradually this book has taken on a life of its own and emerged as something resembling a scrapbook or photograph album: many different windows on the same theme. Ultimately, fascination with the subject has kept us all going.

We all hope that *Free Range Education* will give you a flavour of the variety of approaches to home education, and the information which you need if you are trying to reach a decision or work out how to begin. Of course, in the end, we are simply a group of individuals giving our version of events. Another book by another group of people might follow a completely different path, because there is no One Right Way to do anything creative...

Having come full circle, it is time for me to let others do the talking.

If a man does not keep pace with his companions, perhaps it is because he hears a different drummer. Let him step to the music which he hears, however measured or far away.

Thoreau

For thousands of years, in thousands of places, families educated their own. This tradition changed, not because a better method was found but because economic conditions required it. To work one had to leave one's children; one's children, furthermore, had to be trained for tasks no one in their purview could be seen doing. For these reasons institutionalised schooling was invented, and, while it adequately addressed a set of economic problems, it inspired a new set of human ones that are psychological, emotional, and even spiritual in nature.

David Guterson:
Family Matters – Why Homeschooling Makes Sense

Only until they're seven

Rosemary Charles

'A piece about home educating?' asked Terri. 'About two thousand words?'

'Yes Miss!'

Let's see, two thousand words spread out over, say, sixteen years is only – turn to calculator – about a word for every three days. Phew! That sounds easier. Worry again: will I be able to get everything in? Do I have anything to say? So goes the constant see-sawing between confidence and panic which punctuates the lives of most home educators.

It is only since I joined the UK Home-Education Internet list that I have begun to think of myself as a Home Educator. It sounds too grand: we have always thought of how we live as EOing, EO being the shorthand for not only Education Otherwise, the oldest of the self-help support groups for people who educate their own children, but also the phrase in the Education Act which makes it all possible. Although many folk do not realise it, there are three main educational paths within the law: State (and similar) schools; Independent and Alternative schools; and the fastest-growing group: No School, or Elective Home Education. I use the word Elective to distinguish home education done on purpose from any sort of non-school attendance which could broadly be described as truancy. The two are as different as chalk and cheese, but not so easily distinguished in the eyes of some who profess to be in authority.

My husband and I both had a standard middle-class education and, although I had always detected a mismatch between passing examinations and learning in the true sense of education, a feeling compounded when

I crossed the dais for a few years' teaching, I never seriously challenged what was going on. Had I done so, I would probably have thought such a path was only for people with an 'alternative' lifestyle: something I thought far removed from anything in my experience.

Although children change one's life more than can be imagined, they did not immediately change our outlook on the formal education system. When our elder daughter was two, however, I did start to look at the options for school in the early years. What I was determined to guard against was this obviously alert person going to playgroup, followed by nursery and then infant school, as it was then called, and being required to repeat the same kind of activities three times over. With this in mind we visited the local first school, which would have taken her full-time at five, to discover that, at three, she was already well capable of what was being offered there. From here (what idiots, in retrospect!) we looked at independent provision, hoping to find a more sensible progression, but among other drawbacks it was all too expensive. There was also Number Two, eighteen months younger, to consider; gym, library story time and her other afternoon activities would all be curtailed by the need to collect Number One from school. It was a nightmare.

The more I thought about it the more ridiculous it became. Ever since the girls were babies we had led active lives with outings, friends and all the learning-through-living-and-play which fills the days of all but the most disadvantaged young children. They were, for want of a better phrase, doing fine. Why not continue?

Some time afterwards the Health Visitor asked about schools, and I said something about not going. She asked if I knew about Education Otherwise, but I was so keen to avoid discussion that I said 'Yes', not being at all sure what she meant. Bear in mind that this was many years before the man on the Clapham omnibus had heard of home education: I thought I was inventing it! Subsequently I read an article on the subject in a local newsletter and that is when we joined EO, late in 1986.

What a long way we have all come since then. Initially I thought our home education would continue until around age seven. How wrong I was! An experienced home educator gave me the very good advice to take one year at a time and ask annually: 'Is this still what we want?' However, there were two factors which I had not taken into account at the outset. The first is that the longer you home educate, the more you question, the more constraining and unnecessary you recognise many aspects of the school system to be. The second factor was the opinions of the girls themselves. Very soon it was they who, when we went to visit a school, said: 'No thank you'. Recently our younger daughter, now fourteen, did think seriously about going to school for the first time, but as the only one she would consider did not have a place, that idea was short-lived.

> *Schools have not necessarily much to do with education... they are mainly institutions of control, where basic habits must be inculcated in the young. Education is quite different and has little place in school.*
>
> Winston Churchill

I started home educating with the thought that my children should be able to read, write and manipulate numbers at least as well as their school-going peers, have enquiring minds and outgoing personalities. It is only the last two to which I would subscribe today, and even then I would not want to prescribe it. I am reluctant to admit to my comparisons with school-going now; I reject all of the 'this-at-that-age' strictures, which have become worse with the advent of the National Curriculum, the teaching-to-the-test mentality and even payment -by-results, which ought to have disappeared with the Victorian era. In my family, reality alone has taught me that reading, for example, can occur at widely differing ages despite the same encouragement and access to books.

What is significant in the long run is that I have two teenagers who keep the library service very busy and are likely to do so into adulthood. Handwriting I would now consider a craft rather like screen-printing: fun and expressive in an artistic way, but not for everyday use. What is a word processor and spellchecker for? Although we used workbooks for number work, I would not do maths this way again. Not only do I now think the same concepts would have been met through real life experiences, for many years at least, but separating 'number' off as a subject was a mistake. My elder daughter says she does not like maths, but it was years before she realised other areas could be divided into subjects such as history, ecology, geography or English.

So, what have we done? Well, all kinds of traditional 'subjects', but much more has just happened. As a family we are involved in local life, belong to many groups and societies: the phone goes constantly. Whereas school-going families with lots of evening events barely see each other, after a day together we have always been happy to go our separate ways. Early on these activities included Brownies, gymnastics, swimming, guitar-playing and various sports. Over the years we have also encountered Woodcraft Folk, trampolining, various types of dancing, more sports, Watch group, church activities and many more.

These days, for Number One, home education involves a job as activities co-ordinator at a nursing home, trampolining, Rangers, dancing, British Sign language, talking newspaper (a heavy involvement here), helping at playgroup, guitar and acting with an adult group, whilst Number Two's interests include helping at Brownies, Guides, bell-ringing, dancing, Countrysiders, choir, two youth groups, playgroup, paper round, swimming and gymnastics. Oh – and they fight over whose turn it is for babysitting! We parents have a range of commitments and interests too, plus working (on an irregular basis in my case) so life is busy before home education, in any separate sense, gets a look in. However we have been, and still are, in contact with an extended family of home educators hereabouts and have taken a full part in attending and organising workshops, museum visits, and a wide variety of outings over the years. The best bit of home education is to see children of all ages at an EO meeting, playing and organising themselves, the bigger ones often operating toddler-on-hip as large families must have done in years gone by. Age and gender make little impact and certainly there are no hard divisions as there are in groups of school-going children. It is *wonderful:* would that more children, and parents, could be rid of such artificial barriers.

All these activities and experiences, plus lots of everyday living, are part of home education: each puts another piece in the jigsaw of a babe growing into an independently-functioning human being equipped for the future of this world. In fact the independence can happen at a pace which suits each individual and so it is built on sturdy, real foundations. A home-educated person is much more likely to have her own relationship with library and museum staff, for example. She is more likely to use shops, banks or public transport regularly, and to relate to people of all ages with the confidence of an equal, having not learned 'her place' in the school hierarchy. This means that not only can she operate in the real world; she also has a safeguard against unwelcome adults having an implied authority over her. The avoidance of school-age culture also means that home-educated children are more likely to have friends outside a narrow age band and can thus be themselves, rather than having to conform to narrow peer pressure.

Schoolchildren are under pressure to conform to the values of the group. In contrast, children who do not go to school are more likely to have the freedom to decide if they want to conform or not. Not being constantly subjected to group opinion allows them to develop their own views and values and to stick to them in the face of opposition.

Jean Bendell: *School's Out*

There are as many ways of home educating as there are families doing it, and it is generally assumed that everyone fits somewhere on the spectrum, from school-within-the-home with textbooks, fixed curriculum and timetable, to learning-from-life with nothing fixed whatever. I used to think that most families came between the two, often zigzagging from almost one extreme to the other depending upon who they last talked with! I have also frequently witnessed those whose children have been to school, starting out in a school-style but inevitably finding it inappropriate and almost always taking a year to shed their background before beginning to relax and enjoy themselves. However, there is a repeatedly expressed worry that home-educated children are somehow missing out by not being directly exposed to various ideas and 'facts'. What if they *don't* come into contact with these ideas in the course of less formal learning?

As well as realising the impossibility of deciding upon which of these ideas and facts to include (I started home educating before the National Curriculum was born and have felt no need to make its acquaintance), I have recently begun to stand back from the feeling that I should decide where I sit in the spectrum described above. Until recently, I thought that my background had inclined me initially towards the formal end of things, and that I had gradually got more laid-back over the years. Now I view it slightly differently: it is my children themselves who have prompted the changes.

As an analogy, when children are small they eat from a small range of foods but gradually you expose them to a wider range. Later they take steps to increase their knowledge by eating at others' houses, seeing advertisements and cookery programmes, looking at books and going shopping. Further on still, your children will not look to you for every meal but will perhaps make their own breakfast and snack-meal. One day you will come home to lunch on the table (yes, it does happen once in a while!). In the end, they will shop, cook and provide for themselves, only returning for the occasional piece of culinary advice where your longer experience may prove useful.

Now apply the above to education. At first, although you respond to your children's preferences and tastes, the main responsibility for introducing them to new ideas and information is yours. This does not have to be in any formal way: most will arise from the situations which occur during daily living. Later a wider range of nourishment will be gleaned from books, TV programmes, visits and group activities, enabling their interests gradually to take over whilst you continue menu suggestions when you think the diet has been lacking in one area for too long. Although a child may seem to eat from only a restricted number of foods, studies show that, when a full range is available, something from each food group will be eaten over time: the same is surely true of educational nutrition. Eventually, your children will decide what and when to learn and your expertise will be called upon only for reference. By then they may also be teaching you, which happens a lot!

Our children are now at the stage of providing for themselves, choosing examinations, or not, as appropriate. Someone recently asked me to describe the role of the parent of a home-educated teenager. My reply? Chauffeur when there isn't a bus! Actually, I hope we retain a slightly more significant role in our teenagers' lives. Although we have our loud-voiced moments, I do feel a continuing benefit of home education is that we have closer family relationships than those which many of my daughters' school-going friends seem to have with their parents. The school system puts so many unnecessary pressures on mid-teens, but because parents see it as their role to uphold this system to which they have subscribed for the past ten years, they inadvertently put a barrier between themselves and their children at a time when communication may become more difficult for all sorts of other reasons. With home education, especially when the whole family has grown into it, any examination syllabuses are embarked upon at the request of the person undertaking the course. This means it is not something imposed and so there is no source of friction. Being able to spread courses (or choose not to do any) means that there is still plenty of scope to be involved in other interests and activities, with the result that academic courses are just one thing, not the only thing, in life.

The easier relationship is also apparent in other ways. Our daughters' independence has evolved naturally and in line with their individual confidence. Now aged fourteen and sixteen, they are currently living a junior student type of existence. They study, socialise, do their bit in the community and earn to help fund it all. By contrast, school-goers have not had the same opportunities to become independent and still have their pattern of life imposed upon them, with sharp divisions between study and enjoyment. The kind of knots into which I see other parents and teenagers tying themselves, as to whether X be allowed to do this or that at a given age, simply have not happened here and so we have side-stepped another potential area of conflict.

It is important to combine home educating with some space for yourself too. Times when you can be without your children, or when you have one child separately, are invaluable. I was lucky in that Granny regularly had one at a time for an afternoon (she preferred them alone, too!) or I swapped responsibility with a friend. I also had two child-minder friends and could occasionally pay for an afternoon to myself. However you achieve it, I would suggest that it is essential at least once in a while, particularly if your children are very young.

Would I advise others to go the home education route? Yes, unhesitatingly. Any bad days in the home education situation must be as nothing compared to forcing a child through the school system. Then there are the obvious advantages of being able to visit the dentist or the shoe shop when it suits you; enjoying uncrowded exhibitions, parks and swimming pools whilst the majority of children are unable to do so. One less-known advantage is that HE children are rarely ill: not that they hold a magic charm to avoid germs, but not having to decide at 8 am whether they are fit for school makes a cold seem less of an event, as well as removing the pressure to administer antibiotics in order to catapult them back to the classroom. More and more families are opting to keep 'the ball in their court' over education and many other issues, a trend which I can only see increasing during the early part of the 21st century. My vision is that elective home education will soon become regarded as a norm rather than an exception. However, now that home educating parent (retired) status is edging closer, perhaps I may admit to some satisfaction in having been 'abnormal'!

And finally, if you are still undecided whether home education is for you after reading this book, there is one clinching argument:
You will never have to sew on nametapes!!

What Lloyd did next

Kay Day

'You are making a rod for your own back,' said the letter from the school's educational psychologist. She was referring to us allowing our very distressed son to skip school on the days when his anguish out-stripped ours. It had all started when 'cuddly Mrs Smith', as he called his first teacher, noticed that he was not making progress with reading and writing. A kindly intended observation, but one that gave Lloyd the first of many labels to hang around his neck. Four years later, the weight of these ever-accumulating labels became too much for him to bear. He communicated this in the best way a nine-year-old knew how and demonstrated his pain by bizarre and self-injurious behaviours.

Until then, I had taken little interest in educational issues. Wasn't school the place my children would go to become geniuses, once we had done maternal bonding and salt dough at home, so that I could get on with the rest of adulthood?

'Lazy, slow, disobedient, stupid and wilful,' said the school. 'A boy of overall high average intellectual ability but with severe dyslexia,' said the independent psychologist's report. We thought vindication was in sight. We assumed we could restore our son as a child of good character, even heroic character, once the school realised what the plucky lad had been up against. But, to their lasting shame, the local education authority had a policy of not recognising dyslexia.

What we were offered instead of proper recognition and resources was a token few hours of support with a non-teaching assistant. That was when the punishment truly began. The non-teaching assistant kept Lloyd in the 'quiet of the classroom' for extra reading while the other children were out and about doing the mini-beast safari. Lloyd felt he must be very bad.

Every morning was a nightmare as Lloyd fought with all his physical might to prevent us from taking him to school. Every professional opinion was that we should, at all costs, continue to insist on his attendance. Although my instinct screamed inside me to keep him at home, I had been told that it was my legal responsibility, as his parent, to get him to school. Finally he threatened to hang himself. He had to communicate the seriousness of his situation to us somehow. I called the head teacher and said on no account would I force him to school. The on-call child psychiatrist telephoned us and offered an immediate place in a small tutorial unit and an appointment at her clinic. Dutifully, and still believing in the benign intentions of the state education system, we attended both for a short while.

It was a family crisis and friends rallied with offers of support. One friend appeared with two booklets saying, 'I don't really know if these will be of any help but...' They were the Advisory Centre for Education journal and 'School is Not Compulsory'. As I read the personal accounts of families embarking on home education, I experienced immediate relief and recognised this as the escape hatch for which we had been searching. After months of isolation and inner turmoil I began to hear the voice of friends out there. Their voice, through Education Otherwise, rose with a conviction which equalled that of the orthodox educationalists, who had tried to convince us of our wrong-headedness and who wanted to swallow our beloved son deeper into the interventionist depths of their institution. When we pulled Lloyd out of the system, it felt like pulling him out of the mud just as it seeped in at the corners of his mouth.

Once Lloyd believed that we were back on his side and that he really would never have to return to school again, all the manifestations of his distress disappeared overnight. It was a miracle to have our happy, healthy son back. We soon became established in the home educators' community and learnt about a new way of life for the whole family. When one thing changes, everything changes: my job, our home, our philosophy about children, our friends, our ambitions. We were on a totally new and exciting path.

'Isn't it exhausting, having your child around you all the time?' asked friends and family as they acclimatised to our home education. 'No, it's easy,' was our stock response. 'What's exhausting is caring for a seriously traumatised child.' We quickly realised that part of his trauma had been our fault. Due to our ignorance about children and our acceptance of the rightness and authority of 'experts', we violated Lloyd.

We used our greater numbers, our physical power and psychological bullying to force him to submit to a system of schooling that was destroying him. The priority for Lloyd, post-school, was to regain his self-respect by continuously exercising his right to be self-determining. This meant no reading, no writing and no being 'taught'. We had to accept that the damage sustained in these areas would take years to repair. We were prime candidates for autonomous education, in which the learning is entirely directed by the learner. We learnt to zip our lips, keep our anxieties to ourselves and to keep out of the way of his learning as much as we could.

Life continued in this relaxed and stimulating way for the remainder of Lloyd's home-educated years until, in the Autumn of 1994, we received the standard notification that Lloyd's Child Benefit would cease shortly after his 16th birthday in February, unless we could confirm that he would be continuing in full-time education, at school or otherwise.

I showed the notice to Lloyd and said that whilst it stated in black and white that EO was an official option, I suspected that it would necessitate a visit from an LEA inspector to confirm our status as bona fide home educators. I was already half way down the track of, 'How on earth do we assemble something that an LEA inspector, untrained in autonomous education, would recognise as full-time educational activity?' when Lloyd stopped me mid-step with the announcement that he did not wish the claim to continue. Indeed, it was his intention to get a job as soon as he was legally eligible.

My first-born had sneaked up behind me and grown up without fair warning. A shock for any mother but particularly unnerving for me as I immediately shifted my anxiety state from: 'What have you been doing with your life? What do we show the inspector?' to: 'What have you been doing with your life? What job have you ever mentioned wanting to do?' 'Well that's the problem,' returned Lloyd, 'I've no idea'.

Until then I had enjoyed a strong belief in Lloyd's ability to make his way in the world, but this development had me thinking like an LEA inspector. Where was the evidence that this young man could offer anything of use to the big wide world of work? What did we have to show that an employer would recognise as skills and ability worth paying good money for?

The following couple of months produced no naturally-occurring ideas from Lloyd about his possible vocation, nor even the mere mention of making a buck. He seemed unassailably bereft of inspiration and enthusiasm. Sooner or later I had to intervene with the inevitable suggestion that we use the Career Service's computer to input the things he liked doing (re-enacting the American Civil War, eating meat, talking on the telephone, comedy, painting model soldiers and sleeping) to see what occupational areas it threw back at us.

We had two meetings with a Careers Officer who helped Lloyd to crystallise his interests and abilities: a passion for history, and experience of working with the public at historical re-enactments; experience of dealing with customers (by dint of my working at home); physical fitness; good communication and social skills (because, being home-educated, you mix with all sorts). We were sent home to think up six jobs with the remotest possibility of engaging Lloyd's interest. These were not easily come by: the flip-chart sheet on the dining room wall lay barren. The day before our next appointment, I squeezed butcher and leather-craft worker from the reluctant lad. I wrote it on the flip chart with a dried-out marker pen and felt dismal.

It should have worked, all this 'letting him be', all this trust of his inherent learning skills to lead him inevitably towards exploration, experimentation, discovery and understanding. Why so directionless now? We retired to the sitting room to watch a television programme about supernatural phenomena. It featured ghosts at Dover Castle with testimony from tour guides.

'That's it! That's what I can see you doing. A tour guide!' I enthused at Lloyd.

'Mmmmm,' contemplated Lloyd, 'now that's the sort of thing I can see myself doing too.'

We explored the idea and discovered that, because of Lloyd's re-enactments of the American Civil War, he knew the local Area Manager of English Heritage. Pleased with ourselves, we presented our findings to the Careers Officer who suggested a period of work experience to see if Lloyd and the work suited each other. Sadly, her records showed that no work experience placements had been established with English Heritage in our area but, if we had a contact, we might be able to sort something out on a personal basis.

At this juncture, six years of home educating kicked in. Within an hour, Lloyd had established himself with three weeks work experience at Fort Brockhurst and arranged lodgings with a re-enacting friend nearby. I arranged personal accident insurance cover for him, took him shopping for sufficient changes of clothes to last him a week without a washing machine, and he was off!

After his three weeks, he stayed on as a Volunteer Assistant Custodian. I wrote to another home educating friend, the mother of a slightly younger teenager, about the changes we were witnessing in Lloyd: 'He really spent a lot of time dossing at home: sleeping in until noon then getting up to lie down in front of the TV for hours. Now, without any assistance from me, except in the purchase of an alarm clock, he gets himself up at 7.15 each morning, breakfasts, prepares a packed lunch, then walks 20 minutes to work at the Fort. Here he unlocks, cleans and maintains the property, welcomes visitors and collects entrance fees, promotes English Heritage membership and merchandise in the site shop, provides what historical data he can, helps organise special events and makes tea. He is working hard to create a good impression so that he can stand himself in good stead for paid work when it is available. He has already been offered some casual work at Spitbank Fort, which is out at sea, and hopes this will lead to a seasonal job there.'

At the beginning of May he was taken on for the season at Spitbank Fort, and was very pleased to have the work even though the wages were low. His employer collected him from his lodgings every day and drove him to the marina, whereupon Lloyd ran the boat out to the fort for his day's work. At the end of his first month, his employer telephoned me to say how pleased he was with Lloyd's contribution: 'He's at least 100 percent better than any other nipper I've had working out here,' he said. The things which he valued in Lloyd were strikingly similar to the competencies delineated some years back by Levi Strauss as the most important qualities in an employee:

1. Good time keeping and the right attitude towards work.
2. A willingness to be trained and to learn a range of skills.
3. Social skills and the ability to fit into the existing team structure.
4. Flexibility and a willingness to take on any job.
5. Willingness to be a part of the enterprise and a part of the business.

Lloyd had never been taught these things, either by me or anyone else. I believe he learned them by virtue of being at home in the real world, rather than at school in some academic's version of it which bore little resemblance to his own family's experience.

> *All men who have turned out worth anything have had the chief hand in their own education.*
>
> Scott

I could not fully explain how autonomous education produced such an aspiring teenager, and I still feel it failed him during times of prolonged boredom and isolation. What I am now more confident about is the possibility of parenting a successful home education graduate by doing just as my own mother had recommended when the topic in question was producing a good Yorkshire Pudding: resist the temptation to peek before the cooking time is up. Self-doubt has the same effect on the novice cook as it does on the first-time autonomous educator. The proof is only to be found in the eating so, if you must look at your pudding or your protégé before it's done, don't panic if the sloppy, insipid-looking thing you see is a far cry from the golden, crusted crown you had expected.

Lloyd left the fort at the end of the season and, throughout the winter months, fulfilled his own prediction by working for the local butcher. His hands were stained green from the sage and onion he stuffed into turkeys and special Christmas sausages. The work was repetitive but he often quotes his days at the butchers when talking about team work, customer relations and good management.

From the butchers he went to the local Volkswagen Beetle 'Innovations' garage so that he could hang out with hip young men and be visited, in the course of his work, by young women car owners. He liked that part of the work but not the ingrained grease, the unreliable pay cheques and the workplace lavatory.

Home educating friends running their own business provided the next opportunity. Lloyd helped out converting audio voice-overs into digital CDs during a big project where they needed casual help over a few weeks.

Home education is seen as a positive advantage to some employers. The founder of our local Montessori school got to know Lloyd when we accompanied his younger brother to occasional nursery sessions. When the nursery grew, Lloyd was invited to work part-time. He trained there for six months before moving to a full-time Montessori Assistant post in Chichester (and buying his first car to commute).

As he approached 18, Lloyd declared an interest in taking an Open University degree. He chose Psychology with the long term aim of specialising in Child Development as a Clinical Psychologist. Nobody was more surprised than his parents who had, up until that point, forked out hefty bribes to get him to write so much as a birthday card. Had we thought back to the lessons learnt in the kitchen, we should have trusted that when all the ingredients of his autonomous education had been left long enough to be allowed to work together, the desire to reclaim his intellectual potential would rise within him – but only when he was good and ready.

He is now 20 years old, a third year undergraduate and living with his fiancée, with whom he is buying a flat. In four years he has been unemployed for no more than three months. He does not find life particularly easy, but he does keep going: another essay completed, another pay cheque earned. He loves his old Education Otherwise group, to which his younger brothers still belong, and socialises within it when he can. He is a real, live role model for the home-educated teenagers, and cause for sighs of relief amongst the parents – not least his own!

Children present the best evidence for a psychology of providence. Here I mean more than providential miracles, those amazing tales of children falling from high ledges without harm, buried under earthquake debris and surviving. Rather, I am referring to the humdrum miracles when the mark of character appears. All of a sudden and out of nowhere a child shows who she is, what he must do. These impulsions of destiny frequently are stifled by dysfunctional perceptions and unreceptive surroundings, so that calling appears in the myriad symptoms of difficult, self-destructive, accident-prone, 'hyper' children – all words invented by adults in defence of their misunderstanding.

James Hillman: *The Soul's Code – In Search of Character & Calling*

Nick (aged 15)

I have been educated at both school and home and I much prefer it at home. You have greater flexibility, so you learn what you want and pretty much when you want. So you look at something when you're ready to look at it. This makes learning a lot more enjoyable.

When GCSEs come around, there is not as much pressure put on as there is in school. I am 15 and have been home-educated for six years. I have already passed some GCSEs and am currently taking more. I have done them all on a distance learning programme, where I work from home and then go into college for fortnightly or monthly tutorials.

Home Education, in my opinion, is the most enjoyable way of being educated. You are taught by your parents, so you don't have to deal with problems like not getting on with your teachers, and you feel comfortable with people you know educating you. You do not get unnecessary work piled on top too, this freeing up more spare time to do the things that you are interested in.

Home Education – a great thing!

Sam (aged 8)

I don't know why, but what I learnt in school I seemed to forget but what I learn at home I remember.

Ollie (aged 7)

I'd rather be home-educated because you get to spend time with your mum and dad. You can do maths without being flustered to do it (I like maths). You can make stuff – in fact once we made a tepee. You can read loads of exciting books without having to read them out loud to people, go up the garden and plant some plants. It's just really fantastic. You can do anything that you would do in school, but when you really want to do it.

At school you have to get yourself there for nine in the morning and go to all these different lessons, and you have to get interested when someone else tells you, even if you are more interested in something else that day. At home, you don't have to be told about things to learn – you can always just get a book or something on the computer.

You get a smaller number of friends when you are home-educated, but you get nice ones. You never get bullied, except by some schoolkids around here when you go out sometimes.

You can make bread, and fix yourself meals when you are hungry. You can do juggling practice and play the piano or practise the drums full-go in the daytime when all the neighbours have gone out. You can go places more easily – like the Science Museum. You can learn French and play about on your bike. You can play with a calculator, and get magic books to do tricks on your friends.

Home education thoughts from abroad

Sue Fairhead

I had been interested in the idea of home education for some years before we started. It seemed like something for those perfect parents whose spotless homes appear in washing powder adverts. In the ideal family, I imagined, children would wake early, enthusiastic to get to their books, and would respond eagerly to their mother's teaching by asking relevant questions or writing wonderful stories and reports. They would take part in team sports and delight librarians, museum curators and neighbours with their good manners and intelligent, caring attitude.

Of course, in my view my children were as wonderful as any cereal-munching child in a commercial, but I am an average procrastinating person, inclined to take life easy. Whilst I can enjoy research and explain things when asked, I am by no means an inspiring teacher. Nor could I imagine keeping to a schedule or never having a moment to myself. Besides, we had a lovely C of E school close to our home which most of the boys' friends attended and where I was able to be involved as a parent volunteer. The boys loved being there and gained a great deal from it, including an excellent introduction to playing instrumental music.

We moved abroad at the end of October 1997, when Daniel was 11 and Tim was 9, and decided to try home education for a few months whilst settling in. I was full of worries: would my children miss out academically and socially by being away from school? What about sport? Music? Art? How would we deal with classroom discussions, drama, role-playing? With brainstorming sessions about how to design science experiments? Rather to my surprise, the staff at the boys' school were most encouraging, and helped me to see that there was no point in emulating a school day at home. They gave me helpful suggestions for books and other resources, and pointed out that, for instance, since both boys were fluent and enthusiastic readers, and highly computer literate, I need not worry at all about reading or ICT. They reminded me that learning to live in a new culture was far more useful 'geography' than any amount of text book learning, and encouraged me to give them more freedom to learn at their own speeds with a lot of independent research.

I think we've tied acquiring knowledge too much to school.
Arno Penzias, Nobel Laureate (Physics)

The boys quickly worked out that when one takes account of assembly, break, lunchtime, registration and the general lining up or moving around that goes on in school, there are at most three hours of academic learning in a six-and-a-half hour school day. We could limit ourselves to mornings and still cover everything, probably more efficiently, since I would only have to answer questions for two of them. They would not have to wait around for others' questions to be answered, nor have to work through sections of books they found too easy, or dull.

However, despite everything, I started with a 'school at home' mentality and we did what we could to make our days as like school as possible, sitting at the kitchen table with workbooks, pens and paper, covering different subjects in fixed periods. I read as much as I could about the National Curriculum and worried about subjects I could not manage such as technology, music and art.

Gradually we learned to relax and take one day at a time. I realised that if one of the boys asked a question, then that was the time to follow that topic whether or not it was scheduled. By Christmas we had decided to continue for the rest of the academic year, so I bought some more text books, joined a home education Internet mailing list and started reading about homeschooling as much as I could. Meanwhile our sea freight with the boys' computer had arrived, which meant that they could word process sometimes rather than writing everything, and supplement some of their learning with CD-Rom reference guides and educational software.

Around that time I discovered that in the UK many home educators do not follow any curriculum at all, even loosely. I learned about autonomous or child-led learning, where the parents do little more than make suggestions and answer questions, with the child deciding on the learning subjects and speed. I was amazed to find just how many home educating families there were in the UK, and that no two appeared to function in the same way. Some used formal American curricula, some were totally free and easy, and there were all manner of variations between the two extremes. I wasn't comfortable with no structure at all but I began to ease up, to encourage the boys to spend as long or as short a time as they wanted on each topic and to use computer games that were not specifically educational if they were relevant. I was surprised to find that some of their 'strategy civilisation building' games were full of politics, geography and history, and brought these subjects alive in a way I could not begin to do.

After some investigation, we felt that the local primary schools were not appropriate for either of the boys and Daniel decided that, rather than looking at a secondary school for Autumn 1998, he would like to continue with home education. I panicked again! We had no science lab, no sports facilities and I knew nothing about secondary school history or geography. On the other hand, Daniel was happier and more relaxed than he had ever been. Both boys had been able to continue with music, important to both of them, with outside teachers and we had also heard about a Saturday art workshop.

I began to feel that their learning was more balanced, and agreed to another year. I was delighted that they were enjoying it so much because it felt to me as if I had finally found my vocation. I had always enjoyed teaching small groups of children but knew I would never manage to train as a classroom teacher.

Again I researched, and bought more books and CD-Roms, we also found a second-hand French Linguaphone course. I asked questions on the Internet mailing lists and found out as much as I could by browsing web sites. These seemed to be full of success stories, of 'proof' that home education was more efficient than school and produced happier, more productive adults. I read about bullying and high truancy in secondary schools in the UK, heard of children stressed with hours of homework, pressurised into exams, rushing around from place to place like parts on a production line. I compared that image with Daniel who, at eleven years old, would read computer programming books in bed, ask questions about world events late at night, had joined the church music group despite being the youngest by 25 years, read and enjoyed everything from Asimov science fiction to P.G.Wodehouse, and was half way through writing a novel.

Tim, at nine, was the one who really missed school and his friends. Nevertheless he said that he was learning more at home than he had ever learned at school, and that he didn't think he wanted to go to any of the local primary schools. He made the interesting comment that it would be a good idea if every child could have at least a year of learning at home, at around the age of nine or ten, to consolidate what they knew, 'catch up' on things they had missed, and have the opportunity to follow up their interests in ways not possible in schools.

The object of education is to prepare the young to educate themselves throughout their lives.

Robert M.Hutchins

Gradually, over the months, Tim made some friends and started to enjoy new interests, despite missing his friends and school in the UK. He learned to cook and started to knit and sew. For my part I found that, despite myself, I was becoming more and more enthusiastic about home education as a choice for life. I could see the boys blossoming as they stopped being limited by the school bell. They no longer had to pause in the middle of an interesting project just because it was time for something else. They seemed to squabble less, and were certainly less tired. We could take time off whenever we had guests, and then the boys would build fabulous cities and drainage systems on the beach or role-play for hours with their Lego cities and people.

We experimented with autonomous-style educating. The boys got up when they felt like it and did what they wanted, but it did not really work for us. They felt that they 'ought' to be doing some maths or writing, and if they were not following text books at all they felt disorientated. We found that the Linguaphone French was a good way to start the day, and that if we did two to three hours of reasonably structured academic work each morning, the rest of the day felt more constructive. During April and early May 1999 we did very little, as we had a series of guests, then with renewed energy we got right back into a flexible timetable covering the academic National Curriculum subjects, using appropriate text books and working through in a fairly structured way. Being flexible means that there is plenty of freedom to miss out easy sections, spend longer on harder parts, and do any amount of reinforcement with computer programming, word processing, research and relevant games.

So we came full circle: our home educating now is more school-like in one sense than it was at the beginning. The boys start with French, followed by an hour or so of another subject (biology, history, geography, chemistry or RE) using a text book appropriate to their ages. After this, we spend time on either maths or English, again mainly using text books with the addition of some children's writing magazines to inspire them to enter competitions or write new forms of prose or poetry. They both learn two musical instruments and practise reasonably regularly; they attend art class, go to Sunday School and have a variety of social events with friends. Tim sings in two choirs, Daniel goes to the church youth group and plays clarinet with the worship band, and they have both enjoyed basketball and cricket coaching when it is not too hot.

As well as this, they have seen kittens born and growing, raised silkworms and joined in with the gardening of our wild back yard; they have helped with painting, with making curtains and have generally taken part in family life. We have built a web site all about home education on the Internet, and they have composed music and written lots of letters. They are teaching themselves to play the saxophone, they have made e-mail friends, designed computer art and written computer programs. Daniel still lies in bed at nights reading computer manuals, but now it is C++, far more complicated than his previous Games Factory or Visual Basic. They read avidly and often, and we still read to them at night. About one week in four we take time away from the structure so that the boys can spend concentrated time on writing e-mail, computer programs, web pages, stories, and reports.

I have no regrets about their time in school in the UK. It gave them a good grounding in many things, particularly music, and we all made many friends amongst children, parents and staff. We loved that school and go back to visit any time we are 'home', but I now realise that it was a school in a million and gave us a high standard for comparison. Perhaps, one day, one or both of them will go into another school. If so, it will be their informed decision and I will support them all the way. In the meantime I can see so many benefits to home education, and I enjoy the way we are getting to know each other so much better. The pre-adolescent years do not need to be traumatic when there is no peer pressure or insistence on conformity, and where there is freedom to learn without stress, at the speed the children choose.

As for the future: we will continue taking one year at a time, encouraging both boys to consider all their options and gradually make their choices about which subjects to follow. They are both starting to talk about taking GCSE exams by correspondence: rather than having to work towards seven or eight at once, they can take just one or two subjects at a time, starting earlier than is usual in school. At the moment Daniel wants to be a computer programmer or graphic designer and Tim wants to be a primary school teacher. Both of them also want to be musicians and authors. I hope I can encourage them in whatever career path they wish to follow, whilst helping them to understand what preparation they will need to make.

More important is that they grow up to be mature, thinking, caring adults who are able to challenge the status quo if necessary, research and learn anything they need to know, and deal confidently with a world which is increasingly full of uncertainties.

Knowledge is produced in response to questions. And new knowledge results from the asking of new questions; quite often new questions about old questions. Here is the point: once you have learned how to ask questions – relevant and appropriate and substantial questions – you have learned how to learn and no one can keep you from learning whatever you want or need to know.

Postman & Weingartner: *Teaching as a Subversive Activity*

FAQ no.1   How do they socialise?

This question has probably been answered by everyone who has contributed to this book. Most home educators would turn this question around to ask: does the limited nature of children's social experience at school prepare them adequately for the realities of adult life? Or does the hierarchical nature of school, particularly when combined with restrictions of catchment area or gender, instead merely reinforce a tendency to define others in terms of age, sex, race or class?

It is true that you are highly unlikely to find thirty home-educated children of the same age congregating exclusively in the same place; they tend to socialise far more widely, counting adults, younger or older children and members of the opposite sex amongst their friends. For a home-educated youngster, a peer group is more likely to consist of those who share the same interests, just as it does for adults, rather than the same birth year.

On a practical level, if you need some ideas about finding enjoyable group activities, here are some suggestions. Addresses and contact information can be found at the end of this book.

Make contact with other home educators

✦ **Choice in Education** publishes details of groups and outings in its regular magazine, and can also tell you about local newsletters/people to contact. They run **Hes Fes**, a big annual camp for home educators.

✦ **Education Otherwise** has regular activities and groups in many areas, and organises several camps throughout the Summer. They also offer a contact list of members.

✦ **Home Education Advisory Service** will send you a list of other members in your area.

✦ If you have Internet access, join the **UK Home Education List** – a busy, lively discussion forum for home educators from all over the country. Those whose children have special needs are welcome on the **HE Special List**.

What interests does your child have?

✦ Ask at your **library** or **sports centre** for details of relevant classes, clubs and teams.

✦ If your child is older, is he interested in doing voluntary work? Find out whether there is a **volunteer bureau** in your area. Contact locally-based charities such as animal shelters, city farms, conservation projects – whatever appeals to your child.

✦ If your child enjoys singing or playing a musical instrument, are there youth orchestras, jazz bands or choirs in your area? Ask local music teachers or ring the **County Music Advisor** for the Local Education Authority.

✦ Look at special interest groups such as the **Young Ornithologists Club, Junior Amnesty International or Young Archaeologists Club.** The **St. John's Ambulance Brigade** run groups for youngsters and in some areas the **RSPCA** organises wildlife-related courses for children.

✦ How about **Woodcraft Folk, Guides** or **Scouts**: are they active in your area?

✦ The **National Association for Gifted Children** has a list of local clubs which provide a variety of activities for curious children (no IQ test required!)

What else is going on locally?

✦ Ring the **Leisure Services** department at your Town Hall to ask what is on offer for local children: art clubs? Circus skills classes? Drama groups? There may be play sessions during school holidays, football or tennis coaching, computer courses.

✦ Keep an eye open for activities advertised on notice boards or in local papers

✦ If you have a particular religious affiliation, what does your **Church, Temple, Mosque** or **Synagogue** offer young people? If the answer is 'not much', would they be willing to support you in setting something up?

✦ Collect leaflets about **museums** and **galleries**; ask them what activities they have for children: weekend clubs? School holiday activities?

So, what about socialisation?

Jan Jurczak-George

We had returned home from an evening visiting friends and their two schooled children when our seven-year-old daughter came out with the following observation: 'Children who go to school don't seem to know very much, do they?' Now, she wasn't referring to their ability to read, write, spell or do long division but what they actually knew about life and being part of the world. Up until then, I had not thought that much about it, but I could see her point.

Before we had children, and it came as a pleasant shock when we did, we never envisaged the sort of parents we would become. Heck, we look really normal when you meet us, honest! But our babies were born at home, breastfed until they saw fit to stop, didn't get farmed out to child minders as I was lucky enough to be able to stay home, slept with us as much as they wanted to and, as the time to consider schools drew near (which seems to be around six months of age if you live in some areas) we really began to follow our instincts here too. I could go on for chapters about how our natural parenting instincts are hammered into the ground, but that is not what you are here to read. Reclaiming those instincts, however, may be the reason why many of us begin to question following the herd to the school gates.

Our children are the most precious people in our lives. Why would I want to give them to strangers all day? To tell them what? To instil in them what values, if any, about themselves, about life and the world in which they live? How would we avoid losing touch with each other? How do you maintain a relationship with a child whom you hardly ever see, who is wound up and tired from a day in school? By the time they are ready to relax and talk, it is time for bath and bed or: 'You won't be up in time for school tomorrow.' No, that wasn't for us.

*Education, the great mumbo jumbo and fraud of the age, purports
to equip us to live and is prescribed as a universal remedy for
everything from juvenile delinquency to premature senility.*
                                                    Malcolm Muggeridge

This is not say that we amble around the house all day like the Waltons,
baking bread in jolly bonhomie and basking in the glow of it all. If you
think home educating might be for you, get ready to feel tired, argue,
get on each others' nerves and to wonder just why you are doing this.
But this is OK: families who know each other well can cope with
normal daily emotions. Oh, and forget a tidy house. Home education
is not the province of the houseproud – unless various projects covering
every available surface and a vague memory that you once had a carpet
are your idea of radical chic. I would suggest that, much as I wish it
could be otherwise, the dust will still be there when your children, and
mine, are not. One day I will read what I have written here and
remember all the precious moments I have had with my children,
which I would have missed if they had been in school or I had wasted
time dusting.

Initially, I was the one who was more keen to home educate whilst
Glyn was slightly more cautious. He had a great group of friends at
school, so he held on to some happy memories; my memories were a
little less enthusiastic. At first he rather took the view that, as I was the
parent at home who would be 'doing it', it was my final decision; this
did not rest well with me, however convenient. They are *our* children
and so I reckoned we both had to feel one hundred percent confident
about the decision.

I printed off an article from a website, written by a home-educated
teenager, and arranged for the parents of some home-educated children
to come and visit one evening. Glyn and I had a series of heart-to-
hearts, and gradually he became far more at ease with the whole idea.
In fact, I have subsequently been amused to hear him extolling the
virtues of home education.

We come from such a schooled society that it can be very hard for
some adults to conceive of the idea of not going to school, and it is a
potential source of friction between parents. If you can persuade your
partner to read some books about HE and how children learn (John
Holt is always a good starting point, as is this book!) and can manage
to meet up with parents already home educating, that may help to allay
some of their fears.

It can be difficult to deal with anxiety around what others may think: aghast grandparents, doubting co-workers and the occasional, barely-concealed aggression of those who are jealous that you have had the guts (although they may call it impudence) to take such a step. Arm yourself with some stock replies for when you are cornered. Here, for example, is one of my favourite replies when I get the inevitable: 'And what about socialisation?' I radiate concern as I reply: 'Yes, that must be a real worry when you have a child in school.' Not that I want to be antagonistic of course – I'm a real pussy cat – but it buys me time to think about what I want to say next whilst they are still trying to be sure that they heard me correctly. We are not in the business of explaining our choices to others whose 'interest' lies only in fault-finding, nor getting their approval. On the other hand I have yet to meet anyone who was downright appalled to hear that we home educate, and I have lost count of the number of conversations I have had with people in shops or on park benches who genuinely want to know more. If you do decide to home educate, make sure you always take a supply of contact information around with you to hand out!

Returning to the subject of socialisation, would someone please, please tell me why school is considered to be this great social experience? Take a step back a minute and imagine this: someone walks up to you and tells you that for five days a week you have to go to a particular place, no choice about this, and you cannot leave it until a set time in the afternoon. Once there, you will sit in a room with twenty-nine other people all the same age as yourself. Not much variety here, either. You will have to obey the person who is telling you what to do in this room, and show respect regardless of whether you believe they deserve it. You will be given things to do: usually work-sheets to keep you occupied. This is because the person in charge of you will find it hard, if not impossible to give you any individual attention. Thus they will not know you very well, but will nevertheless write reports about you for others to read.

You could try asking questions about what you are meant to be doing, but thirty people all asking questions at once is not particularly encouraged, so you might eventually give up on curiosity. You are no longer allowed to spend large parts of the day with the people you have most wanted to be with for all the previous years of your existence. You may even begin to wonder why they do not want you around anymore. Eventually, many bells later, you will be allowed to leave. Oh, and if you need a pee whilst there, you must ask, so that everyone else in the room knows what you are doing: bodily functions by permission only, please. Once out, you can practise what you have learned – mainly how to pester the person with the spending power in your family to buy you the right trainers, clothes and toys so that you can fit in with all those others with whom you spent the day being processed. Dare to be different and things can get a bit unpleasant. Now, do you want to be there as an adult? Then why would you want to send your children there?

Soap and education are not as sudden as a massacre, but they are more deadly in the long run.

Mark Twain

I like my children and I enjoy their company. I want to give them the time and space to be who they want to be; encourage them to be strong and confident about what they feel and also about their ability to make informed decisions. I hope we all get twenty years or so down the line, still liking and respecting each other.

Having decided to try home education, we had to sort out how to approach it. Our children were four and two when we decided to go for it, so it was pretty much a matter of carrying on as before. They had managed to learn to crawl, walk, talk, feed and dress themselves and express their opinions within our family and group of friends, so obviously something was working. Children learn almost in spite of themselves unless they have their natural curiosity and desire to learn knocked out of them. Give a child a sense of security and love, the certainty that they are being listened to and their ideas valued, combine it with a rich environment to explore and you have a recipe for successful home education. Rich doesn't mean in monetary terms: yes, have plenty of interesting things around, but above all be prepared to give your time to them. That is a gift beyond measure.

If you are looking for ideas about timetables and course work, you are probably reading the wrong chapter! Truthfully, it is only in the last six months or so that we have become slightly more organised and maybe not as 'unschooled' as we were. Our days broadly fall into mornings where we do more 'formal' work on reading, writing and numbers in a variety of ways. We also read together, listen to music, practise French, bake and watch 'The Magic School Bus' or some of the schools TV programmes, plus so many other things as well. It usually involves eating lots of biscuits too. 'Morning' is a loose term for any time between when we get up and when we go out.

One great benefit of home educating is the freedom it gives you to follow the flow and do what you fancy. A sunny day? Let's take our stuff down to the beach. You're interested in the Tudors? Let's visit a nearby town with an Elizabethan house that belonged to Anne of Cleves. We are lucky to live in a town with plenty going on, and almost daily activities for local home educators. We dip into these as we want; one of our problems is having almost too much to do.

We had a wonderful home educators' get-together at our home one summer day which included fifteen children and eight adults, all making potions in the garden using herbs, rose petals, essential oils, water, food colouring and cornflour. The results are still decorating the patio with stains, and we have some vivid orange splashes on our sofa. When I see them, I also see a group of free, happy children and adults having a lovely time just being themselves and having fun. Incidentally, they also learned how water, oils and cornflour mix, how to negotiate for what they wanted to use if another child already had it – and they made some pretty weird 'perfumes' into the bargain!

In the course of our days, my children come into contact with all kinds of people and age groups within our community, and we also have three generations of our family living in our home. I enjoy it when someone tells me that my children are different because they are so confident and equally happy to talk to adults or other children. Of course, they might have been like this if they had gone to school, but my experience of seeing children whom I have known since babyhood going into the school system, and noticing the way they change, makes me think not. A friend whose child is in school, has several years-worth of school photos on the wall. The first shows the big, bright, happy, open smile of a curious four-year-old. Sadly, over the subsequent years the pictures gradually change to a guarded and much less happy face.

What is the worst you can do if you decide to educate your child at home? Remember, if it is not right for your child and family, the schools will still be there. So what have you got to lose?

The opportunity to develop and practise social skills in school is quite limited. Children spend nearly all their time in school with other children born during the same academic year as themselves, and a great deal of time outside school as well. In school, there is little social contact with younger or older children and even less with adults. It is easy to see how peer mores, values and codes of behaviour become entrenched, resulting in considerable pressure to conform and the threat of ostracism or exclusion from the group for those who do not. Moreover, up to one and a half hours a day in school is specifically set aside for social recreation in the playground, where children are thrown together with nothing much to do. It is not surprising that playground hierarchies emerge and bullying is rife.

The consequence is that the 'social' skills acquired are those which may be essential for survival in school but have little applicability in the outside world. There is virtually no opportunity to relate socially to adults in school in order to learn wider social skills. Ironically, such skills can only be learned outside school hours. Teachers do, of course, set up social scenarios and discuss with children how to behave in given social circumstances. But these are no substitute for learning through real-life, dynamic social contact.

Alan Thomas: *Educating Children at Home*

Just tell me why

Clare Murton

When I started to think about what led us to home educate our two children, one word leapt out: 'Why?' It is a very powerful word which children use endlessly almost as soon as they can speak and it drives many parents and teachers crazy. I spent years of my youth asking 'Why?' with my heart, mind and actions. Now I am home educating because I have developed a lifelong habit of asking 'Why?' and demanding a reasonable answer before I follow the crowd.

About eight years ago, when my first child was two years old, I began considering his education. I asked:

- Why do parents send their children to nurseries and playgroups from such a young age?

- Why is age five chosen for the start of schooling?

- Why do people think that children will become antisocial if they don't meet with twenty to thirty children of similar ages every day?

- Why should I force my child to be separated from me for hours at a time when I don't believe he is ready and he expresses a clear wish not to leave, and what will happen if I do?

- What is the real reason behind the social pressure to push your child away ever earlier?

• Why is a parent, who has nurtured her child for five years and knows him better than anyone else, not trusted by 'professionals' to know what is best for him?

• Does education need to be the unhappy experience it appears to be for so many children?

• What evidence do the 'professionals' have that schooling is essential?

I want all parents struggling with these sorts of questions to know that thousands of home educating families have asked similar questions before them. They have found no answers that warrant forced school attendance between the ages of five and sixteen years. You are not over-protective, clingy, misguided, inadequately versed in child development issues or even plain stupid. It is perhaps the same survival instinct that stops you putting your hand into the flame, which makes you baulk at sending your little one off to start school, or continuing to send your older children when they are clearly unhappy there.

Luckily, I read about the home education option in a magazine. At first I was naïve and had an ignorant idea that home education must be for hippies, travellers, the very rich or maybe children unable to attend school because of severe special needs. I never imagined 'ordinary' people did it. After reading some of the home education support group publications, I went along to local meetings and slowly things changed. Home education was then 'in reserve' on my school choice list. Over two years it gradually moved into first place. I had many doubts along the way, all of which were fed enthusiastically by friends, relatives and strangers alike. My husband, who had enjoyed his own school years much more than I, and who worried about the academic aspect at first, was slower to be convinced. However, he was willing to give it a go and, after a year of observing the process in action, he too was convinced that, at least for the 'primary' years, this was the best choice.

We had listened to and worked through criticisms such as: 'Your child will be a social misfit; he'll never let go of you; he'll never learn to take the rough with the smooth; you'll make a rod for your own back; he'll never want to learn if you don't make him; he won't be able to work in a team; he'll have to go when he's older because you can't teach him everything he needs to know.'

Have confidence in the evidence that none of this is so. Check out a little research or meet with some home educating families, and it will be clear that most critics have not done either of these. Also have confidence in your child and in your own understanding of him because no one knows him as well as you.

I expect that many readers will have a child who, like my first, is quiet, thoughtful and slow to trust new people and new situations. Nursery or school seems like the last thing such children should be facing. However, the armchair experts out there assure us that we need to pack them off and ignore the tears if we don't want them to grow up hanging onto the apron strings.

'Go on Mrs Smotherlove, leave him with me, he'll be alright as soon as you've gone', the teacher says with a smile.

'Rubbish', says Mrs Why, 'You don't need to make him go. I have trusted my child to develop social skills at his own pace. Instead of being forced to "get used to it" and becoming resigned to the fact that he has to do this whether he likes it or not, he has grown over his ten years of life into a child who socialises well with males and females of all ages, with a confident maturity that appears to be rare in ten-year-olds. He is a very discerning judge of character and I trust his decisions, never forcing relationships or situations upon him that he resists. My trust in him, against the "expert" advice, has been more than proven and I know he will be a confident and sociable young man who will show people the same respect that he has been afforded. I have little doubt that had I forced him into school, he would have been either rebellious or withdrawn.'

I have not the least doubt that school developed in me nothing but what was evil and left the good untouched.

Edward Grieg

I see the process of trusting development in the way, for example, my children have been left to toilet train or move into their own bed when they chose to try these things themselves, rather than being pushed at a particular age. This is the cornerstone of my understanding of all aspects of their development, education included. When they are ready and showing an interest in something themselves, the learning process is simple, speedy and successful with no tears on their side or mine.

There were of course times when doubts popped up, and I regularly reassessed my decision. I occasionally attempted to get my son to join clubs that would widen his younger social circle but he declined. He was almost eight when he started to show more interest in joining in with group situations and I admit to feeling a certain relief when he did. Somehow, it is acceptable for a school-going child to be the quiet type who likes to spend time alone, but when a home-educated child is like that, people think it the result of isolation caused by home educating. Sadly, anything that the home-educated child does which society considers 'a bad thing' is blamed on their unusual education.

There are also those times when friends or relatives suddenly feel a need to convince me that, although it is quite clear that my child is happy out of school and doing academically and socially very well, he would more than likely be doing even better and be happier if he went to a good school. I waver. I listen to their reasons, to the description of the laboratories, the sports facilities, the school orchestra and the wonderfully enthusiastic teachers. I waver a little more. I go off quietly and think about it. I consider sending my son to school. I ask him if he would like to go. He wavers.

Then I start to put the whole picture together. There are also many negative aspects to school life, any of which could tip the balance alone, not least the likelihood that given a choice, most children would jump at the chance of not going to school. What does that say about their learning experience? However, I don't need to put that into the balance. I just look at the many wonderful things we've all learned together over the past years and the freedom my children have to learn in their own way, at their own pace, about whatever it is that they find interesting at the time. I watch them enjoying the great outdoors while school children are sitting at their desks; I witness them learning and mastering a principle of physics as they build a den, for example, and I see that formal instruction would have been so much more boring. I value the time we have together as a family, which would be swallowed up by schooling. When I remember these things, the school facilities suddenly hold no attraction and my wavering stops.

I used to worry occasionally that, given this freedom, children might not learn the basic skills they will find so necessary in life. My boys have shown me that the opposite is true. I believe that so long as they are not stopped from learning these things, they will want to make sense of the community in which they live. If that community is full of words and numbers, they will want to understand them in the same way they want to understand how to ride the tricycle in the garden or use the TV remote control. My children understand the same mathematical and literary concepts as their school-going counterparts despite having had no formal teaching and never having been made to labour over a page of sums or spellings. They have learned them and apply them during the course of their work and play, in situations relevant to their own lives. They are not super-kids; I am not super-woman; it is not difficult. It really is as simple as answering their 'Why's'. This involves making sure you have time to listen and to answer, and that they live in a stimulating environment where there is something about which to ask 'Why?'

Of course they sometimes ask questions to which I don't know the answer and I expect, as they get older, these will increase. This is one of the concerns that many would-be home educators and critics raise. I am not a qualified teacher of all (or any) subjects they may choose to study, how will I cope? I simply do the same for them as I do for myself. First, acknowledge that I do not understand, then show them how to go about finding an answer. Schools do not have a monopoly on knowledge. Chemistry teachers do not have a monopoly on chemistry. I ask friends and family, check out books at home, go to the library, check out the Internet, ask the local butcher/baker/candlestick-maker, find out what clubs, groups or societies have an interest, search out an 'expert' in any of these places.

I also think it is important to remember that choosing to home educate need not be a one-off, irreversible decision. It is something that can constantly be reassessed. If tomorrow I decide that my children's learning experience would be improved by school attendance, I still have that option. I have not amputated a limb.

My five-year-old has always been more outgoing. No one tells me that I should send him to school to mix with the other children. Outside opinion appears to be that he will not hang on to mummy's apron strings for too long. The uninvited panel of experts tells me it is because he is a second child. Who knows? Maybe it's his star sign, or what I ate when pregnant! He reinforced my growing understanding that there are so many reasons not to send your child to school, other than just the belief that this country expects it far too young. Both of the boys were learning so well, as most children do, way before school age. They were bright and enthusiastic to know everything. They asked 'Why?' from the moment they woke until the moment they fell asleep. They amazed me with the knowledge they absorbed from the world around them without a single formal lesson in anything.

I am awe-struck at the capacity for learning that young children have. I could not bear to interrupt that natural process by forcing some learning regime on them. I do not want my second son to have to timetable his sociability, to have to sit down and practise writing his name when he wants to dig a hole or hammer some nails. Once again, the 'panel' say, 'We all have to do things we do not want to do, he needs to get used to it or he will never hold a job down when he is older.' Many people in our society are spending far too much of their lives doing things they do not enjoy and they have been well trained to accept it. I hope for a better life for my boys. For some bizarre reason many people's thinking is that if it doesn't hurt, it isn't doing you any good. Why? I am sure that a good psychologist would tell me, but for now I trust my suspicion that it simply isn't true. Children are smart. They can learn to value their freedom without having it taken away from them, in the same way as I can appreciate my food without being starved. Children are so smart, in fact, that so long as you don't neglect them, I don't believe you have to 'teach' them much either. They 'teach' themselves.

> *When you make the finding yourself – even if you are the last person on Earth to see the light – you will never forget it.*
>
> Carl Sagan

What we actually do each day
When people first learn that we home educate, after asking about the social and legal aspects, they often want to know how we do it, what the children actually spend their days doing. The style of learning we follow is labelled 'autonomous'. This means that the children are in charge of their own learning and I am their guide, companion and chaperone. Their education consists almost entirely of honouring their need and wish to ask, 'Why?' about everything and anything they meet in life.

Most children quickly learn to regulate their verbal 'Why's, especially when they start school. They find out that they will be told what they need to learn and that there is little time for anything else. The system is such that children are fed a complete syllabus of the information they are required to absorb and will be periodically tested to see if they have absorbed it. Children soon learn that to ask why they have to do any of it is pointless. As the years go by it simply isn't cool to ask 'Why?' It just gets you labelled as a trouble-maker or shows the 'knowledge police' that there's something you don't know. Showing a flaw in your understanding of a topic earns reprimand or humiliation and children learn to avoid it by not bringing any lack of understanding to the teacher's attention. Tests and exams instil in young people the idea that to be 'OK' they have to know or recall 100% of the knowledge someone else expects them to know. For us, the opposite is true: asking 'Why?' is essential.

When I first planned to home educate, I thought I would need to be prepared with lots of books, materials and ideas for how I would cover the work my son would have done in school. I worried about how I would know what he should be learning. I invested in a few commercial SATs examples to reassure me, along with a dozen examples from a reading scheme. They are all gathering dust now.

Meanwhile, the student continued merrily with his 'Why's, and I continued to answer them. In the first five years of life, the questions children ask are not trivial. They are attempting to make sense of this incredible planet. 'Why is the sky blue? Where does the wind come from? Why are flowers all different shapes, sizes and colours?' In between the big questions are all the 'Why are you/they doing that, mummy?' questions that lead to discussions about every aspect of life. It has taken time and retrospect for me to realise that all I need to do in order to prepare my children for an adult life in which they will be valuable contributors to society, is to continue to accommodate their 'Why's.

It sounds so simple. It is so simple. On those days of doubt, I start to think that I only follow this path because I am too lazy to teach the boys properly and that a decent mother would be more concerned about the content of their syllabus. The school system makes it look so difficult, and so much emphasis is put on producing reams of paper, that I worry my boys must be neglected because they don't have books full of their work to prove that they have learned something. I have slowly learned that there are other ways of recognising progress and development which don't get charted and evaluated by a national yardstick. The real progress is so difficult to put into words and measurements. A school report says nothing of those intangible 'Einstein Moments' I love to witness.

Every day, my boys get up when they wake up, unless we have prearranged for me to wake them for some early outing. The time they rise is usually later than the local schoolchildren. I like this because it gives me an hour or two of free space for myself in the morning. This is an essential element of a home educating parent's day and I would suggest anyone embarking on this lifestyle considers carefully how they will find this time. I say 'lifestyle' because it is not a simple change of education plan, but a level of living together that most parents and children do not experience. From what I have observed, I think this takes some time to get used to for those whose children have been in school for a while. To give myself a little extra space, I have occasionally made arrangements to leave the boys with another family for a few hours while I do something alone, and then I reciprocate the favour.

Once up and breakfasted, the boys do whatever takes their fancy, unless we have an outing planned. Outings include social and educational visits with other home educating families, shopping, library visits and any of the other trips that a parent may make in the course of a day. If I have an appointment with the doctor, hairdresser or bank manager, they accompany me. If I have a tradesman calling to give me an estimate for work, they are part of the discussion and decisions. If I have to buy a new carpet or sell the old sofa, they take part in the process. Instead of going off to school to prepare for life in the adult world, they spend every day experiencing it first-hand.

I believe that school makes complete fools of our young men, because they see and hear nothing of ordinary life there.
                                                     Petronius: *Satyricon*

In some ways this makes them very worldly-wise and mature. However, it doesn't deprive them of their childhood. Instead of being made to sit at a desk, fill pages with writing which gets thrown away or finish their game when the whistle blows, they can jump on the bed until they are bored with it, play hide and seek at any moment they choose and read books about cars and aeroplanes, with a picnic in a tent in the garden.

I know other children do these things at weekends and in holidays, but I believe my fortune is in having realised that proper learning is taking place during these activities and they are not just valueless play. As an example, I recall the time my son had been reading every book he could get hold of on the topic of aeroplanes. He then spent days drawing his own designs for a plane, working out the number of seats he could fit into the space, how much petrol it was going to use to get to other countries and how much he would need to charge his passengers. He had chosen the time and setting for his own learning of design, economics, mathematics and much more. This setting may have bored another twenty-nine children in a class and they may have been unready for, or gone past, this level of understanding. His calculations, at age seven, were a little naïve, but he was happy with them and I was impressed with how much he learned and laboured over his work.

I consider one of the most important aspects of this process to be that he was the judge of his own work. He didn't do it because someone was waiting to see if he was capable of it, nor did he take it to anyone to see if it was good enough. He came to me with many questions, our discussions were stimulating and he enjoyed himself. He also stopped when *he* was ready.

It took me about four full years of home educating, before I relaxed enough to stop the occasional attempts to sit my children down with a page of 'schoolwork'. I am a slow learner. Every such attempt ends in boredom, argument, frustration on one side or the other, or absolutely no intended learning. I'm still not completely rid of the social pressure to check out now and then how the children compare academically to their schooled counterparts, but thankfully I have read enough research and theory, and practised enough quiet observation, to constantly increase my confidence in autonomous learning.

I have noticed that, so long as I don't interrupt the natural flow of 'Why's by suggesting contrived educational exercises, the boys will keep me busy providing one natural lesson after another. One tiny interest leads us on to so many things that we constantly have a list in the back of our minds of things we must find out or practise when we have time. I have learned not to be shy about asking friends, relatives and strangers if they can enlighten us about topics I don't understand myself. I have learned to speak up about the boys being home-educated, because most people are very interested and eager to share their skills and knowledge with enthusiastic children.

I have become used to announcing nonchalantly that my boys will be with me when I keep appointments and that I will be with them when they pursue their interests. My eldest, for example, at the age of nine, wanted to attend an early evening computer class where the children ranged up to fourteen years old. He didn't feel ready to attend alone, so I accompanied him, chatting quietly or reading with his young brother at the back of the room. Some people think we are odd for such things, but we feel that if odd means confident to stick out for what you really feel happy with, then we are more than happy to be odd.

I know that many people wonder how I can be confident that the boys are learning enough to be able to take GCSEs if they choose to, or that they can possibly learn a wide enough variety of topics from this laissez-faire approach. Once again, it is really retrospect which does the trick for me – and I know that doesn't help anyone just starting out. I have trusted the theory or trusted my gut feeling and, when I look back,

I can see that my trust is, so far, vindicated. The boys' dad, who used to think we would have to send them to secondary school, is now happy to carry on home educating too. He was again slower to reach that decision, and that is perhaps due to the fact that he is not as lucky as I am to spend so much time witnessing their growth.

It is a common understanding that mature students in colleges are more enthusiastic than those fresh from school. Perhaps this is because they have had more self direction in their timing and course of study. I believe that this is how it works for the home-educated child. We don't have to worry that they will not be able to reach their goals, because they are setting them themselves and are not being dumbed down. They *are* mature students.

Before I learned to trust the process, I used to keep a journal and write down what activities we had done each day. It may have said, 'Read in bed til 10am, discussed who writes books, why, how etc. Went to library. Boys looked up way home in street map – got lost. Mowed lawn. Discussed nettles and dock leaves. Friends called, played ball games. Boys made tea – discussed germs. Watched TV.' Sounds like a typical family day. On days when I worried that the Local Education Authority may ask what my children had learned this week, I would make a mental list of what 'subjects' we had actually covered. The above day would include: reading, comprehension, English, spelling, history, literature, geography, co-ordination skills, technology, plant biology, herbal medicine, PE, domestic science, microbiology and media. Looked at in these terms it seems a little tongue-in-cheek, but this is just because we are so used to thinking that learning involves sitting at a desk and absorbing information passed on by a professional teacher, that we don't always appreciate the value of the simple activities of life. It is usually in conversation about something else at some later date, that I become aware of the learning that has taken place during what to *me* had seemed a mundane activity.

This is not to say that the children only potter around doing house chores and learning what these offer. Their curiosity has led us to pursue some highly intellectual topics and some very off-beat projects. My ten-year-old is currently compiling a file of local and family history, involving visits to the Local History Library and the Family History Society, perusing old books and photographs and asking questions of people with good local knowledge. My five-year-old spends hours writing important messages on scraps of paper and 'posting' them all over the house, or being a waiter and taking our orders from the menu.

Some of the spellings he checks with me, some he makes up and some of the 'writing' is lines of 'scribble' which he can write quickly.

The newer and broader picture suggests that the child emerges into literacy by actively speaking, reading, and writing in the context of real life, not through filling out phonics worksheets or memorising words.

Thomas Armstrong

That reminds me to mention how important I have found letting the children be their own judge of what is interesting. Naturally, I want to introduce them to all kinds of topics and I have a personal bias towards some. It can feel quite disappointing when they turn their nose up at an outing I thought would be fun, or a book I thought they would love. A little persuasion has sometimes stimulated a new interest, but there is clearly a point when I have to let go. I have to ask myself who I am trying to satisfy: them, the critics or me?

There is no National Home Education Curriculum. Every child's home education is personal to that child and I believe the only way to find out what to do is to follow the child. This is what I have relaxed enough to do, and I look at my children, see how happy they are, what they have learned without a day of formal education, and then I ask my trusty question: 'Why?' Why would I do anything else?

We are now top of the European league table in at least one respect: our children are subjected to more national school exams than those in any other country... Parents may comfort themselves with the thought that, however badly educated their children may be when they leave school, they will at least be able to do exams.

The Independent: Editorial Comment 7/1/2000

I have not done a full survey or review of education systems around the world, so that the views I express are based on personal experience. I would say that all education systems I've had contact with are a disgrace and a disaster.

Edward de Bono

FAQ no.2   Don't you need a lot of money?

If you bear in mind that home education almost inevitably reduces a family's earning power, the answer has got to be: 'No'. A great many home educators are on low incomes or state benefits and gathering resources is largely a matter of ingenuity, know-how and, sometimes, luck. Here are a few suggestions which have been road-tested and recommended by other home educators; no doubt you will discover plenty more.

Resist the urge to buy stacks of books and equipment (or to feel guilty if you can't)

+ Wait to see what you need – only buy what is necessary now
+ Can you get it secondhand?
+ Borrow it?
+ Share the cost with other home educators?
+ Bear in mind that stationery may be cheaper from an office supplier

Get to know your local library system – what do they offer home educators?

+ Can you get extra tickets? Project loans?
+ How does their book-ordering service work?
+ How often do they sell off their old stock?
+ Can you borrow tapes, music, videos, software?
+ Do they offer Internet access? Tuition in using the Internet?
+ Does their information desk have a list of local activities?

If there are some reference sources which you prefer to have at home:

+ Look at introductory offers for book clubs, especially if there is no commitment to buying more books: there are often excellent bargains. At the time of writing, one book club could let you have a good atlas, dictionary, thesaurus and biography dictionary for a total of £5.

+ Try library sales or remainder tables in bookshops. These are also good places to pick up quirky books on subjects you might never have considered: African Hunting Dogs? A Field Guide to Toadstools? Castles of Wales? You never know what will catch your child's imagination or spark off a new passion.

✦ If you have a computer, keep an eye out for CD-Roms on the front of PC magazines. It is possible to find good software for the cover price of the magazine. For example, one magazine costing under £3 recently offered over a dozen different Oxford Dictionaries and reference sources on CD-Rom.

✦ If you also have Internet access, go surfing for free games and software, and to find good search engines for use as an alternative encyclopaedia.

Is there a scrap-store nearby?

✦ These are places where schools, playgroups and, often, home educators can get all kinds of free materials, donated by local businesses from their surplus stock. There is usually an annual membership charge: does your local home educators' group have membership?

Cast a creative eye over your own (and others'!) household rubbish

NB. Check before you remove anything from skips/beside dustbins – who needs a criminal conviction for theft?

For example:
✦ Keep the card from cereal packets
✦ Elastic bands the postman dropped, paperclips, treasury tags etc
✦ Old wrapping paper (decoupage?)
✦ Chunks of polystyrene (make great printing blocks)
✦ Leftover emulsion paint (to prime the models made out of the cereal packets)
✦ If your iron/toaster/washing machine is certified dead, would it be fun to take it apart?

Trawl charity shops, car-boot or jumble sales and junk shops regularly

✦ Apart from being a good source of cheap books, once in a while there are some real finds.

Join your local LETS scheme

✦ Short for **Local Exchange Trading Scheme**. This is a register of people willing to swap skills: 'You lay my carpet, I teach you guitar'.

Make the most of your TV and radio

✦ **BBC** and **Channel 4** will let you have a free guide to schools broadcasts.

✦ Check out the TV and radio listings for plays, poetry, documentaries and general interest/current affairs programmes, plus music of every kind.

✦ **English Heritage** allows home educators to borrow videos under their free 'teachers' loan' scheme.

Consider getting an allotment

✦ For cheap vegetables, with plant sciences and PE thrown in.

Let's get out of here...

✦ If you join a home education support organisation, the membership card will entitle you to free or concessionary admission to many galleries, museums and places of interest. Alternatively, the **National Arts Collection Fund** card offers similar benefits.

✦ I probably don't need to sing the praises of the various types of rail/bus saver cards, but keep an eye out for new, improved deals.

What is on offer to schools in your area?

✦ Can you get low-cost tickets for performances by touring ballet, opera or theatre companies?

✦ If you live near a large city, find out whether resident orchestras or theatre companies have an education department. There may be special free or cheap performances/workshops at which home educators are welcome.

✦ During British Film Week, and for occasional previews, **Film Education** offers free cinema tickets to schools and home educators.

Wherever you want to go, always ask if there are concessions available for home educators. Even if the answer is 'no' today, it draws attention to the existence of home education and makes it more likely that the answer will be 'yes' next time around.

Lessons from the leg-break fairy

Terri Dowty

When we took the plunge into home education three years ago, I had no idea what to expect. My experience of education was limited to schooling, so it had never occurred to me that they are not the same thing. I assumed that home education would involve creating a more sophisticated version of 'playing schools' and that I would spend my evenings predigesting knowledge for regurgitation the following day. I never anticipated the changes which lay ahead. Not just the obvious, practical effects on our everyday life, but the awakening of my own curiosity, the strengthening of my political beliefs, the shifts in all our relationships and in the way Ian and I each view the world: home education has been an eye-opener for us, too.

We had started out along a conventional route: Biggs, our older son, went to school because we knew that is what children do. We also accepted, albeit doubtfully, the prevalent belief that children must separate from their parents in order to be 'socialised' – rather as wild animals need to be domesticated – and, like any educational target, the earlier the achievement the better.

I often wonder now if there is any connection between society's apparent queasiness around attachment, and the alienated, damaged culture in which we live. Is it healthy for small children to be removed from their community of family and friends for most of their waking hours? Does the man-made environment of school, where a peer group is merely a large crowd of those who share the same birth year, honestly provide a better alternative? Is it right for our children to learn social rules from the most domineering, aided and abetted by a rampant consumer industry? Can a sense of morality and purpose be nourished through a school curriculum? Do these concepts even have any meaning if they are divorced from participation in real, diverse community?

By the time Ollie, our younger son, reached five, we had begun to ask many such questions. We had also met several ordinary, concerned parents whose resounding 'No' to those same questions had led them to home educate. Biggs was now eight, and our uneasiness was fuelled by his restless boredom at school, combined with a growing conviction that it was not the right place for either of our children. Our decision to home educate was inevitable, although tentative enough for us to limit it to an initial trial of one year.

The decision made, we felt as if we were waking on the morning after the revolution: what next? I had no clear idea of how to set about educating the boys and was only too aware that the responsibility was largely mine because Ian was now the main breadwinner. I panicked, floundered, bought text books and made ambitious curriculum plans. Sometimes I would go cold with fear, convinced I was caught up in an aberration, if not barking mad. What had possessed me to agree to this? I silenced my anxieties by redoubling my time-tabling efforts and buying still more books.

As I was preparing to 'start the school year', fate, clearly irritated by my headless-chicken antics, took a hand in events. I had a serious fall. Following an operation to rejoin the wayward bits of my right leg, I was sent home to lie in bed for a few weeks with my plaster-encased leg sticking up like Everest on a pile of pillows. Those acquaintances who had disapproved of our decision to home educate were quick to move in with grim predictions of our inability to cope and suggestions that school was now the only option. Mercifully our friends disagreed. Seeing Ian's heroic juggling act, they arrived to whisk the boys off for games of football and trips to the Science Museum. We emptied out our savings to pay for a part-time helper who took the boys to swimming pools, galleries and workshops. When they were at home we read stories, played games and talked for hours at a time. My timetable plans were out of the window and, had I not been dazed with painkillers, I probably would have panicked.

By Christmas I was able to hobble around the house on crutches and my head was at last clear enough to survey the aftermath of the past three months. The boys' faith in my indestructibility had taken a battering and this was reflected in their sometimes unpredictable behaviour, but they had also grown in confidence by contributing vital skills to our family. My relationship with them had altered from one of benevolent authority on my part to a respectful companionship. I was humbled by the devoted care and friendship which they had given to me, and astonished by their competence. The house resembled a bear-pit and I could not have found all those text books if I had tried – but I was not trying. What struck me most forcibly was that, despite the chaos, the boys were learning. The evidence was all around me in the shape of open books on every subject imaginable which had been raided from our shelves, their beautifully produced newsletter, drawings, sculptures, models, the pile of music on the piano and, above all, in their lively and informed conversation. They were bursting with knowledge and curiosity. Suddenly my curriculum plans seemed rather foolish: the boys were up and running, and I was the one with a lot to learn.

As far as I could see, the only thing remotely like 'teaching' which I had offered was in maths, and even that had been very low-key. It was largely a matter of showing Biggs how to calculate angles and circles for his model-making, helping Ollie to tell the time and doing puzzles with them. Any kind of 'age-appropriate' book was a complete waste of time. The boys did not need to weigh and measure imaginary ingredients or add up pictures of coins because they were actually doing all these things in the course of cooking and shopping. Their excellent mental arithmetic had developed quite incidentally, courtesy of a snakes and ladders board, some dice and a pack of cards. There was no point in coaxing Ollie to separate little coloured shapes into piles when he could single-handedly stack the week's shopping in exactly the right places in the cupboard or sort a load of washing and put it in the machine at the correct temperature. The text books seemed rather a pale substitute for everyday life.

Education is an admirable thing, but nothing that is worth knowing can be taught.

Oscar Wilde

Biggs was reading voraciously, as he does now. He developed a habit which I have since copied, of keeping several books on the go at once: one to suit every mood. Today a glance in his room tells me that he is currently reading *Moonfleet*, a book about the Stone Age, *Chemical Chaos*, a biography of Marcos and *The Diary of a Nobody*. Realising that reading must be a good thing, Ollie began testing the water, although it was to be the *Tintin* books a year later which painlessly transformed him into a fluent reader.

Trips out obviously sparked the boys' curiosity, and my role was to listen as they described what they had done, to throw in snippets of information and to answer their questions. If I did not know an answer, I would ask them to fetch a dictionary, book or atlas and then show them how to find the information they wanted. Biggs quickly reached the point of doing this for himself and will now automatically look in the Biography Dictionary if he hears an interesting name or the UN Reports if a country's economic or health statistics are mentioned. Again, Ollie has picked up the idea. This morning he staggered into bed with me, toting a large atlas so that I could show him the Great Wall of China. For us, easy access to reference books and the Internet, either at home or in the library, has proved vital.

Conversation is a very important ingredient. During the hours when they had been curled up on my bed, we had talked about castles, Antarctica, poetry, babies, volcanoes, windmills and everything else under, and including, the sun. We had discussed imponderables and constructed theories, answered each other's questions, told stories and laced it all with knock-knock jokes and limericks. I had not taken the lead in these discussions, I had simply enjoyed the tangential ramble. Nevertheless they had learned and remembered an enormous amount.

The authority of those who teach is often an obstacle to those who want to learn.

Cicero

I am convinced that they retain so much knowledge because it is gained in an order which makes unique sense to them. When information is not divided arbitrarily into subjects, they can steer along their own path, relating one piece of information to another in a perfectly logical sequence. It would be a mistake to think that a child's learning is unstructured if an adult is not imposing the structure. Let me give an example of what I mean. Recently, Biggs asked me what 'nom de plume' meant. After I had explained, we thought of a few examples and considered the different reasons why an author might use one. Ollie asked if William Shakespeare was a nom de plume, so Biggs checked in the dictionary and read out a few biographical details. This prompted a question about Stratford-upon-Avon which needed the map book. We traced the Avon to Gloucestershire and reminisced about visiting my parents who had lived near Newent when the boys were small. Having found Newent on the map, Biggs noticed the source of the Thames and we followed it back to London. Ollie pointed out the bridges which we cross regularly, relating them to nearby buildings. We wandered past the Houses of Parliament, pondering on democracy and elections, and on to St James's Park with its pelicans and memories of a friend whose guide-dog had decided to take a dip in the lake. We talked about blindness, my Grandfather and the Somme. We paused for Biggs to read out a couple of Wilfred Owen poems, remembered the D-Day beaches we had visited on holiday and the glow-worms we had seen in a Normandy garden. Eventually we found a satisfactory place to stop for lunch. These mental meanderings can last for hours with each new idea prompting more opinions and questions. What do MPs do? I'd vote Monster Raving Loony. Why do pelicans have such baggy beaks? How do they train guide dogs? What is shrapnel? Why did they land in Normandy? I bet the Germans could see them for miles. Do glow-worms glow all day as well? Maybe you only notice it at night.

If you think this sounds exhausting, you are right! This way of doing things can feel exhilarating and seamless, but it is rarely effortless. Even when they are busy with an activity which does not need my direct input, I am on call to unscramble Sellotape or rummage in the hedge for a lost ball. Because we work with the ebb and flow of the boys' energies there is no bell to signal the end of the day, nor is there any demarcation between 'work' and 'play'. Education never starts or stops, it is simply a part of life. Often, the boys want to take advantage of Ian's presence in the evening for help with woodwork or a tricky computer programme. Perhaps they want to talk about Madagascar, build a periscope or go outside to look at the stars. We frequently go to plays and concerts with them, something which would be impossible if we had to follow a routine of bedtimes and early rising. If I am to keep my energies at a level where I can meet the boys' needs, it is important that I also make room for my own, either by going out for the evening or letting Biggs and Ollie know that I want some undisturbed time to follow my own hobbies and projects.

It is easy to become too busy, particularly in our social lives and outside activities. The boys belong to several clubs and sports teams, they are keen musicians and spend the whole of Saturday at music college, they visit friends or have them to stay, we go on day trips, to talks, workshops and the regular meetings of our local home educators' group. If we are not careful, we run out of space for another essential ingredient: time to do 'nothing much'. Solitude and the opportunity for private thought are also important if Biggs and Ollie are not to swell the ranks of adults incapable of passing unstructured time in their own company. The boys both benefit from periods of apparent inactivity to flex their imaginations, to play fantasy games together or separately, and to give attention to their inner voices. Sometimes they need simply to recharge their energy or resolve a problem, at other times their silent abstraction precedes a noticeable step forward in their understanding or precipitates searching questions about human nature, eternity and what life might be about. Their capacity for creative thought can stretch me to the limits of my own abilities, challenging me to look deeper, question further, think harder.

> *It appears, therefore, that some development of the capacity to be alone is necessary if the brain is to function at its best, and if the individual is to fulfil his highest potential. Human beings easily become alienated from their own deepest needs and feelings. Learning, thinking, innovation and maintaining contact with one's own inner world are all facilitated by solitude.*
> Anthony Storr: *Solitude*

Ian and I owe our own revived enthusiasm for life to Biggs and Ollie. Without their encouragement I might never have started learning the double bass, raising butterflies or making soap, let alone going to concerts of Vietnamese Chant, Cuban Jazz or Sitar recitals. It is their example which has taken me to the 'new non-fiction' shelves of the bookshop and made me bring home books about William Morris, Tibet and global economics. Thanks to them I am willing to try anything, and if I hesitate they urge me on: 'Go on, Mum, give it a go!'

I don't know where the boys got their anarchic idea that you can cheerfully reach out on the hoof to grab life, gobbling knowledge down without first chewing it to a tasteless pulp. They certainly did not get it from any school, but then neither did we, their parents: two well-trained, pruned and pollarded products of an academic education. With any luck, Biggs and Ollie will never discover just how easily the sources of their spontaneous pleasure can shrivel up into the dusty, grey stones of work and duty.

It is our privilege to watch our sons growing into likeable, thoughtful and confident young men: our only hope is that we never fail in our task of nurturing their joyful exploration of the world in a way that ensures it will last a lifetime.

As things stand, many children – and many adults too – see education and school as inseparable with the consequence that, when they leave school, they want to put it all behind them. We should see education as being life-long, as going on all the time, and not something we can turn our backs on gratefully when we leave the school gates for the last time.

Jean Bendell: *School's Out*

An orchestra requires men with different talents and, within limits, different tastes; if all men insisted upon playing the trombone, orchestral music would be impossible. Social co-operation, in like manner, requires differences of taste and aptitude, which are less likely to exist if all children are exposed to the same influences than if parental differences are allowed to affect them.

Bertrand Russell

Emma (aged 9)

My name is Emma and I've been home-educated for around four years. I used to go to school but I left when I was 5. I think home education is much more fun than school, I get to go to lots more exciting days out that I should only rarely get at the weekend while I was at school. I get ill a lot less now, and I get to see my little sister Molly and my Mum and Dad much more. I am much more happy now and I think I have more friends! I have more fun working at home and I play with Molly a lot more.

At school the work was too easy and I had baby books, even though I could read very well. Because the work was easy the teacher sent me to do project work in the library. I always got lost. So I'm really glad I've come out of school.

In Education Otherwise, we go to lots of outings, like going to Oxborough Hall and Amazonia which is a place where you can feel snakes and lizards. Once we went and got dressed up to go in a thing called Y.N.T.T. We were dressed up as Victorians and we did lots of interesting things like a Victorian dance. Also every month we go to

Frettenham Village Hall to have a meeting and all the children get to play and have a nice time. Sometimes we have special events at Frettenham, like a storyteller who came and as well as telling stories, he made masks with us and pictures with bits that moved.

Jeanna (aged 13)

I have been home-educated for my whole life. When I tell my friends that, they usually come out with things like; 'Oh, cool!' and ask me all about it, what it's like not having to go to school and: 'What do you do all day?' Most adults, on the other hand, when you say you don't go to school, will probably say 'What about your social life?' Most of my friends envy me because I don't have to get up at 6:30am every morning to get to school on time.

I love homeschooling. I think I would describe it as having the freedom to learn what you want, when you want to. It doesn't matter if you can't read when you are nine, or don't do your GCSEs at 16, or at all. You can just pick a topic that you are interested in and start learning about it. I know that most of my friends know a lot more history than I do, but I will learn it in my own time, even if it is three years later.

A lot of people who find out that you are home-educated will say stuff like, 'Oh, school is brilliant, you really don't know what you're missing', and then go on to complain about it. Actually I do know what I'm missing, but a lot of it is peer pressure or bullying. There was one girl I met who actually thought I didn't know anything and picked up a pencil, showed it to me and asked me if I knew what it was.

We have moved quite a lot – mainly because of my dad's job – from America to Australia and now in England. It has given me a chance to learn a lot about where I have lived, and taught me about different cultures. I sometimes find that if one country that I've lived in bad-mouths another, I get quite defensive because I feel like an international student. I have lived in almost as many houses as years I have lived. I think that if I had been in school, moving would have been a lot more disruptive for me. Moving around has created some natural geography and maths lessons for me. As a result, I have many friends to write to.

When people ask me if I would want to go to school, most of the time I reply, 'No, I don't think so, I'm quite happy learning at home.' Right now, I am content doing what I am doing, learning at my own pace. My parents help me out, and I know it was their idea to homeschool me in the first place, but if I had the choice in the beginning I wouldn't have done anything differently.

Learning at home gives me the chance to learn from people I want to learn from and helps me to respect people for who they are. So many of my friends who go to school have little respect for their teachers and adults in general. Because I have always had the freedom to choose what I learn, I see learning as something positive and maintain my interest in learning.

A natural style of learning works best for me. I feel supported by my parents and have the resources to learn what I need and want to. I'm glad I don't have to learn in a structured 6-hour-day style, like some of my friends (at school or not). I like learning with as little structure as I choose. Being self-directed also helps me learn what I am interested in and means I will probably retain what I have learned.

I am a happy home-educated person and I think that being home-educated will help me to be more confident and independent in the future.

EDUCATING ARCHIE
What is structure? Mrs G ponders....

Working it out

Jackie Mason

When I started out to write this article, I hoped that either I would be able to give it a unifying theme, or at least a structure. I think it was the memory of school and university essays coming back to me: here is your topic, now say what you are going to say (introductory paragraph), then say it (more paragraphs, one point clearly made in each), then say what you have said (final paragraph). I found instead that the topic (well, at least I have a topic if not a theme) resisted this treatment. Or maybe I resisted. Perhaps that is the underlying theme after all. I'll leave you to decide.

To start with, a story. The other weekend I went to a reunion, held at my old school, of pupils who had left the school some twenty-five years previously. Most of us had not seen each other throughout that time. There was instant recognition of faces and remembering of names in most cases, a perturbing blankness in a few others (how could we have spent seven years at the same place and have absolutely no recall of each other?) The noise level was incredible – everyone had so much to say to everybody else. Once we had got past the old school hymn (in case you're interested in these things, the first verse went 'These things shall be, a loftier race, Than e'er the world hath known, shall rise, With flames of freedom in their souls, And light of knowledge in their eyes' followed by many more verses in a similar vein), we settled down to the serious business of catching up. Or rather, getting to know each other. For me, the pleasure of the reunion was tinged with a sadness that here were so many people with whom I had spent so much time, and with whom I was having such great discussions now, but also with whom I had barely exchanged a word throughout those seven long years.

And why was that? Well, firstly there was the girl/boy divide, which seemed to have persisted pretty much throughout those years. Then there was the gang/clique (aka group of friends) culture which cut the number of contacts down still further. In terms of social education it left, in my book anyway, a lot to be desired.

I guess this sort of brings me back round to my starting point – or rather our family's starting point, as far as home education is concerned (family being myself, and my daughter aged 10. And the two cats). It was for social reasons that I withdrew my daughter from her nursery at the age of three. She 'failed' to settle in. Thanks to reading John Holt's books *(How Children Fail, How Children Learn* and many others) I eventually learned how to decode that word. I decided to keep her out of nursery, and then out of school, because I did not feel that emotionally her needs would be met by going to these places. Home education was for us, as it is for many families, a pragmatic rather than an ideological decision, born out of a feeling that there has to be a better way.

Now that I have mentioned ideology, a word of warning to families setting out on the home education route. The risks of succumbing to a totalitarian viewpoint exist in the home-educating world just as much as in the schooling world: 'Home education is a universally good thing!' 'School education is a universally good thing!' I have read many books and articles on home education over the last seven years which have given me much food for thought, but which have also, I have to say, tempted me from time to time to seek safety in dogmatic thinking: 'If we do or think this, we will be OK'. I then have to remind myself that it was gut judgement which forced the decision all those years ago, and it continues to be gut judgement which influences our decision now about whether to continue to home educate or not, depending on our current circumstances.

I have just thought that I am writing here about a child's emotional needs, assuming that everyone will understand or agree with me about what this means. Perhaps I need to say that for me this means that a child will be cared for, be valued, be respected, be encouraged, be challenged. I am still not convinced that this happens for most children in schools. Actually, that is inaccurate. I actually don't believe this happens for the majority. How can I know this? My experience tells me. Not only my own from all those years ago (yes, things may well have changed in twenty-five years!) but also my daughter's current experience. The majority of children we know go, or have in the past gone, to school. We only have to listen to them, see how they behave (and when did the word 'behaviour' start to take on its negative connotation?) and see the consequences of lack of care and respect. What are these consequences? Well, they include mistrust and even hostility towards adults, the defensive tactic of banding in cliques which I experienced as a child, a lack of self-esteem and no confidence in their own judgement.

> *We shall never learn to feel and respect our real calling and destiny, unless we have learned to consider everything as moonshine, compared with the education of the heart.*
>
> Scott

So if that is the problem, what is the answer? Well, for us, the short-term answer lay in doing it ourselves. I believed that my daughter needed to feel emotionally secure in order to be able to enjoy learning from the experiences around her; I think the years since that time have justified the decision taken then. I was just about to write that I think she is now better placed at the age of ten to return to the formal learning environment of school, when I realised the inaccuracy of that statement because she has had formal learning experiences during her time out of school: in music classes, for example. What I mean is that I think she is a strong enough person now to go to school, if she chooses, to benefit from what is on offer there and to withstand the worst of the pressures. This may be tested out as she is considering going to secondary school next year.

What has home education and our contact with other home educators given us over the years? Well, the encouragement to try new things, for example. Whilst my daughter has taken up horse riding and French horn, I have taken up the violin and Flamenco dancing, to name but a couple of things. The opportunity to learn from each other: I have learnt so much from being with my daughter over the years, both in terms of 'knowledge', because her interests don't always overlap with mine, and in terms of personal insight. Flexibility: if something is not working, it is time to change tack or shift gear or whatever. Effectiveness (if that is the right word): if this is what I want to learn or achieve, what is the best way, given our resources and what is available out there?

At this point I can hear faint voices saying: 'That is all well and good, but we're sitting here trying to decide if we want to home educate our child, or children, and we need to know what it is that you actually do!' Or: 'I'm on my own, have little support or money and I don't know if I can do this'. To the first I would say that there are plenty of stories of what different families do, out there in the home education newsletters; I have always found the USA newsletter, 'Growing Without Schooling', a major source of inspiration and ideas. Make contact with as many home educating families as you can and see how they go about it. To the second I would say: 'Yes, me too!' Or at least, I would have done back in those early days; I have more support now, if not more money. Perhaps it would be useful to other single parents if I did say a bit about some of the issues which home education has raised for us because I think it does feel different, doing it on your own.

One main issue is money: how do you afford to home educate when you live on a low income? Everyone's personal circumstances and priorities are different. For us it means using our bicycles, or legs, as much as necessary and public transport if we have to. Borrowing books (project loans from the library are useful) rather than buying. Working holidays in youth hostels and on organic farms, or camping trips. Reducing the space we live in and taking in lodgers. Being members of our local LETS (Local Exchange Trading Scheme). Growing food on our allotment. These changes have all taken place since we began to home educate and there have been benefits and things to be learned from each. I don't want to belittle how hard it can be when there is something you want, or your child wants to do, and there is no money to fund it. It is a situation we are currently facing ourselves, and we haven't stopped brainstorming ways of raising funds, nor of cutting back on the cost of what it is we want to do, so I think something will come out of it for us anyway.

Another issue is work: how do you combine work and home education, particularly when there is no partner to help look after the children? I have always felt the need to work, to have some outlet outside the home, to be with other adults, to be doing work I value which is not only about caring for children, whether my own or those of other people. To meet this need, I have worked part-time, either taking my daughter with me to the creches which were part of my work (running effective parenting-skills groups) or, where I could not do this, relying on the support of relatives, friends and neighbours, swapping childcare whenever I could. When I have not been able to do paid work, I have volunteered for organisations sympathetic to the idea of my bringing my daughter with me and involving her as far as possible in the work I was doing. Again, there have been benefits for her as well as for me; she has a better understanding of what certain jobs involve, and has met a wide range of adults in the process.

And what about social life, time for me? Well, the same child-swaps allow me to go out and follow my interests on a regular basis; I also try to make sure I have the odd day or days to myself, as I need that space to recharge my batteries. As my daughter gets older and does more things independently, it's becoming easier to do this.

I have chosen to focus in this article (now there is a bit of summing up, if ever I heard it!) on the things which are closest to my heart when I think about home education. I hope it encourages you, if you are a parent, to think about what you and your children want out of life; and whether school is the best way to achieve that, or whether, like us, you might find another path more congenial.

We live in a hierarchical world in which we defend ourselves ... from our eternal infancy and childhood by insisting on a graded, necessary elevation through learning and technological sophistication out of the child into the adult. This is not a true initiation that values both the previous form of existence and the newly attained one; it is a defence against the humiliating reality of the child.
Thomas Moore: *Care of the Soul*

FAQ no.3   Don't you have to be a teacher?

If you mean: 'Do you need to be a qualified school-teacher in order to home educate?' the answer is, 'No'. Sometimes people are surprised by this, but consider for a moment what a teacher's job entails.

Teaching in a school involves getting information over to thirty people, often comparative strangers, simultaneously. Although roughly the same age, they will have very different needs and learning styles; some will not even want the information at all and are consequently bored and restless, others need to ask a lot of questions in order to understand. As a teacher, you are aware that a certain amount must be done before the bell goes. Classroom teaching undoubtedly demands a high level of particular skills, but they are skills which are largely irrelevant and unnecessary in home education.

Another way of answering the question is to say: 'You already are your child's teacher.' Consider the things your child knew, the skills she already possessed before 'education' was a consideration. How did she learn so much? Because she wanted to and you were there to answer questions, offer help and share her pleasure. This is at the heart of home education; you are simply continuing the journey of discovery together. Knowledge is out there waiting to be found, whether in books, computers, on TV, in museums, theatres and workshops, or from friends and family who have particular skills or experience to share.

If a time comes when all of these potential sources are no longer enough, there are colleges, correspondence courses and tutors. Your child will be well-placed to benefit from these because she has already gained another vital skill from you – by learning alongside you, she will have learned *how* to learn.

Actually, I do have a social life

Ann (aged 16)

Here's a piece (complete with spelling error) I wrote for a magazine eight and a half years ago:

I would like to introduce my-self, I do not go to school and will be telling you about EO. My name is Ann and I feel strongly about those of you who don't know about the legal side of HOME EDUCATION.

THE LAW
The law says that you MUST have education either in school or otherwise. We/I are the otherwise part.

WHAT WE/I DO AT WORKSHOPS.
We have lots of fun at workshops.
Once we did a History chain/line. When we got into groups and had a BIG list of very famous dates and four groups who chose a date and acted it out. There were a lot of other times we did splendid things. Like the time we had a circus day. We tried things that are in a BIG CIRCUS, like plate spinning and Tightrope walking. (Note to Animal lovers, There were NO ANIMALS involved.)

As you can see there is a lot of fun for everyone, so please start home educating your child. (if you have one.) There is so much fun from these and other events, that we just need more peple to do it and help with their skills. Please join us soon.

Your sincerely
Ann (age 7 and a half.)

I suppose I remain as evangelistic about home education (HE) today as I did then, and am still a fervent supporter of animal rights! EO (which is an interchangeable term with HE as well as standing for Education Otherwise, a national support group for home educators) is such a good way of learning, and of life, that it is a shame some people miss out on even considering it as an option simply because they don't know it is possible.

I have been home-educated all of my life. Originally my sister and I were only going to be at home until we were seven. Nine years later...

I always knew that I was not going to go to school, and was perfectly happy and accepting of that decision. Before the age of five, my younger sister and I had attended playgroup one morning a week, as well as doing activities such as pre-school music, gym club, library story time, seeing friends, going out to play, NCT swimming group, shopping with our parents, and we have built from there ever since. Home education in our case is, in a nutshell, learning from life.

For the first few years, our family followed a very vague plan of what we were going to do and when. A 'typical' (I use the word very loosely: in reality it should *never* be connected with *anything* to do with home education!) week would have included maths, doing something 'Englishy' (e.g. writing a letter to a pen-pal) and guitar practice twice a week, a space for something different twice a week and a weekly morning for French. We also watched numerous schools' TV programmes (actually, I can remember learning how to spell the word 'school' by copying it down whilst it was being displayed on a Channel 4 test card). I used to write stories and poems, and my sister did a lot of drawing. We had a computer and became computer literate from a very young age. I learnt about capitals using a computer (the keyboard shows capital letters, but what you get when you depress 'A' is the lower-case 'a'). We used programs such as PC Playtime (in its numerous incarnations) and Brown Bag Outline (an early word-processing facility) – all for fun, but that is when you learn the most. We also enjoyed a regular dose of 'Australasian/Antipodean Culture Studies' (aka 'Home and Away' in the afternoons). Every other week there was an EO workshop ('workshop' is the term used locally when groups of EO families get together to share an activity) as well as regular visits to local museums for talks on various periods of history, the latest art exhibition, object handling sessions and so on.

In recent years, our approach has become much more autonomous. Whereas in the past we worked from books and Mum checked the answers or coerced us, now we are older we look after ourselves. We don't work from books in the way we used to. As we got older, Mum thought that we had reached a basic level of understanding and if we wanted to take that further, it was down to us.

When I was twelve, I decided that I wanted to work for my first GCSE. I worked via a correspondence course over an eight month period, and took the exam when I was thirteen. Since then I have done three more GCSEs, and hope to add on several more, plus my first 'A' level this year. People often ask about exam arrangements. Of course, there is no legal requirement to do exams (I know several people who didn't take them on principle, and have done extremely well for themselves) but if you do want to, it is relatively easy to do so from home. The advantage of home education is that you can spread exams out and take a subject when you are ready, which does ease the pressure somewhat, as well as allowing you to go into the subject quite deeply. Options for exam arrangements include: doing them via correspondence, where you receive a pack to work through and send assignments to a tutor who marks them and sends them back with comments; enrolling in an Adult Education or evening class, if you live in an area which allows under-16s to do so; or simply finding out the information you need on your own and getting a syllabus. So far I have used or am using *all* of the above methods! One advantage of correspondence over 'own knowledge' is that course-work arrangements are sorted out, as well as a centre to sit the paper (the only bit you can't do at home!) and on a good course several marked practice papers should be included. Taking the actual exam (after a few trial runs so you can get the hang of 'playing the game') is not usually a problem for HE children – it is usually the silly things like how to fill in the front that nobody explains, though the invigilators are usually extremely helpful.

One of the problems with exams is that home educators tend not to split experiences into subjects as schools do. We don't tend to 'label' activities as History, Art, Science, Mathematics, English. (We would actually call all the above activities done at once 'going to the museum', but there you go...). On the other hand, school friends of mine don't tend to make connections between these 'subjects' and the real world either – I have lost count of the times I have been standing next to a trampoline and someone has asked me, 'So what do you do about PE?'

*English is not history and history is not science and science is not
art and art is not music, and art and music are minor subjects and
English, history and science major subjects, and a subject is something
you 'take' and when you have taken it, you have 'had' it, and if you
have 'had' it, you are immune and need not take it again. (The
Vaccination Theory of Education?)*
    Postman & Weingartner: *Teaching as a Subversive Activity*

Apart from my EO friends, I have lots of friends (of all ages) who go to
school. This seems to be the opposite of what people imagine – the one
question I am asked *without fail* is a variation on: 'What about your
social life?' The fact is that I sometimes get so busy, I hardly have time
to breathe.

I have been involved in various different groups and activities all of
my life, and tend to make most of my friends through them. Some of
the things I did when I was younger included belonging to Red Cross,
Woodcraft Folk, Circle Dancing, Brownies (and later Guides), music,
swimming, and a singing and drama group. At the moment I do a
German class, trampolining, Rangers, maths class, dancing, sign
language class, help with the local Talking Newspaper, guitar and
lifesaving during the course of a week. I am a member of a local
community theatre group, and occasionally volunteer at a project
aiming to set up a television station for Deaf people. I also babysit for
a few families. I worked in a nursing home for a year and, up until last
term, my sister and I worked as volunteers for four years at the same
playgroup which we used to attend! Those are just the regular activities,
never mind the EO trips and outings, meetings concerned with the
Talking Newspaper, rehearsals for plays, gang shows or dance shows,
shopping with friends, and other special events.

Mum wrote this poem about our schedule in 1994 for one of the
'newspapers' our group produced as an EO workshop:

Now another year has passed
Each one more busy than the last.
Numbers; writing; guitar too
There is always so much to do.
Shopping; cleaning; bake a cake;
For gymnastics, we must not be late.
Museum; UEA; EO workshop
And back for dancing, we can't stop!

Brownies; swimming; trampoline; chess;
(Shame the house is such a mess.)
I've Rainbow Guides; Heritage Society;
Will someone get the tea for me?
Tomorrow's 'Watch', can't find a boot?
We'll search after Family Reading Group.
Granny's; singing; ringing; when...
Will we all be at home again?
Do tell me – I may be a fool –
But how do most folks fit in school?

It is precisely because we *don't* go to school that we have such a bustling life – we don't have to deal with the mountains of homework that infringe on the social lives of so many of our school-going friends. The other thing that puzzles me is *why* people assume that going to school is the only way you learn how to interact with others – not only is it such a false environment anyway, but *when* are you ever in your life again only going to be mixing with people who are within six months of your own age?

HE, by its nature brings people up to be very independent, free-thinking, talkative *individuals.* HErs tend to be very confident, friendly and outgoing people. A former EO co-ordinator once told me that she didn't understand why some people wondered if it would be hard for home-educated people to get a job in later life – her theory being that any HE person could simply talk themselves into a job, leaving some bemused interviewers in their wake. She is probably right!

One of my favourite things about home education is when groups of HErs meet each other. When we started to home educate, workshops were held fortnightly. Sometimes a theme would be chosen (e.g. the world, the body, festivals) and each family would prepare a 'stall' about a country in Europe, the pancreas, Judaism. Usually each family would have prepared a quiz or craft and then everyone would wander round visiting everyone else and generally having a lot of fun. On other occasions an 'outside' person might run the session (such as the circus group which ran the workshop mentioned in the first extract) or we might have a single theme. Then everyone would play during lunch, before going to a nearby playing field for a game of hockey or rounders, depending on the time of year. Once a year there was 'EO Sports Day' which was excellent fun!

However, the real reason I enjoy meeting with other EOers is the sense of community you gain – it is like one big family. There are no distinctions of age or sex – everyone is included. Definitely not a case of: 'I'm not playing with them because they're older boys/younger girls/grown ups'.

There are regular museum trips arranged for local EOers, and we have been going to these for so long that we know most of the talks by heart and are on first-name terms with all the education department. The same is true of the staff of the local university's 'schools talks'. I think a big factor behind the reason that home educators tend to enjoy looking round places of interest is that we can do it in its own right, without hours of busy-work and preparation, or mountains of projects and essays to write afterwards. Therefore we don't instantly connect, say, going to a museum with being dull, or 'boring'.

Although the format for HE activities has changed a bit since we were first involved, there is still a thriving list of events taking place, including a recent singing group which has been set up. If you want to meet with other HE people, there is almost always something going on near you. If not, take heart: after a while you develop a knack of *knowing* if someone is home-educated at one hundred paces – even if you've never met them before!

In the future, I would like to do some more 'A' levels and go to university, and am seriously considering a career in television. I enjoy being home-educated and would recommend it to anyone. I certainly plan to home educate my own children. However, I can't really give you a picture of what home education is *like*. The beauty of EO is that it is different for every person, because every person is different. The above is just a cobbled history of my EO life so far. I know for a fact that other HE families reading this will be saying, 'That's not how it is at all'. This is because every family has a different approach and everyone (in the nicest way possible) assumes that their way of doing things is normal (as with 'typical', this is not a word to be used lightly in connection with HE) and it is everyone *else* who has a slightly 'unusual' way of doing things.

So, if you want to be able to sleep later in the mornings, go to museums, libraries and shops when they are not busy, see a group of (HE) children scatter on reflex when they see another group of children in an 'alligator' (and find out what 'alligator' is slang for in HE-speak), never fill in a questionnaire again without scribbling extra boxes all over it, find out about the joys of EO Standard Time, and why all your friends collapse in heaps of laughter when the careers computer tells you that you are destined to become an Education Welfare Officer (it happened to me!) as well as generally have an outgoing, friendly, talkative, curious and downright ODD family (and be proud of it) then home education is for you. WELCOME!!

It is tempting to impose our goals on other people, particularly on children or our subordinates. It is tempting for society to try to impose its priorities on everybody. The strategy will however be self-defeating if our goals, or society's goals, do not fit the goals of the others. We may get our way but we don't get their learning. They may have to comply but they will not change. We have pushed out their goals with ours and stolen their purposes. It is a pernicious form of theft which kills the will to learn.

Charles Handy: *The Age of Unreason*

It seems to me that anything that can be taught to another is relatively inconsequential, and has little or no significant influence on behavior.

I realise increasingly that I am only interested in learnings which significantly influence behavior.

I have come to feel that the only learning which significantly influences behavior is self-discovered, self-appropriated learning.

Such self-discovered learning, truth that has been personally appropriated and assimilated in experience, cannot be directly communicated to another.

As a consequence of the above, I realise that I have lost interest in being a teacher.

Carl Rogers: *On Becoming a Person*

Education to go

Gill Wilson

Ed and I first heard about Home Education when Martin was just two and we went on a holiday to Wales. At the Centre for Alternative Technology in Machynlleth, we found a publication called 'School is Not Compulsory'. 'Hey look at this,' we said, 'we don't have to send him to school.' It all seemed a long way off, but the information proved more useful than we expected at the time.

Martin was quite definitely the most clingy baby in the world. He was never happy when I went out of sight and even followed me to the loo, though he was pretty good at the old potty-training, having seen the demo enough times. Home education by example, I guess!

Playgroup was an absolute disaster. He cried and screamed, then tearfully sat on one of the helpers' knees. I walked home, heartbroken, and phoned after an hour to see how he was doing. 'Come and fetch him,' they said, 'we've never failed with one yet – they always settle in eventually'.

After two days of this, we had nearly had enough. On the third attempt it took three staff to carry him in when Ed dropped him off; on the fourth morning he hid under the bed (Martin, that is, not Ed, though I'm sure Ed and I felt like joining him there).

This playgroup was in familiar surroundings, and he loved it so long as I was there to play with him. Looking back and thinking from a tiny child's point of view, it must be terrible to be left in the company of a lot of noisy children and a bunch of adults whom you don't know. Imagine having no one to turn to in a sea of faces; having to make an announcement to a complete stranger's knees at the top of your voice whenever you need something and then being misunderstood because your grasp of the language is a bit shaky. It's no wonder that the child who is 'backwards in coming forwards' feels intimidated.

Suffice to say he never went back there. We simply continued at home in much the same way as before. We played board games, baked cakes and stirred things on the stove – carefully supervised of course. He loved to feel important, helping to make our evening meal. We did lots of gardening, nature walks and playing in the park. We made playdough, we painted, crayoned, cut and pasted. We played cards or chess and re-enacted all the Postman Pat stories. We weighed, sorted, poured and mixed. Hours were spent sitting inside cardboard boxes going to the moon in a rocket. A walk down the road would take ages as we stopped to look at cracks in the pavement, leaves, patterns of bricks in walls. We even managed to fit in NCT coffee mornings and Gymtots.

Evan arrived when Martin was three, and at four, Martin and his friend started at another nursery group. I'm not saying it was dire, but a lot of the so-called art work was cloned and the children had to drink full cream milk, slightly warm, out of those tiny bottles whether they liked it or not. Pretty soon both Martin and friend, being the bright boys they are, asked if they had to go to nursery. Well of course they didn't, so they stopped going.

We continued with lots of activities at home, and in fact our house became a Mecca for all the neighbourhood kids. They flocked in to do art and craft activities, dig holes in the garden, play in the sandpit and on the climbing frame. It seemed that they all came round to do the things they were not allowed to do at home, and for which there was no time in school hours.

I suppose it is because nearly all children go to school nowadays, and have things arranged for them, that they seem so forlornly unable to produce their own ideas.

Agatha Christie

There were 'jam sessions' round the battered old piano with all the simple instruments we have accumulated over the years, mega art sessions spent painting large cardboard boxes; one summer they even painted the outside walls of the house with poster paint and then spent many happy hours up ladders washing it off with soapy water. We have a small zoo of pets to play with and these became popular with children who were not allowed to have pets at home. It is almost impossible to keep your house tidy when home education is going on.

Evan tried playgroup for one morning. When I asked him if he liked it, he said: 'Yes, but I'd rather stay at home with you and Martin'. I am pleased to say that he has been at home ever since.

We did have a little look round the local primary school, if only so that when the LEA got in touch we could tell them that we had seen it and 'thanks but no thanks'. The school was not at all to our liking. The policy seemed to be 'Parents keep off'. To quote a particularly telling phrase from their charming brochure: 'After the fourth day infants will be left at the gate'. Hmm... not mine, matey! I was equally unimpressed by the school nursery. All the tables and chairs were large and I could see none of the things which I would consider essential for young children; no paint, sandpit, playdough or books. To me, it looked more like a waiting room for the tots until they were old enough for school.

There is no choice about which school your child attends around here. If you have religious beliefs, you may get your child into a C of E or Catholic school rather than your designated one, but that is the extent of the options. Since we are not religious, and we didn't like the school, we waded gently into home education.

We pretty soon got involved with the local Education Otherwise group, which at that time had only one child of 'school' age. The group grew up together and we have seen a lot of people come and go. For many years I organised activities, meetings, talks, visits.

At the same time, by a process of trial and error, the children have learned to read and write and are pretty confident with maths, thanks to a very good friend who bailed me out by consistently and heroically taking them through the subject. Now she has moved away and we are on our own for maths work, which has been a little difficult.

One of the things I have found tricky with home education is in providing motivation. Having someone else set work and expect to see it done by the next week helps to a certain extent, although that has the disadvantage that you can rather lose touch with where they are up to.

We have done a lot of hands-on, kitchen-sink science, and we discuss the weather, the seasons and things in the natural world. There are always lots of books around and we are lucky enough to have a computer, which gives them access to the Internet and all sorts of CD-Roms.

Evan is particularly good at art and has been able to pursue this at any time the mood takes him. (This 'being in the mood', even for things which interest you, is important. The great thing about home education is that if you feel like drawing at midnight for hours on end, you can just do it without having to worry about getting up early in the morning for school.) It broke my heart to see one of the boys' friends, who is also artistically gifted, only able to do art at school if it was raining and they were unable to go outside to play. Needless to say this child spent a lot of time at our house after school, drawing and swapping ideas with my two boys. We have also been going to art classes at our local art gallery for over six years now and have learned a great deal from our wonderful teacher there.

We should use kids' positive states to draw them into learning in the domains where they can develop competencies...You learn at your best when you have something you care about and can get pleasure from being engaged in.

Howard Gardner
(Quoted in Goleman: *Emotional Intelligence*)

Both children had the opportunity to play a musical instrument at the Junior Strings scheme run by the Royal Northern College of Music. Evan decided to give up after a couple of years but Martin still continues to play his cello. Although he has now outgrown Junior Strings, and would in any case rather play for himself than take exams, the scheme gave them a good start. Nowadays Martin is rediscovering his confidence in art and drawing whilst Evan can be found experimenting with his electronic keyboard.

The boys are now older, and the thought of GCSEs looms on the horizon. Martin attended the local college for GCSE Biology at the age of twelve and was doing very well. However, when the teacher left, the course fell apart and he did not take the exam after all. I was so impressed with his ability to take notes and manage the homework: he got many As in tests and generally kept up well with the seventeen-year-olds who made up the rest of the class. I feel confident now that, when the time comes, he will cope with whatever exam courses he wants to follow.

Colleges certainly vary in their willingness to take on pupils who are under the age of sixteen. I thought we had struck lucky with the local establishment; however they do very few subjects at GCSE level and you do have to pay for them. Another drawback is that the GCSE courses are often re-sits for those who have already failed the exam at school, so you have to consider the possible effect on your child of going into a class of disillusioned seventeen-year-olds. There are also correspondence courses for GCSEs, although these can sometimes be expensive and don't always cater for the under-sixteens.

As the years have gone by, we have found fewer children of the right age in the local home educating group. Those with whom we started out have either moved away or gone off to school. Without exception, those who have begun school after many years of home education have done very well and fitted in without difficulty; our two, though, have to some extent been left high and dry, and we have to search hard for opportunities to work in a group.

Both boys have belonged to many clubs and groups over the years: drama, Scouts, art, home education meetings, gymnastics and Young Ornithologist's Club, to mention a few, but nowadays they do not seem to want this sort of thing. They seem reasonably happy with each other's company and still see their friends when they return from school. It is worth thinking about the difference between one or two deep friendships and a large number of passing acquaintances.

Certainly something to bear in mind when embarking on home education is that this small child will become a large and potentially stroppy adolescent one day. If you choose to home educate, you may have to go on with it until your babies reach the age of eighteen. At any time they might decide to try school, or they might be happy to stay at home throughout their 'school age' years.

It can be hard to work out how to bring in the money: home education usually means that one of the parents has her (his?) options somewhat limited. It is difficult to find work which can fit around home education and often such work is low paid and part-time. I would have found it impossible to go out to work when the boys were younger but now I can manage an uninspiring job during the evenings and weekends. Ed's desire to 'spend more time with his family' has inevitably led to his avoiding any advancements at work which would have caused him to spend more time away from home. On the plus side, you do have more time to shop around and find educational bargains in all kinds of places: the small ads of newspapers, in charity shops, educational suppliers' bargain corners and scrap stores.

I could not say home education has all been a doddle, but it does feel like second nature now. I do worry that the boys might not be learning the right things, but then who is to say what those 'right' things are? A lot of the stuff children are presented with at school has to be learned by everyone in the class, and as set out in the National Curriculum. Yet how can you expect an entire class of children to be interested in the same thing at the same time? How many of them will be bored and not paying attention? On the other hand, how many of them might want to continue with the subject after the bell has gone, but they have to move on to something else?

At home you are free to study something for just as long as you have an interest in it and no longer. Because the educational day doesn't begin at nine am and finish at three-thirty pm, home-educated children are learning all the time; even when you think there is nothing going on between their ears, the little cogs are whirring away and taking in information when you least expect it.

Much of the literature about home education tends to dwell on the marvellousness of it all; quite often the children are portrayed as paragons of virtue who cheerfully and voluntarily learn astro-physics before breakfast, gain grade eight in the Indonesian Nose Flute by the age of six and had picked up their times tables in utero. I am afraid I can't tell you any fairy stories like that. Mine have minds of their own and if they do not want to do something which I think is a good idea, then they will certainly argue their corner. In consequence they are terrific at compromise, persuasion, discussion, evasion and disappearing at the rustle of a work book. They are also kind and considerate, terrific at looking after children younger than themselves; they give up their seats on buses and they help people with heavy bags of shopping or pushchairs.

Although I am not sure what the future holds as far as exams, degrees and the like go, I am only too aware of how quickly children grow up, how fast they are pushed nowadays to become adults. I am glad we have managed to avoid the worst of the pressures, that our sons have been able to enjoy their childhood and can take on adult responsibilities as and when they are ready. Meanwhile they have plenty of time to play and dream.

Ed takes up the story...

Day to day, if you have the time, you can experiment and see what works best with a particular child on a particular day. Sitting down with a book, pretending the sofa is a rocket, drawing on the blackboard, cleaning out the rats, staying in bed, watching the schools programmes on TV, downing tools and going on a train trip: you can try them all to see what keeps you inspired. The one thing you cannot do, though, is leave your children to take their own path until they are somewhere around fifteen, before deciding it has all gone wrong; you cannot go back to try again.

I hear a lot of faulty logic in this game. For instance, I remember somebody quoting John Holt, or Ivan Illich, to the effect that a child in school might only have an hour's attention from a teacher in a week, and arguing that you therefore only have to put in a weekly hour to get your child educated. The point had been missed that this was a criticism of school, not a recipe for an alternative!

Similarly, I hear people discussing child-centredness and wonder whether any two of them mean the same thing by the term. By all means let us agree that the best learning experiences and (arguably) the best-remembered knowledge come from an activity in which the child is interested, and perhaps even because s/he selected or initiated it. However, too often it is argued that you simply have to wait for the child to do just that, then you support them in it, whatever it is, and all is fine and rosy. Children are naturally inquisitive, the argument goes, and I agree; but children are naturally more than one thing: lazy, for example. I can't sit around until they are old enough to leave home, just waiting and hoping that they will ask the right kind of questions and that I will know how to answer them.

Many of us feel we have to become a bit of a teacher; no bad thing, because we fool ourselves if we think that we automatically know enough to do the job. We have to learn to help our children learn. Sometimes we are driven into a corner and feel that it is us against the world, that we have to do everything with and for our children. Sometimes we can spend so much time relishing the existence of like-minded people in the area, and organising get-togethers, that we miss the fact that this apparently important social interaction is wasting a lot of time and the kids don't like it.

One thing Gill and I dreaded about school was the social pressures, but the kids are, like me, fairly urban animals. They have a handful of friends who go to school. They hang around in the street playing football and eating all sorts of things I don't want them to eat. They swear and talk about pop music. They watch far too much TV. There again, I think they have a pretty good grasp sometimes. Although Nike footwear would be nice, it is something they can drop in favour of something else, or because we own up to not having the money. It is not a matter of day-to-day face-saving. They can make their own choices sometimes where other children can't.

In other areas their choices are made by us. We are self-destructively child-centred and yet we define the world they live in: sometimes it feels like a very small one. The contradictions are endless. I would like Martin and Evan to be able to avoid wage-slavery and consumerism and all the rest, but I also want them to be equipped to choose to enter the same world as everyone else rather than sit outside it, lonely and looking in.

The work goes on.

FAQ no.4   Do you need a special schoolroom?

Whilst some families may choose to set a particular space aside for 'work', especially if they are following a full curriculum, this is not essential. Indeed, many home educators feel that having a set 'work space' actually creates the very division between living and learning which they are trying to overcome. To regard learning as something which can *only* happen at a fixed time and place is to miss out on one of home education's great strengths: the opportunity to live curiously and thus lay the foundations for real life-long learning.

The 'education' part of home education is going on the whole time, much of it in the course of ordinary conversation. Children ask questions on the bus and in the garden; they are learning as they do the shopping, plant seeds or cook dinner. Talking about snow whilst walking the dog is no less valid a way of learning about climate than sitting at a desk studying it in a book and, for many home educators, frequent trips out to museums, art galleries and special events provide rich food for thought and conversation.

Easier than expected (so far!)

Jos Underhill

I am Jos, married to Tony, and we have three children: Robert (9), Emily (7) and Matthew (4). Tony works as a printer. He left school at sixteen with no qualifications but later took 'O' level English, 'A' level art, and a degree level life-drawing class. I have worked as a library assistant and in an accounts department; I now work a few hours a week as a maths tutor. I left school at 17 with some 'O' levels, then went on to take more, plus a BTEC National Certificate in Business and Finance and, a couple of years ago, a maths course with the Open University.

Our decision to home educate evolved gradually over a year or two. I have always read a great deal but, until I had children, it was usually fiction. When I knew I was pregnant, I began ploughing my way through library books on pregnancy and the development of the unborn child. After Robert was born I started on books about child development and learning. It was during one of these trips to the library, when Robert was nearly two, that I came across books about home education.

I had already seen occasional local TV items about parents teaching their children at home. The children were always seated at desks and seemed to work set hours, just like a school. The usual reason for home education appeared to be a feeling that they, the parents, could do a better job of school than the schools themselves. Tony, on the other hand, had gained the impression that home educators were well-off eccentrics living in the Outer Hebrides. Thus, although home education as a possibility was not completely new to us, it did not seem relevant.

I worked my way through several books, including Jean Bendell's *Schools Out* and a few John Holt titles, and through one of these books

I found out about Education Otherwise. We vaguely considered home education then, and I even went so far as to visit the local Education Otherwise co-ordinator, but at the time we found the idea too daunting. I think that, despite the reading I had done, I still had the picture of 'school at home' swimming around in my head. We decided to follow the usual pattern and accepted a place for Robert at the local state nursery. When we went to look around, they seemed to have so much equipment available that we felt as though we would have been depriving him had we decided not to send him.

He went to nursery happily for the first couple of weeks, but then began to resist. We had been told that we would be able to stay with him if necessary but in practice there was pressure to leave him, even though he was crying and asking me to stay. I was told: 'He'll stop crying and be fine once you've gone,' but whenever I went early to collect him and had a chance to watch him, he never looked happy and involved as many of the other children did. Instead of improving and getting used to nursery, things deteriorated until I was eventually carrying him in and giving him to the teacher to hold, kicking and punching, until I had gone. The staff seemed to take it very matter-of-factly. One helper mentioned that her son had been the same for a whole year, presumably thinking that this would encourage me!

I worried that I had caused the problem. Many magazine articles about starting nursery suggest that this type of separation anxiety is caused by the child's mother not being able to let her child go, yet he happily climbed into the coach for the nursery trip to the woods, and ran into school on the day of the Christmas party. Except for the first couple of weeks, however, he did not like the normal nursery sessions. I came to the conclusion, after talking to Robert, that it was a combination of boredom and a dislike of being told what to do and when to do it.

After a particularly gruelling trip to the nursery gate, which included prising Robert's fingers off our front door post and struggling to get him into the car, I decided that enough was enough. We went home, never to return again. Looking back, I find it very hard to understand how I could have been so cruel as to keep taking him to nursery when he so obviously did not want to go (I have since apologised). I think it was due to my concern that he would have to get over this problem some time if he was to go to school; I had hoped that part-time mornings would ease him along this path. In the event, a term at nursery was enough to convince us that home education was for us, no matter how daunting it seemed. It couldn't be worse than forcing him to go to nursery, and later school.

Our ideas about how to home educate have gradually evolved through a combination of reading books, talking to other home educators in person and on the Internet, and then finding out what works in practice for our children. One of the first things I tried when Robert left nursery was to do some maths and reading work every day, but he soon made it clear that he was not interested. I put the words from an early reader book on to flash cards: he learnt those and read the book, but it was like pulling teeth. It soon became evident that this type of organised and directed approach to learning just did not work for at least one of our children: it simply resulted in arguments and stress. If I was to have any kind of relationship left with my children, we were going to have to find a different way forward.

I started reading again. Before Robert tried nursery I had found out about autonomous education from John Holt's books, so I began re-reading some of them. There were also relevant articles in the Education Otherwise newsletter and in some of their literature. What I read certainly seemed to tie in with our experiences of education as adults.

Tony and I have both done far better educationally since leaving school and taking control of our own education. We have been able to follow our interests and, when we have taken courses and exams, have gained much higher marks than those we gained at school. We do not feel that the results can be explained purely by the fact that we are 'older and wiser'. I gained much better grades in the 'O' levels I completed during the year after leaving school, using correspondence courses, despite the fact that I studied the subjects for one year instead of two.

We had also seen how well our children had learned up until then without formal, planned lessons. For example, Robert had learnt to count to a hundred very casually, just by asking what came next. Maths arose quite naturally through our asking him if he wanted two slices of toast or three, for example, and whether he wanted it cut into halves or quarters. He went through a period of quite intense interest in number and would say things like: 'Five and six make eleven, don't they?' while doing apparently unconnected things like riding his bike around the garden. He was obviously thinking about numbers a great deal for a period of time and just asked for information when he needed it.

What we want to see is the child in pursuit of knowledge, and not knowledge in pursuit of the child.

George Bernard Shaw

Robert's resistance to formality, combined with our reading about different approaches, our personal experiences of education and our observations of how our children learned, pushed us towards a more autonomous, child-centred way of educating. We gradually began to realise that children learning at home do not need set things in a set order at set ages – not even reading, writing and arithmetic.

We have come to the conclusion that the rush for literacy in schools is mainly necessary because teachers in the later primary years rely on children being able to read. This view is supported by recent research conducted by Alan Thomas; his study of a hundred home educating families in England and Australia shows that, whereas late readers in schools generally fall behind their classmates in all subjects, late-reading home-educated children do not fall behind in other subjects. Moreover they rapidly catch up, and often pass, their age mates in reading once they are ready to learn. In other words, late readers in school are held back in other subjects by their poor reading level, but home-educated children are not. Our guess is that school children have to be able to read and follow written instructions so that teachers can set work for them which can be completed with very little further help. Children at home are able to learn without great reading skills: through conversation, adults reading to them, visits and outings, and through seeing and experiencing the world at first hand.

We now believe that when children choose to learn to read, they will learn more quickly and easily than those who are forced into it before they are ready. John Gatto, author and 'New York Teacher of the Year', believes that basic numeracy and literacy can be learnt in about one hundred hours if the child is ready and has chosen to learn. We have certainly found that Emily is mastering reading with very little time and effort, and feel this is because she has made her own decision and is able to take it at her own pace. I would say that she probably spends less than ten minutes a day on reading and writing, yet she is making good progress.

Another thing we have noticed is that improvements seem to happen after periods of apparent inactivity. Writing is suddenly neater even though the children have barely put pen to paper for several months; friends have described exactly the same experience. One of the side benefits of this, and something I love about home education, is that it gives children more time to play.

Our current approach to education, then, is that the direction, content and methods of learning are fully controlled by the child. We try to follow our children's interests through reading and through relevant visits and activities. We have a wide range of materials available of which they can take advantage if they wish, and we try to avoid telling them what they should learn, although we do make suggestions. Our children have always enjoyed going out and about, so it seemed only natural to expand on this. We go to castles, Sea Life Centres, zoos, beaches, mountains and rivers, as well as on trips and activities organised by other home educators. Recent trips have included an Egyptian afternoon at a local museum, making casts of our hands in glass, going to watch two blocks of flats being demolished and a tour around a sewage works. We have also been swimming, rock-wall climbing, ice-skating and canoeing, and have done various art workshops and pond-dipping expeditions.

We hope that seeing so many things at first hand will help them if they choose to study any of these areas further. I am sure that history and geography books will make more sense to them if they have had first-hand experience of the things they read about.

Experience is the child of Thought, and Thought is the child of Action. We cannot learn to be men from books.

Disraeli

Stages in the course of a river, for example, or particular types of castle will hopefully be easier to understand and visualise when they have seen and played in examples of most of them! Their learning happens through these trips, their day-to-day experiences, conversations and reading together: much as it does for most children before they start school. Although I have mentioned history and geography here, in practice we do not think in terms of separate subjects.

Structured text books and workbooks can have their place alongside more informal ways of learning, if that is what the child wants. I have always found good textbooks useful when following an interest myself, as the subject matter is usually laid down in a logical, structured way, making them easy to follow. We are happy to include structured approaches to subjects as one of the options when an interest is shown. For instance Robert has learned most, if not all, of his maths through conversations and asking questions. He may not be able to write out maths problems conventionally yet, but he has a solid understanding of numbers and how they work and also has good mental arithmetic skills. Emily, however, quite often asks me to help her with some workbook pages in maths or writing and has asked to be taught how to read. I have used a combination of phonics and the Oxford Reading Tree books.

The hardest thing we have found with this approach to home education is trusting that our children will learn all they need, particularly in the areas of literacy and numeracy. In the past, we 'encouraged' Robert to read one book each night. He had said that he would like to be able to read but would prefer it to be instant! On many nights he would happily read the book, on other nights he took a little persuading and on yet others, he could not be persuaded at all. When asked about this he would say that he *did* want to read a book each night, but then often changed his mind in the evening. It is difficult in this situation to resist applying pressure: there is a fine line between persuasion and pressure and I am sure we get it wrong at times.

Another problem I encountered initially with home education was the intense nature of my relationship with the children. I found that I was losing my temper far too often and realised that something had to change, particularly as we were going to be spending so much time together in the future. I decided to take a Parentlink course not long after Robert left nursery. These courses are run by Parent Network, a charity which: 'Aims to make family life more enjoyable through helping parents to get on better with their children.' The course covered self-esteem for parents and children, understanding your child's behaviour, listening skills, assertiveness skills, and dealing with feelings. It definitely helped me see things differently and improved my ability to solve problems before things become too heated and out of control. Tony took the next course.

Socialisation is often suggested as a reason for going to school. There seem to be two areas of concern, one of these being the chance to learn how to behave in society and to cope with problems and conflict with others. We have found that children learn to socialise more rapidly if they have easy access to adults with whom they can discuss any problems as they arise. Possible solutions to difficulties with friends can be suggested there and then by adults who know the children involved. Ideally, the adults are able to work with the children to find a solution which works for everyone, and they are demonstrating problem-solving skills at the same time. It is generally accepted that children learn most easily from older children or adults, yet when it comes to socialisation it seems that they are expected to learn from a class of thirty of their age-peers, who presumably have a similar level of social skill themselves.

The other concern for many parents is that their child will not get enough opportunity to play with other children who are in school for much of the day. Children vary widely in the amount of social contact they need: some are happy to play occasionally with other children and enjoy having space to do their own thing. If, however, a child enjoys playing frequently with others, it may be necessary for everyone involved to work quite hard to ensure that this happens. A lot depends on where you live and on how many other home educators live nearby. Home educating children often have to travel further to meet up with their friends, and this can be difficult if they have to rely on public transport. I have heard of children returning to school because they want to see other children more often, particularly during the teenage years. Maybe this will become less common as home education grows, increasing the number of children available to meet up during the day.

We are lucky to live in an area with quite a few home educating families within a few miles; one family lives around the corner within easy walking distance. The children play with their cousins quite often, and we still meet up with friends who are now at school. They can play with children living nearby after school, and Emily has recently joined the local Brownies group, partly in order to meet more local children. We go on most of the trips organised by the home educators' groups around our area and, as a result, they have good home educating friends with whom they can play for long uninterrupted periods, particularly when they stay overnight at each others' houses.

We have been home educating now for five years, and even the negatives have become positive. The problems I experienced at the beginning, in coping with the constant close contact, have been resolved as we have learned and grown together.

I am sure that we are more relaxed and far closer than we would have been if the children had gone to school. Obviously we have our ups and downs, as any family does, but on the whole we are finding home education a very enjoyable and worthwhile experience. It affects the whole structure and pattern of our lives: because we do not have to be up early for school, the children stay up in the evening and Tony gets the chance to spend more time with them than he otherwise would. We all enjoy our home educating lifestyle and feel it is one of the best decisions we ever made. As for the future: there is always the option of school and, if they decide to go, I am quite sure that they will gain far more from the experience by virtue of having made their own choice.

*That there is some standard definition of education is a myth too
often promulgated by local education authorities and politicians;
despite popular misconceptions, however, the right not merely to
home educate children, but to nurture the autonomy of that
education is a valid, legal and sustainable one.*

Jan Fortune-Wood: *Doing it Their Way*

School forcibly snatches away children from a world full of the
mystery of God's own handiwork, full of the suggestiveness of
personality. It is a mere method of discipline which refuses to take
into account the individual. It is a manufactory specially designed
for grinding out uniform results. It follows an imaginary straight
line of the average in digging its channel of education. But life's line
is not the straight line, for it is fond of playing the see-saw with the
line of average, bringing upon its head the rebuke of the school. For
according to the school life is perfect when it allows itself to be
treated as dead, to be cut into symmetrical conveniences. And this
was the cause of my suffering when I was sent to school …my mind
had to accept the tight-fitting encasement of the school which,
being like the shoes of a mandarin woman, pinched and bruised my
nature on all sides and at every movement. I was fortunate enough
in extricating myself before insensibility set in.

Rabindranath Tagore

*I think children can be very cruel especially in adolescence and if
you are slow, and I was (I was in a school which was quite
competitive) you do get a lot of slamming about from the other kids.
I don't know about girls, but I know that boys are very cruel and
very tough. It built up a tremendous resentment in me because I
was also bad at sport and athletics and all I could do was play the
piano. So I always got the sense in my adolescent years that 'Oh,
Hopkins, you know he's, well he's not worth much, or he's a failure.'*

Anthony Hopkins
(In The Psychiatrist's Chair, Anthony Clare)

Journey to an education

Judith Clare

Austin Powers went on a journey back to swinging sixties London to find his lost mojo. Our home education experiences have the same feel, if you define 'mojo' in the way the writer, producer and star of the film, Mike Myers, did in an interview as:

> *...essence, right stuff, what the French call a certain 'I-don't-know-what' as well as ...um ...mojo, baby, which I don't really mean. Confidence, assurance, knowing you are on the right path despite the obstacles and difficulties, faith in yourselves, excitement in learning, feeling you are really getting to the core of things, clearing away all the rubbish, doing what you want and trusting your inner voice; that is what I mean. Yeah ...mojo.*

'When I use a word,' said Humpty Dumpty 'it means just what I choose it to mean – neither more nor less.'

We are very affected by films in our household; cinema is one of my sons' passions. Recently we were watching a documentary about the making of *Star Wars* in which George Lucas was discussing mythology and the hero's journey. When the work of Joseph Campbell was mentioned, the hairs on the back of my neck began tingling because I am reading his books: *Myths to Live By* and *The Hero With a Thousand Faces*. Our family had earlier become enthralled by Arthurian Legend; my eldest son had been reading Frazer's *Golden Bough* whilst my youngest son and I had recently been to a lecture where David Rohl, author of *Legend* and presenter of television programmes, was giving fascinating insights into the philosophy and religion of the ancient Egyptians. One thing leads to another for us ...and back again.

When watching that 'Star Wars' documentary, I thought: everything links together. You can't decide what is 'knowledge' and what is not; what is suitable for a respectable curriculum and how and when it should be delivered, nor put set times aside for learning and leisure.

However, the Local Education Authority asked me to do just that when I first withdrew my then twelve-year-old from the secondary school, whose doors he had been unable to face going through for some time. They wrote me a letter and demanded detailed plans. They even asked me where he would be doing his learning.

Nowadays I might write back and say 'everywhere', but back then I was scared of what might happen to him: a special boarding school had been threatened and I had been a teacher for long enough to know the mind-set. I was even a little sympathetic, realising that they had a job to do and that children might be being kept out of school to work in sweatshops or worse. Although that is a welfare rather than an education issue, I was in no state to worry about rights or principles. I just knew I had to protect my child. So I researched at the library and got out my old teacher-training notes. I read books, worried, and wrote voluminous justifications and plans for the 'authorities'. Having cloned our home into a school, I waited anxiously for the Inspector to call.

We had been through difficult times as a family. My ex-husband had become disturbed and dangerous, and we had all suffered. I had sought help from our doctor, a Child Guidance Psychologist, even Social Services at the very worst time. Certain protection from my husband and resolution of the situation had to be won through the courts when all else failed, and those were extremely stressful experiences.

In some respects I was left a bit of a nervous wreck for a while, but in other ways I was stronger. One thing I had learned was that relying on the 'caring' professions has its dangers. The resources just are not there, in terms of money, time or sometimes even understanding, and yet you can be at their mercy. You can lose your dignity and the conviction of your own responsibilities.

One day I was sitting in the Child Guidance Psychologist's little room, very worried and unsure, asking his advice. He explained to me that most children realise that school is not good enough for them, and that they are not always treated properly, but they put up with it. They do not have a way out and so they make the best of things.

I looked at him, this man who had helped me so much, whose judgement I respected, and I thought, 'No, he's not right here, it's not right that our children have poor quality education with no way out if it gets excruciatingly boring for them, or if they get bullied, or even if they just can't explain why they hate school'. I thought of my son who was turning our lives upside down by refusing to go, an unhappy and difficult boy to live with, and I felt the first stirrings of admiration for his bravery and his sense of his own self-worth. He had asked me to educate him at home, the Education Welfare Officer had even suggested it, but until that time I had held back, believing in the myth that it was impossible because I was an inadequate divorced mother coping on my own with adolescent boys.

Looking back, I think the psychologist was caught up in a different myth: that 'school-phobic' children are suffering from the effects of 'separation anxiety'. He was not really a text-book sort of man but he was constrained within his system and by the resources at his disposal. He later told me he thought he had been wrong and I had been right, and I told him he had helped me enormously. We parted friends and I got on with my task alone.

So that is how I came to be compiling documents about my philosophy and plans for a school of one pupil, and preparing the house and myself for a vetting. It was very hard dealing with the Inspector's visits although he was a nice enough man, and approved us. Having tried to point us in the direction of learning tables and doing dictations, he said that he would not be back for a year, which was probably the thing we liked hearing most of all. Too much was at stake for us to be able to relax or to make use of anything he could offer. You are in any case very much on your own with home education and the responsibility, especially financial, is all yours.

Many people, friends and family, have helped us and I am so grateful. I did not join Education Otherwise for a while. I had come out of the school culture and I did not want to be part of any group, I just wanted to think for myself. I discovered an Internet list of UK home educators where I read good advice and was relieved to find encouragement from like-minded people. Much later we met local EO members and wished we had not left it so long before joining in their activities and enjoying their support.

I had a degree in Psychology and had spent years teaching in secondary, middle, primary and infant schools and bringing up my boys. I had lived by certain formulae, but challenging life experiences shook me up and made me deal with things as they were. 'People are so complex, so convoluted, getting to know them is like being a spelunker, feeling his/her way downward into the cave, by feel alone', wrote a dear friend in America whom I met on a Baha'i homeschool list. I assumed a 'spelunker' was a caver or a potholer. It is not always easy understanding even your own children. You need support, and his has been invaluable.

Sometimes it is a boon being a home educator, sometimes it is an ordeal. The myth of being inadequate is one you have to overcome, as is the one where you have to be the little red hen and do everything all by yourself.

Myths do not always obscure reality: sometimes they uncover it. The journey of the hero, or the heroine (although she was usually being rescued) is a myth to grow with, finding your strength by overcoming obstacles and trying to choose the right thing to do. It has felt a bit like that. I knew that I had to keep my sons happy and healthy, that their true education was our ultimate aim and we had to search out the way ourselves.

To find yourself, think for yourself.

Socrates

My boys do not really want me to write about them, and it devalues their learning to document and pigeon-hole it. They are not factory products and do not need to be quality-controlled. They are not objects, neither are their thoughts and insights, nor is the growth of their understanding. Their talking, their writing, their puzzling out with numbers, their use of computers and other technology, their hypothesizing and experimenting, their art, their drama and their sport: I do not see all these things which they make and do as 'outcomes' or evidence to be measured and compared. Moreover I certainly would not want to document their friendships under 'social skills'. They are themselves and what they are becoming is up to them, with help and guidance from me and other relatives and friends. This seems to be a lot about me: not out of self-centredness, I hope, but out of respect for their integrity and privacy.

A quote from the Baha'i Writings has inspired me. It contains a mythological word that makes me think: 'talisman'.

'Man is the supreme Talisman', says Baha'u'llah. 'Lack of a proper education hath, however, deprived him of that which he doth inherently possess.'

A talisman in legend is a magical charm, something which gives you strength and protects you, but I am beginning to understand from this phrase that the real magic is not something you can hold in your hand or wear round your neck, not something strange or weird, not even some truth 'out there'. It is not something you can be given or lose or find. It is our very selves. What is 'a proper education'? That is what our hero's quest in life seems to be, for ourselves and for our children. Sometimes the burden of responsibility for educating your own child weighs heavy, especially when you are carrying it alone, but it is the same responsibility that any parent faces, even if they choose to use schools. Two of my boys have chosen to stay within the state education system and I feel my responsibility towards them just as keenly.

I recognise it as a natural law, and of course the law of the land, that children be educated, but that does not mean that they have to be forced to attend conventional institutions. Education is a wonderful adventure rather than a duty and, at times, full of fun. It is a tragedy to make it seem like punishment for young people, just as it is sad if they are not given opportunities or helped to tackle challenging work that requires perseverance. I do not feel it should all be a lark, but it is the source of real happiness.

I have had to be brave, but I think my sons are braver. As Mike Myers said about 'Austin Powers 2':

The maybe-shouldn't-be-spoken-of-truth of what the movie is about is: you can let somebody take away your power, or you can maintain your own power. I'm not having a seminar here. We're going on a nice little journey and having a few laughs. But the journey is rooted in something. My belief is that no one can take away your mojo.

That is my belief too.

Childhood placed at a tangent to adulthood, perceived as special and magical, precious and dangerous at once, has turned into some volatile stuff – hydrogen, or mercury, which has to be contained. The separate condition of the child has never been so bounded by thinking, so established in law as it is today…How we treat children really tests who we are, fundamentally conveys who we hope to be.

Marina Warne: *Managing Monsters*, The Reith Lectures 1994

Daniel (aged 13)

One of the things I didn't like about school was that someone would *always* stop the whole class just to ask, 'I don't understand...' At home, you go at your own speed, and when you want to stop, you stop. If you want to spend all morning working out fractals, you can. Not to mention the fact of getting up late! I like maths, but in lots of school maths books you have to do hundreds of questions just to prove you understand it. Now I can just do a few and go on to more interesting things. If I don't understand, I can spend longer at it, without feeling stupid if other people are faster.

We do lots of IT at home, and I've been doing loads of programming, which I wouldn't have been able to do at school. I have my own website, and put some of my games and programs up there. I am part way through writing a novel and have won two short story competitions. I wouldn't have had time to do these if I was in school. I have read more books at home than they have at the school library!

It is very difficult to do PE or sports at home and also, in Cyprus, there aren't any children's orchestras that I can join. But I can be in the church music group, which would be more difficult if I was at school.

Teaching means different things in different places, but seven lessons are universally taught from Harlem to Hollywood Hills. They constitute a national curriculum you pay for in more ways than you can imagine, so you might as well know what it is.

1. Confusion
2. Class Position
3. Indifference
4. Emotional Dependency
5. Intellectual Dependency
6. Provisional Self-Esteem
7. One Can't Hide.

It is the great triumph of compulsory, government monopoly mass-schooling that among even the best of my fellow teachers, and among even the best of my students' parents, only a small number can imagine a different way to do things.

John Taylor Gatto: *Dumbing Us Down*

There is one thing at least of which there is never so much as a whisper inside the popular schools; and that is the opinion of the people. The only persons who seem to have nothing to do with the education of the children are the parents.

G.K. Chesterton

FAQ no.5

Don't you have to be a really patient person?

Yes and no. Home educators do have to adjust to their children's pace and take the time to answer questions or involve children in activities which might be quicker done alone, but sainthood is certainly not a requirement for home education. Things sometimes get fraught and it is easy to panic as the day degenerates, convinced that you are crazy to home educate, if not a thoroughly obnoxious parent. Well, perhaps you *are* today, but tomorrow will be different.

You may be surprised by how much patience you actually have, once the pressure of rushing to meet deadlines and others' expectations has been lifted. Generally it is stress which makes us impatient. When the stress eases it is possible to enjoy pottering along at your children's pace, not to mention seizing excuses to forget about boring things like adulthood, good sense and dignity!

If you constantly find yourself stifling your irritation or involved in shouting matches with your children, don't beat yourself up. Instead take it as a message that something needs to change. What sparks off the rows? Do you need more time for yourself? Do you feel under pressure to produce 'results', whether for unsupportive relatives or the LEA? Talk to other home educators about it because many will have useful insights gleaned from their own difficult times. Would you find a **Parentlink** course helpful? Above all, discuss it with your children: home education works best as a partnership and their perspective on the situation may lead to all of you finding a better way of life.

Reclaiming Tom's childhood

Ali Edgley

When my baby, Charis, was eleven months old, I let her play with a lighted candle. She protested so strongly when I tried to take her away from it that I took a deep breath and decided to watch her instead. She moved her finger slowly towards the flame, held it there, and moved it away again. She carefully put her finger into the melted wax, took it out again and examined the wax on the end of her finger. Then she waved her hand from side to side through the flame, sat down and crawled off to investigate something else. Since then she has shown no interest in candles, except to tell me that they are hot.

This is how home education works for us, on the good days. I aim for a kind of benign non-interference, watching my children without appearing to watch, and constantly trying to resist the temptation to offer unsolicited help and advice.

Tom is seven, and has been out of school since nursery. He is an energetic, physically confident and insatiably curious child who demands a lot of stimulation – on his own terms. I have found him easier to deal with since I discovered a wonderful book called *Raising Your Spirited Child* by Mary Sheedy-Kurcinka, and learned to think of him as 'spirited' rather than just bolshie and in-your-face. Although we still have days when I get cold feet and try to 'persuade' him to buckle down to the Three Rs (usually when his schooled friends have displayed their fluent reading, neat handwriting and – wonder of wonders – spelling skills) they invariably end in disaster with Tom belligerently refusing to do anything and me impotently threatening to send him to school, where they will *make* him co-operate.

Everyone, at present, is in favour of having students learn the fundamentals. For most people, 'the three Rs', or some variation of them, represent what is fundamental to a learner. However, if one observes a learner and asks oneself, 'What is it that this organism needs without which he cannot thrive?', it is impossible to come up with the answer, 'the three Rs'.

Postman & Weingartner: *Teaching as a Subversive Activity*

For me, the over-educated product of a grammar school, university, teacher-training and a family who regard academic achievement as a jewel beyond price, the last three years have been a revelation. I have had to learn to trust Tom when he asserts that he just isn't the kind of person who draws and paints much, despite being surrounded by children who come home from school with reams of masterpieces. I have had to keep my faith when he refused to learn tables or to spell anything, and when he told me that he didn't want to read yet, but would when he was seven.

He did! He discovered the Traveller's School reading books at HesFes and asked for the whole set for his birthday. He tore the parcel open excitedly and read six of the most difficult ones straight away. He has recently discovered 10-squares and the interesting patterns that tables make on them when he marks them with different coloured blo-pens. He has also just learnt to tell the time, which helps no end with tables and fractions, and is currently giving me a running commentary on the interesting relationship between his digital watch and the kitchen clock. Money is another passion: he loves working out how long it will take him to save up for things, and honing his negotiating skills trying to persuade me to give him an advance.

I am still waiting for the spelling breakthrough, and for his handwriting to progress beyond kindergarten level, but I know it will happen because he is beginning to discover the power of the written word. I keep finding 'No Smoking' signs on my bedroom door, and 'No Entry' signs on his, and he has started writing letters to people whom he really loves. He is articulate (he gets plenty of practice) and he has a large vocabulary which he uses accurately, if idiosyncratically. Sometimes I worry that he is turning into a Dick King-Smith story tape. We listen to Radio 3 and 4 a great deal and I am often surprised to find him absorbed in something which I had assumed was way over his head. He can climb anything, ice-skate, chop wood, swim and dive; he is working on swimming a length under water. I take credit for very little of this: all I do is provide resources and respond to his cues. If I try to do more, I usually end up getting in his way.

It is hard not to, sometimes. If I could see into the future and catch a glimpse of Tom as an adult, it would all be so much easier. Home education is a huge and often daunting responsibility, and on the bad days I do wonder if I am depriving him of opportunities and experiences. Yet, he is learning and adamant that school is not for him at the moment, so all I can do is try my best to nurture his curiosity, his self-esteem and his confidence that he can find out anything which he needs to know.

I do try not to be coercive but I am not libertarian, either. I have always insisted, for instance, that Tom cleans his teeth and eats good food because, as an adult, I can see into the future more easily than he can. Now, as Tom gets older, I can see that he is changing and am beginning to encourage him to equip himself with the basic tools of learning because he is an intelligent person who deserves to succeed in life.

In retrospect, my decision to home educate Tom was an inevitable consequence of other decisions I made when he was a baby. His early babyhood was difficult for both of us; he was colicky, slept badly and yelled whenever I put him down. He was bewilderingly different from the babies in the books. My first decision was that our relationship was not going to be the constant battle of wills that well-meaning friends and relatives were beginning to predict for us, so I set about finding out how to change things. I discovered Deborah Jackson's books: *Three in a Bed* and *Do Not Disturb* and Jean Liedloff's *Continuum Concept* and, through these, I found the La Leche League and the Natural Nurturing Network. I realised that Tom was telling me what he needed and I had to learn to listen to him. He needed to be carried, to share my bed, and he needed me to stop trying to wean him.

As I began to take back the responsibility for my child's well-being from the 'experts' whom I had assumed knew best, our relationship was transformed, along with my attitude to parenthood. So later on, when Tom made it perfectly obvious that he was unhappy at school, I could not then suddenly stop listening to him (although I tried for a while!) And I had to take responsibility for his education as well.

It wasn't always this clear to me. I had Tom when I was thirty-five and confidently expected to resume my career within a few months, while Tom's father looked after him. Instead, I subsequently found myself single, on income support and living in a rented flat in Hackney with a sixteen-month-old baby. Although I was interested in home education and already had serious doubts about the direction which

State education was taking, I felt I had no alternative but to start Tom on the path to school, with playgroup at three and nursery at four, whilst I started the slow process of getting myself back to work.

Tom had other ideas. He was happy to be minded by a friend, but never managed to settle at his carefully-chosen playgroup. I am still not sure why; maybe I was more ambivalent about it than I thought, and he sensed my doubts. He found it difficult to separate from me and I found it equally difficult to leave him crying at the door and go home. I couldn't bring myself to ignore him and get on with my own life. It didn't seem right to give him no choice, so that he gave up hope of being listened to or taken seriously. We tried various strategies to help him to settle, but the bottom line was that he could not cope with playgroup if I was not there.

When he started nursery, it was the same story. Although I had been given the impression that the nursery was a free, happy and non-coercive place where the children were at liberty to follow their own interests, during the many hours I spent there I found this not to be the case. There was so much subtle pressure to conform, to join in with everything – particularly activities which involved pre-reception class skills such as number and letter recognition – and I saw children being told off for not sitting still and concentrating when a story was being read, when they clearly needed to go and burn off some energy.

> *The teacher who has been deprived by his superiors of freedom,*
> *initiative and responsibility cannot carry out his instructions except*
> *by depriving his pupils of the same vital qualities.*
> Edmond Holmes: *What Is and What Might Be*

Above all, there was such a lack of emotional support, the children were expected to be 'happy' and co-operative all the time; and my attempts to offer the children some acknowledgement of their difficult feelings were politely discouraged, or even sabotaged.

Perhaps if I had been totally committed to the education system, I could have helped Tom to work through his problems, but my own experience of school was not a happy one. My abiding memory is of being unheard and unacknowledged, and feeling that I was the one with the problem. At nursery with Tom, I realised that I still found schools intimidating: I couldn't stand up for him against teachers half my age. On several occasions I left him at school when I should have taken him home again, simply because I could not cope with the teachers' disapproval.

By half term, we had reached crisis point. Tom needed to be allowed to be himself and to be proud of being an individual, and we needed our old honest, supportive relationship back. He came out of school, and I had my confused, bewildered little boy back home. It took him a year to recover. For the first few months, he often behaved like a much younger child. He would not let me leave him with anyone, not even his Dad. He would not pick up a pen, even to draw a picture, and refused to join in with any group activities: in fact he would deliberately disrupt them. Instead, he played, listened to story tapes and watched television. We went for long walks and I read to him for hours. Gradually, he began to tell me about things which had upset him at school and which I had not known about at the time. He still found some incidents so traumatic that he often ended up in tears.

Tom came to work with me two days a week at the cafe in the local park and made friends with a lovely group of pensioners. He had plenty of children to play with during the summer holidays and we also went back to the One O'Clock Club, where he had spent many happy afternoons before going to nursery. I learned to avoid situations in which he would feel powerless because they invariably led to tantrums.

It wasn't easy at first; I often wondered if I was doing the right thing. Was I being neurotic or over-protective? Was I encouraging him to be self-indulgent? I really felt that I had no choice but to trust him: if I tried to coerce him in any way he became either very distressed or very angry. I was lucky to have the support of two home educating friends who assured me that he would recover, and gradually he did. The first sign came when he accepted an invitation from his step-dad for a 'boys' night out'. After debating with himself for some time, he managed to let go of me and returned triumphant, having had a really good time. Before long, his old confidence had come back and he was inviting himself to friends' houses and suggesting more nights out with his step-dad. His curiosity began to get the better of him, too: when we were out and about, he would go up to anybody who was doing anything interesting – mending a car, building a wall or fiddling with wires in a hole in the road – and interrogate them. He would also march up to complete strangers and say: 'I'm home-educated, you know.' Usually, people reacted very well and if they didn't, Tom was not in the least put off. 'He wasn't very friendly, was he, Ali?' And off he would go to startle somebody else.

Towards the end of the summer holidays, I began to wonder how he would cope when everyone went back to school. A friend suggested that we start a new EO group in the park, and we held our first meeting on the first day of term, which helped us over a big psychological obstacle. The group is still meeting two years later.

We were lucky to be living in London then, because there is so much going on for home educators. We went to meetings in East London and also joined Leslie Barson's 'Otherwise Club'. Leslie was running a science class there for the younger children, doing a project on endangered animals. Tom couldn't help getting involved, and soon did not even need me to sit with him. He made puppets for the end-of-term show, although he didn't manage to take part in it, and he also broke through his block around painting after watching some of the adults painting the scenery. Gradually, he joined in with the drama class. Although he was at first determined to have nothing to do with it, before long he was a keen participant.

By this time, Tom was also enjoying a gymnastics class; he had enjoyed PE at school and it was the only thing he missed. I found a class with an enthusiastic and inspiring teacher, who was strict and pushed the children quite hard, but was also sensitive to their limits and gentle with Tom, allowing him to join in at his own pace. I felt Tom had reached a stage in his recovery where he needed me to encourage him to move outwards and rise to the challenge, and it worked. Tom loved it. We have now moved away from London and Tom goes to a different gym class, but he still enjoys it and has recently got his first two BAGA badges – entirely on his own initiative.

> *To teach a man how he may learn to grow independently, and for himself, is perhaps the greatest service that one man can do another.*
> Benjamin Jowett

Ironically, I think if I had not pushed Tom to separate from me and to go to school before he was ready, he would probably be able to cope with it now. However, he is quite clear that he does not want to go and I have had many reasons to be glad about his decision. When Tom's sister, Charis, was born eighteen months ago she was very ill in special care for ten days. Tom was able to spend those days with us, getting used to her, and the nights discovering that he could manage without me. A few months later, we moved to Dorset at the start of a very difficult year during which we moved four times and spent six months living in a caravan with no electricity or running water. Tom's step-dad and I separated, and then we moved again to our present home. Tom has been with me throughout these upheavals and has been involved in all of our decisions. I have been able to give him the attention which he needed to help him cope at his own pace and in his own way.

Tom is very happy and well-adjusted now. He has plenty of friends, both home-educated and some who go to school, and his best friend is a girl – which I am pretty sure would not happen at school! He has time to go for long walks, hunt fossils on the beach and go on adventures with his friends on the twenty-acre farm where we live. He gives the hens flying lessons, feeds carrots to the pony and makes friends with the cows. He is involved with life in a very physical, earthed sense.

We still don't have any money and I often feel stretched to the limit trying to make sure that all our needs are met. I have made sacrifices and compromises, but the rewards have been unexpected and enormous. Okay, so my clothes come from charity shops, my car has a stagnant pond under the back seat and a hacking cough, and I have 27p in my purse. Who cares? I have kind and generous friends, a beautiful place to live and the freedom to stay up until 3am writing this while the kids are asleep.

When I am sleeping in the mornings, Tom has been getting up by himself, lighting the fire, listening to the dawn chorus, teaching himself to tell the time and making me a cup of coffee. I think he should have the last word: 'Home education's fun and I love it.'

Children are natural learners, in the sense of being born as rational, creative thinkers with unimpaired minds. Whilst coercion destroys that natural learning ability, parents (and other trusted adults) still have an enormous role to play in helping children to achieve their ends and in introducing children to a wide range of possible interests. A child who is never forced to learn an academic subject still stands every chance of gaining academic knowledge if this is what he or she desires, but a child whose parents never engage with him/her will be severely hampered in gaining any kind of knowledge. Autonomy is not neglect.

Jan Fortune-Wood: *Doing it Their Way*

Education everywhere

Angie Pullin

I am Angie Pullin and I live in Kent with my husband, who works for BT, my son (11) and my daughter (9), although if our house were another 500 yds up the road we would live in London. My last job before I had children was as branch manager for a chain of estate agents. I misspent my youth living in Canada and California, and bumming around the beaches of France and Spain. When I left school at fifteen, I hated the way school had killed my thirst for knowledge. It took me five years to start learning, and another five before I could face taking 'O' Levels.

Within three weeks of his starting school, my son, who had asked questions all day at home and wanted to know everything about everything, stopped asking questions. He became aggressive and withdrawn. We could not simply stand by and watch the school system destroy him, so we took him out of school and discovered the joys of home educating. His sister has never set foot in school.

About three years ago, I started helping out with the 'Choice in Education' newsletter: I used to edit every alternate issue and do half of the printing. As I became more involved, people started contacting me for information about home education and passing on my phone number to others. I then became a local contact for one of the home education organisations for a while. Now, I just manage the 'Choice in Education' database, distribution, some publicity and providing general home education information, write bits of book, decorate, grow organic veg – and home educate.

How do you home educate?
With great difficulty. Sometimes.

There are so many ways to home educate. You can have school at home or entirely child-led learning, and lots of variations in between. None of them is right or wrong – it is important to do what suits you and your children. Like many others, I started off fairly formally and became more relaxed when we realised how much children learn without formal teaching.

As with the rest of life, you have good and bad days. Occasionally nothing goes right: all the children want to do is use the playstation, everyone is grumpy and all you can think of is to threaten them with school. If we have days like that, I have found the best thing to do is go out, even if it is only a walk to the park or a trip to the supermarket.

Actually, that trip to the supermarket can have a lot of educational possibilities. English? Ask the children to write the shopping list. Exercise and co-ordination? Just try pushing the trolley in a straight line. Economics? Why are you buying own label digestive biscuits, not the famous brand chocolate variety? Seriously, particularly for older children, give them x amount of money and tell them how many meals for y number of people you need, then let them loose. Ask your children to estimate how much your shopping will cost by rounding the prices up and down, then compare the difference at the till: a much more meaningful way of learning maths. History? Discuss what shopping was like when you were their age and ask grandparents or elderly neighbours to relate their experiences. Geography? When my children were smaller they would fill in on a map of England or the world where all the items came from. I am sure there are lots of other ideas which we have not thought of.

A few months after I had taken my son out of school, I was reading to him and his younger sister in the garden. He asked me how a strawberry flower got to be a strawberry and, taking advantage of the moment, I rushed indoors and got the little Usborne book that we had, all about pollination. We spent ages wandering around the garden following bees from plant to plant, talking about the process and naming the different parts of the plant. Because we were home educating, my son's question could be answered and demonstrated when he wanted to know. When they learn like that, it sinks in and stays.

My children like watching some of the schools programmes, and some mornings when it is really cold, we all sit in bed together thinking of the poor children arriving frozen at school. Radio 4 sometimes broadcasts children's plays; my daughter has really immersed herself in 'Swallows and Amazons'. She has made up miniature books for the children (dismembered Barbies!) to take to the Island, drawn maps, looked at atlases, found out about Amazons and spent hours acting out the play.

> *It is hard not to feel that there must be something very wrong with much of what we do in school, if we feel the need to worry so much about what many people call 'motivation'. A child has no stronger desire than to make sense of the world, to move freely in it, to do the things that he sees bigger people doing.*
>
> John Holt: *How Children Learn*

Both of my children enjoy educational computer games; inexpensive ones can be bought from places like Wise Owl Shareware, or you can download a lot from the Internet. (But do check to see how long you need to be connected to download the program, it can take ages!) My son's spelling and typing have radically improved since he has started playing fantasy role-playing games on-line with other children.

We play a lot of board games which make maths and English fun, things like Scrabble or Monopoly. Card games like poker and cribbage also help with maths, while Bingo is great for number recognition for younger children. You can buy good, cheap books of number and word games very easily.

We cover local history and tie in different historical periods with educational visits, either near home or while on holiday, and with TV programmes like the '1900 House' and schools broadcasts.

At the moment most of our Geography is UK based: we have an excellent jigsaw puzzle of the UK, with all the counties as separate pieces. We make full use of the library, and Tourist Information Centres are good for finding out about educational opportunities if you are going on holiday.

We have plenty of Science books from many sources, and buy electronics kits from a mail order company called 'Opitec'. We also get the 'Science Experiment of the Week' from the Internet. There is an excellent Internet site called 'How Things Work' where they strip down everyday items such as cars, computers or cameras, and they also have a question and answer section.

How much does it cost?

As much or as little as you want or can afford. The income of the average home educating family is as diverse as the different ways of educating. I have friends who are single parents on benefit, couples bringing in only one low income and others who seem to have plenty of money, and all do a brilliant job of educating their children.

Being on a low income does not stop you from home educating: you can order any texts or special books from your library. Some libraries allow you to have more books out for a longer time, and offer special rates for hiring educational videos or CD-Roms. One of the best ways of getting books is from charity shops or boot sales. Some families club together to purchase educational resources to share, and other home educators in your area may be willing to lend books or equipment. If you or a friend have access to the Internet, this can cost 50p an hour or less at weekends. There is so much information available, and many sites have worksheets or quizzes which you can print out.

Most educational suppliers will take orders from home educators, but tend to be expensive and very school-mentality biased. I would not recommend buying books that you have not inspected first, but some companies will let you have goods on approval. WH Smith and Waterstones offer an ever-improving range of educational and workbooks, with regular special offers. County bookshops sell permanently discounted workbooks and are good for fun, educational books. Some of the best general workbooks I have found are produced by the Travellers School Charity – they cost around £5, and offer 135 pages of worksheets in science, maths, history and English, teaching children about the world in which we live now. They cover environmental issues, wildlife, traditional crafts, recipes and enjoyable activities.

One of the most important resources for home education on a budget is cereal boxes. You can make board games targeted to your child's ability, multiplication charts, flash cards relevant to your children, counters, bridges, quiz cards – the list is endless. My children used to love playing shops (you can buy ready made small size counters or, better still, make them yourself from matchboxes and corks, covered and decorated). To start with we priced everything at 2p then, when they had learnt their two times table, we moved on to 3p. It was a great success. Once they can read, another essential item is the Argos catalogue: a couple of months before Christmas and birthdays, my children are browsing through the toy section, calculator and paper to hand, working out what they want and listing it in order of preference!

A computer or frequent access to one is essential, in my opinion. Anyone who cannot use a computer will be at a great disadvantage in the near future. They are rapidly coming down in price and a few Internet suppliers will even give you a free computer if you sign up for a couple of years with them. Some suppliers offer free weekend access, and it is now very cheap to use the Internet as long as you stay off it during the week.

There are no tax allowances for home educators. There are no grants, nor is there any financial help available from LEAs. On the plus side, you don't have to fork out for expensive uniforms or fares to school, and you would have to provide stationery anyway.

What about socialisation?

As the first contact for many parents thinking of home educating, the above question is the one I can guarantee they will ask – as will anyone who discovers that I home educate. Meeting others can be a problem in some areas of the country but is becoming less so, due to the huge increase in home education during the last few years.

Our family has the opposite problem: we could go to a different home education group every day of the week! Some groups are purely social gatherings for children and adults, others are more formal and the children work or do projects and crafts together, some are a mix of both. Then there are all the other educational visits, children's workshops and outings. In the last year we have been to National Trust and English Heritage properties, the Tower of London, the Golden Hind, the National Gallery, the Design Museum and many others. Visits generally provide plenty of discussion or ideas for work.

The whole family enjoys camping and meeting up with home educating friends from all over the UK, starting with the biggest and the best – HesFes in May – and ending with Debden at the beginning of October. HesFes, The Home Educators Seaside Festival, started in 1997: 44 families went camping for a long weekend, with plenty of activities and workshops laid on for the children. By 1999, it had grown to 144 families from all over the UK and Europe – and by an extra couple of days. The children love it. They have friendships which pick up where they left off, and they always manage to make new friends. Often they correspond afterwards by letter or e-mail (English and ICT!)

The difficulty for children at school is that they only learn to socialise with children of the same age, and even that fails if there is a bullying problem. Peer pressure does not permit children to play with others who are older or younger.

It is a joy (most of the time) to watch home-educated children playing together. Last year I was at a friend's open house meeting with fourteen children aged from nine months to fifteen years old. They all played together, taking turns (boys as well as girls) in looking after the younger children and including them in the games as much as possible. They were noisy purely from enjoyment, there was no fighting or the dreaded 'I can do that better than you can', or the putting each other down which you hear from so many schoolchildren. The same is true of most of the local groups.

Overview

Would I have still taught my children at home if I had known what I know now? Yes, without a doubt. I think the hardest part is lack of time for yourself, just to be at home alone. If you don't have a supportive partner or family nearby, it can be very tough. For me, the other bugbear is the mess: there is always some craft activity or science experiment on the go that can't possibly be moved, and I have forgotten what the dining table looks like. I dream of a bigger house, of being organised with loads of storage space, but we manage.

The best thing is being with my children. I would hate to miss that look of bliss on their faces when something clicks into place. I am constantly amazed at what they seem to learn without effort. School never had the chance to kill their desire to learn.

> *The majority of parents feel affection for their children, and this sets limits to the harm they do them. But education authorities have no affection for the children concerned; at best, they are actuated by public spirit, which is directed towards the community as a whole, and not merely towards the children; at worst, they are politicians engaged in squabbles for plums.*
>
> Bertrand Russell

What use is it to pile task on task and prolong the days of labour, if at the close the chief object is left unattained? It is not the fault of the teachers – they work only too hard already. The combined folly of a civilization that has forgotten its own roots is forcing them to shore up the tottering weight of an educational structure that is built upon sand. They are doing for their pupils the work which the pupils themselves ought to do. For the sole true end of education is simply this: to teach men how to learn for themselves; and whatever instruction fails to do this is effort spent in vain.

Dorothy L. Sayers: *The Lost Tools of Learning*

Getting a life

Lara (aged 14)

I have been home-educated for a year now, and I can honestly say that I haven't looked back. When I came out of school I was stressed, unhappy and in a state of permanent exhaustion. These days, however, my life could not be more different.

My journey into freedom started several years ago when I came down with glandular fever. Over the next few months, I became the target for every passing cough or cold, and my teachers and classmates became used to my regular absences from school. I was constantly anxious and tired, and felt very depressed.

Back then, homeschooling sounded like something for child prodigies or the elaborately non-conformist. Not quite fitting into either of these groups, I didn't think I could ever be a homeschooler. But there was something inside me that stopped me from abandoning all hope. Somewhere in my heart, I knew there had to be another way. After all, education is a blessing. I knew it shouldn't be something that made my life a misery.

As the weeks rolled by, my desperation grew. Thanks to the global community of the Internet, I was becoming more aware of the home education movement. It had a much stronger presence than I had anticipated – I couldn't believe there were so many people just like myself who didn't go to school! I armed myself with information, exchanged long e-mails with homeschoolers around the world, and thought hard. School certainly wasn't getting better, and neither was my health. But what chance did a twelve-year-old have of getting her parents to let her leave school?

I count myself lucky that my parents are open-minded people. Somewhat sceptically, they agreed to look into homeschooling. Certain they would say no, but wanting to be fair, they joined me in a research effort that dominated the latter part of my Summer holiday. Books were consulted, websites were scoured, and phone calls were made as we scrounged for information. Packages from EO, HEAS and others came through our letterbox each morning and, slowly but surely, I saw a change in my parents' attitudes. Like me, they were surprised at exactly how much homeschooling had to offer, and when decision time came they gave me full permission to leave school. With my parents backing me at last, I was on cloud nine.

My parents did, however, leave the final decision up to me. Whilst my heart begged to be free of school, my head was contemplating the enormous changes that homeschooling would bring; but, armed with so much knowledge about the world outside of school, I don't think I could have gone back for good. I said yes to home education, and attended school for one final term before saying goodbye that Christmas.

Goodbye to school, and hello to freedom.

After a year at home, I'm starting to find my niche in the home education community. When it comes to my academic objectives, I am usually in the driver's seat. After deciding which GCSEs I will sit at the end of each academic year, my dad and I scrutinise the appropriate syllabuses and draw up lists of plans to act on and deadlines to meet. The closest thing I get to a school timetable is my termly schedule, which my dad draws up a few weeks before the start of a new academic term. It outlines my objectives for the coming weeks, including things such as lists of books to read, videos to watch and sources to consult. Mentally, I break the schedule down into things to accomplish each week, and then, finally, tasks to get done every day. Let's just say that my time management skills have improved dramatically over the last year!

Many home-educating families see GCSEs as a stumbling block where parental expertise just isn't enough, but I beg to differ. I study by correspondence course, which gives me the freedom to do the work as and when I want, but get guidance when it comes to coursework deadlines, recommended reading and exam preparation. Yes, there is a lot of work to get through, but the flexibility of homeschooling provides the perfect conditions for just that. You learn a lot more about self-motivation and discipline than you would at school. When the goal is your own, nothing can stop you.

I will be sitting my first two GCSEs this summer, and I feel strongly that home education has been a major bonus during my studies so far.

I can give as much time as necessary to assignments, coursework or revision, and really immerse myself in each subject. When do you get the chance to do that at school?

Over the last year, my mind has become free again and I have been able to ponder over so many views that would once have seemed set in stone. I have definitely started to query this wonderful socialisation thing that schools are supposed to offer.

Say the word 'school' and you automatically think of rows of children sitting at desks, books open and pens poised. Despite these academic associations, I sometimes wonder what school is really for. Though I have been questioned over and over about the status of my social life now that I am free, people tend to be surprisingly accepting of the fact that I am capable of teaching myself. If school is about learning rather than socialisation, how come it is the latter that receives the most attention? It always confuses me slightly that people think a school-based social life is so wonderful. Show me the good in being made to turn around, quieten down and sit up straight all day. You may be with people at school, but there's a big leap to take before you are actually socialising with them. Sitting side by side in forced silence doesn't seem like much fun to me.

It is true, however, that home education has had a significant impact on my social life. School allowed me to resent the forced contact with my peers, and left me physically and mentally shattered by the early afternoon. Weekends and holidays were sacred – I rarely wanted to waste my precious hours of freedom by seeing the people that I was expected to spend all week with anyway. 'Friendship' was often little more than chatting to someone by the Coke machine during break.

And now? My diary is overflowing with social engagements, weekends rarely pass without seeing my friends, and the school friendships I have held on to have deepened beyond belief. My friends and I have learned to make time for each other out of boundaries imposed by the institution, and it must be said that they have been wonderful about including me in parties, sleep-overs and shopping trips. I value the time I spend with them now, and really appreciate the fact that they've stuck by me and still include me in so many of their activities.

As well as this, my social circle has widened far beyond a cluster of classmates born in the same year as me. I'm free to mix with people of different ages and from different backgrounds. I am a firm believer that the age-segregation imposed by today's school system is unnatural and unnecessary. Age has little to do with maturity or academic ability, which is another factor that home educators are free to recognise.

You see, home education isn't just for child prodigies or those with special needs, and you don't need to be a millionaire, a superstar, or wildly eccentric. Plenty of us ordinary folk are homeschooling too – and loving it.

I do sometimes feel the urge to rescue my comrades from the stifling world of our school system. I can see everything so clearly now, but they are still stuck in the daily grind of academia. Thanks to my persistent illnesses, few people were surprised when they heard I was leaving school, but some of them looked ready to faint when they discovered I wasn't having a regular tutor. I might as well have been speaking in Ancient Greek when I told them I was an autodidact. My friends are bright, interesting, intelligent people – but school is all they know, and it's likely to stay that way.

Many adults, of course, think school is 'good'. But why? Because it's what children are supposed to do? Because it gets them out of the way for six or seven hours a day? I rarely hear an adult say that school is an enriching and fulfilling educational experience for their offspring but, sadly, I have heard people say that they couldn't bear to be around their children all day.

Parents who send their children to school are often loving, caring, open-minded people, but they might have their eyes opened a little if they really knew how their children felt. None of my friends has uttered a negative word about home education, and many have openly expressed their envy.

Home education is not necessarily right for everyone, but neither is school. Adults, who will never be forced to return to school again, think it's 'good'. Many of the children who go on a daily basis dislike it. Who is really the most qualified to judge?

Home education is a different world from that of the hectic school day. For me, it is much more intellectually stimulating, and allows me to make time for personal interests that range from yoga to writing. I am no longer bound by the four o'clock school bell. If I have a goal that matters to me, I will do everything in my power to achieve it, rather than only being allowed to work on it in a stuffy classroom during a forty-minute lesson. If I take the time to visit friends or relatives during the school day, I can simply put in an extra hour each night until I feel I am up-to-date again. I have my overall objectives in mind all the time, and this keeps me on the right track.

Home education offers me a kind of physical and mental freedom that I never dreamed possible. My life is my own again, and I have lost that sensation of swimming against the tide. I'm free to live and learn as I please – and I can honestly say that I have never been happier.

Molly (aged 6)

I have been home-educated for all of my life. Because my sister is home-educated I thought I'd like to be with her. Since I was two I have been going to Education Otherwise things. I like being home-educated a lot. I like my work, I love doing maths and I think I can read very well. I have lots of friends in EO I see a lot of people who are much older than me who I wouldn't see if I went to school, I like them a lot and I think they like me. One of the people we know had an Indian fashion show and we were in it. We are going to be in another one this year. I liked being in it very much and I think we were good because we are going to be in more dances this time. I have a friend that I like very much, she is called Katie. I have been round to her house on my own.

Trying to get more learning out of the present system is like trying to get the Pony Express to compete with the Telegraph by breeding faster ponies.
Edward Fiske: *Smart Schools, Smart Kids*

Leaving school behind

Penny Clarke

Our children are all boys: James (18), Nick (15) and Alex (9). The older two both went to school until six years ago, when we began home educating.

James and Nick both went to a very traditional C of E primary school, the nearest to us which seemed suitable at the time. James always struggled academically whilst Nick just went with the flow, but they were both happy at school and generally enjoyed going. When James was twelve, and at secondary school, we realised that he was not going to do anything much academically and might well suffer all the social consequences. The school could offer only inappropriate disciplinary measures and a lack of text books. We needed to do something to help him, but what?

I knew that home education was an option, so we joined Education Otherwise and avidly read their literature, and any other articles about home education which we could find. We contacted people who lived reasonably near to us, or who had children of similar ages, and talked to them about their experiences. In consultation with James, we finally decided to de-register him from school with the initial aim of getting him set with the basics, before reviewing the situation and deciding whether he should return to school. Well, he didn't return and within weeks his younger brother was also de-registered; our youngest has never been to school.

Having taken James out of school, and with Nick, at his own request, following close behind, we wondered what to do next. I knew that if we pushed James in directions he did not want to go, we would end up with a real rebellion and problems on our hands, and so we let him go his own way. With hindsight, I think he really needed the next four years to de-school, get rid of all the negative messages which teachers had thrown at him and simply recover. He watched TV, listened to CDs, played his drums and did bits and pieces of 'work.' In contrast, Nick is quite conscientious and worked hard in a school-type way for a couple of years. We purchased several curriculum schemes for both James and Nick because, with three lads of such differing ages at home, it was too time-consuming trying to plan work. We decided to cut our losses and buy in ready-made schemes. James worked at them half-heartedly, whilst Nick was quite keen to 'keep up with his school mates', and worked hard.

Do you know what? Over that period of time James's handwriting, spelling and presentation skills all improved immensely; I cannot describe how bad they had been. He enrolled on three GCSE courses (due to my panicky attempts to appease our LEA) but hated them. However, he chose to do a Saturday course at the local Further Education College when he was fifteen. It was at BTEC level and he passed with merit, having hardly ever passed anything before. He has just gone on from there. He is at college (has won an award and passed two maths exams!) and loves being a student; he plays in several bands, works with his Dad installing computer systems and earns some money designing web sites – all self-taught (apart from the drum lessons).

> *One of the many great advantages of home-based education is that children not shut up in school have a chance to see their parents and other adults work and if they wish, as many do, to join in.*
> John Holt: *How Children Learn*

I tell you all this to illustrate that at one point we really wondered if we had done the right thing in taking him out of school: he spent years being reasonably happy, but with no real sense of direction and apparently doing nothing.

Nick is quite different: he is the one who started doing GCSEs at fourteen and is keen to do more. He has really enjoyed the GCSE course work, but was very nervous about the exams. He did a CLAIT (Computer Literacy and Information Technology) course at a local Adult Education Centre a couple of years ago and now, like James, works with his Dad and is beginning to get to grips with web page design. He is also doing the same BTEC module that James did a few years ago.

Alex has never been to school. He toyed with the idea a while ago but when I explained that he would have to spend time each day sitting down, listening to the teacher and doing as he was told, he gave me an incredulous look and said, 'I'm not doing that.' He can read quite well, although I have not really taught him – we have just read books together and I have pointed out sounds like *ch, st, oo* – but he prefers me to read to him. He can dictate letters and e-mails fluently, but prefers not to write or type them himself! He loves sport, playing with his friends, watching TV and playing computer games, and is also a whizz at deciding which are the best buys in the supermarket.

Like many families new to home education, we originally tried to duplicate school at home in those early days. However, after joining a newly-formed local home educator's group, we began to go out a lot on visits, to workshops, meetings and to see friends. As we became busier, somehow the 'work' side of our lives became less important. Although our main aim was to get the boys to GCSEs, we felt that as long as they had the basics and knew how to present their ideas, they would cope with GCSEs later on, if they chose to take them.

I tend to collect anything which I think may be of use at some time, such as leaflets, books and special offers. Consequently we have loads of resources which I can use to get things started whenever an interest is expressed. We may only end up reading a story, going on a visit or starting to build a model Roman Villa, but the amount of information which seems to go into heads and stick there makes me realise that we do not necessarily need to spend hours working on anything in order for it to be of long term value.

Education is too important to be left to the educators.

Francis Keppel

To give a good illustration of this: Alex and I waited in the car one day during his brother's music lesson and we began talking about nouns, verbs and adjectives. I told him what they were, giving him a few examples, and we then made up sentences in which the other had to identify the parts of speech. A good game which we repeat periodically for a couple of minutes. In school, he would probably have spent half a term doing daily worksheets on this, whereas we just have occasional conversations; yet the end result is the same. He does not do any 'work'; most of our 'work' is done orally, but this does not prevent the older ones undertaking academic work and passing exams.

We have always tried to offer the boys as wide a variety of experiences as possible so that they can seek out where their strengths and weaknesses, skills and interests lie. We let them try something out so they can get an idea of what is involved, but we make no great financial outlay in terms of buying special kit or equipment until they are ready to commit themselves. If they decide not to continue, that is OK with us.

They all like music and we have financed many lessons and instruments for them, often at the cost of doing something for ourselves: our pleasure comes from seeing them developing their talents and enjoying themselves. They have also helped purchase some of the instruments, mainly by doing paper rounds. I spend hours in the car driving them to places, lessons, events and to see friends. Luckily, most of their friends have parents with whom I also get on, so enabling them to socialise has not been a chore for me – it has allowed me socialising time as well.

At times I get into panic mode and think we should be doing something, thinking about workbooks and projects, but then I look at James and compare the lethargic, uninterested and under-confident boy he once was with the young man who is now enjoying life to the full, going out in the world confidently, living his own life, and I know that we were right to let him do it his own way. He is not 'academic', but does this matter?

Much learning does not teach a man to have intelligence.
Heraclitus

When I look at some of my non-home educating friends and the perceived problems they have with their teenagers, whom they seem to feel they have to control, I feel thankful that we 'deviated from the norm' with our family before the teenage years. By opting out of the system and educating the boys at home, it made life so much easier for us in choosing to bring them up in our own way. Not only have the boys been free from peer pressure, so have we as parents.

We do have a few rules, important ones which the boys are expected to stick to, however none of them has ever done anything bad enough to warrant being 'grounded'. We have good relationships with our boys (yes, we do have arguments sometimes but they always blow over very quickly) and absolute trust in them. Since he was fourteen, James has been going all over the country on his own to visit or stay with friends, with no problems. Nick has just started going about on his own locally. He is not quite as confident as James at the same age, but they are different and need to be treated differently.

I have tried to illustrate how we spend years 'doing nothing', and yet how, in spite of this, the older boys are being successful, each in their own way. It just so happens that they have both chosen fairly conventional routes – but that alone, to us, does not necessarily spell success. What is important to us is that they have made their own choices. They have both chosen their own way of life and we respect them for that.

There is no 'right' way to home educate. Every family does what is right for them. You may well find that, as time passes, you need to reassess what and how you are doing things. We started out in a fairly structured mode with regular visits from our LEA. We tried timetables of various kinds, workbooks and schemes, 'lessons' and so on. We were actually being a school at home. Gradually the emphasis shifted and the boys learned quite informally until GCSE syllabuses dictated otherwise. We no longer accept visits from our LEA, instead offering them written reports, which I find much less nerve-wracking.

If we feel the need to become more focused, we have a family brainstorm to explore areas of interest to everyone. Even if we don't follow up all of the suggestions, we find that this process of exchanging ideas often fires our enthusiasm.

We have always found it of great help to join in with HE activities, both locally and nationally. We are very active members of our local group, getting involved in all sorts of things, from playing and chatting to workshops and camping holidays. Alex and I, especially, have contact with many Education Otherwise members and other home educators, and now have friends all over the country. We find this contact with others vital, not only for the boys but also for us, their parents.

Looking back over the last few, home educating years, I feel so pleased with the decision we took to remove the boys from school. I feel that our lives have been enriched by the experience. We still have 'bad days' (doesn't everyone?) but they are in the minority. If something is not working out, we can leave it and put it aside for another time. The main down points are an inevitably reduced family income, with only one of us working full time, and the (very) occasional need to have some child-free time. There are no great pressures other than the self-induced ones of trying to fit too much into each day. We live our lives to suit ourselves and have the pleasure of knowing that we are at nobody's beck and call.

The single most important contribution education can make to a child's development is to help him towards a field where his talents best suit him, where he will be satisfied and competent. We've completely lost sight of that. Instead we subject everyone to an education where, if you succeed, you will be best suited to be a college professor... And we evaluate everyone along the way according to whether they meet that narrow standard of success. We should spend less time ranking children and more time helping them identify their natural competencies and gifts, and cultivate those. There are hundreds and hundreds of ways to succeed and many, many different abilities that will help you get there.

Howard Gardner, author of *Multiple Intelligences*

By bells and many other similar techniques they [schools] teach that nothing is worth finishing. The gross error of this is progressive: if nothing is worth finishing then by extension nothing is worth starting either. Few children are so thick-skulled they miss the point.
John Taylor Gatto: *The Curriculum of Necessity*

FAQ no.6   How do you make time for yourself?

By giving your own needs sufficient priority. In practice it can be difficult to take time out from your family, particularly if you do not have a partner to share some of the responsibility, and it is also easy to feel guilty about your 'selfishness' in making yourself important. However, if you are exhausted, overwhelmed and irritable, then nobody is going to enjoy home education very much. Far from being selfish, it is vital that you have some space to call your own.

Do you have friends or family who would be willing to help? Can you find other home educating families with whom to child-swap? Sometimes, having other children round to play with yours can give you a few hours relative peace, if not quiet! Can you afford a minder or babysitter once in a while? If you want to do a course or play squash at the local leisure centre, are there childcare facilities?

If your children are in school at the moment, bear in mind that their behaviour may be very different when they are home-educated, especially if you are contemplating home education because they are unhappy at school. They will no longer come home stressed and miserable, desperate to 'fill up' on parental comfort whilst they have the chance and vying with each other for your attention. Once their confidence returns, they will be more likely to get engrossed in their own projects for a while, giving you some breathing space.

It is perfectly reasonable to ask older children to sit with a book, game or story tape whilst you have your eyes tested, teeth filled or hair cut. If your children have not reached an age where they can wait for you, or if they have particular needs which make it difficult, can you plan an MOT day for yourself whilst somebody else looks after them?

Probably the most important thing is to discuss with your children what it is that *you* need if home education is to work for the whole family. Shopping trips, uninterrupted phone calls, time to get on with your own interests: all these can usually be negotiated. (If that were not true, this book could never have been written!) Like anyone else, most children are remarkably reasonable when they feel that their views are considered; you can depend upon them to treat you with the same respect which you offer them.

Joe (aged 7)

In school you do all this work but you never have any time to think about it.

Biggs (aged 11)

It's funny how, when I say I am home-educated, other kids always say 'You lucky dog.' Nobody ever says: 'Oh, you poor thing.' On the other hand, loads of adults say: 'Wouldn't you like to be at school?' Well, if they are honest, would *they?*

Tim (aged 10)

When we were living in The UK, my brother Daniel and I went to a wonderful primary school in Bournville, called Saint Francis School. It was beautifully situated, with a nice big playground, big playing fields for the summer, and just before we left they started building a nursery for younger children. The teachers were all lovely and, because it was a small school, I knew everybody.

When I first left SFS to move to Cyprus, I thought that home educating would be very lonely, because at school it all seemed to be planned. I had lots of friends at SFS, I had chatter all around me while I worked, and the school had lots of good teachers. At first I missed choir, recorders, chess club and all the other after school clubs. Now I have joined: a choir (Greek), Cubs (in Greek), I have kept up all my piano playing, and have started learning guitar. At church, I am in a lovely Sunday School, and while all the adults are having their coffee, we all play together. The Sunday School is a good mix of cultures (Canadian, Greek Cypriot, Russian, American and English). Every week we have friends round one afternoon, and we play in our wonderful, huge wild garden.

One of the things that used to irritate me a lot in school: you've just got started, you're digging in and suddenly, one person says: 'I don't understand', and the whole class has to go through the whole explanation, and you completely lose the train of thought.

Now we have been Home Educating for 16 months, I am enjoying it a lot, I enjoy having more time for cooking, reading and gardening.

One of the main things I enjoy is that there are no time limits. At school we had maybe half an hour per subject and then we had to stop whether we wanted to or not. But with home educating, I can spend all morning writing my story or, if we had a question, like Daniel wanted to know about Newton's Laws, or we wanted to learn about silkworms, then we can spend all morning looking in encyclopaedias, or on the Internet. Another thing I like is that you can learn languages much earlier, I'm currently learning Greek and French with Linguaphone. In science, we are following a wonderful biology course, which I totally enjoy, and are using Daniel's chemistry kit to do some chemistry experiments. I think I am learning more than I did in all my years at school.

At first I really wanted to go to school but some of the schools round here are not very good. I wanted to go to secondary school when I'm older but some of the reasons I'm not sure that I want to go to secondary school is that there might be: bullying, teasing, too much homework or the fact I don't like fixed assignments. Like if I'm told to write a two-hundred word story by tomorrow, my brain goes blank, I do it, and just as I'm handing it in I think of loads more stuff.

The end of the tunnel

Mary Rose

'Ooo! There's a mouse!'

The smartly dressed woman edged closer to the edge of the crowded Underground platform and leaned over the rails.

'There he goes!' she screamed. 'Poor little chap! We must help him!'

And before anyone could stop her she was on her knees, head down, bottom up and reaching toward the line...

So what was I doing on Euston Station platform at rush hour on a Friday evening anyway? What had possessed me to leave the comfortable home which I love and bring my husband and five young children to the City? And what psychological damage was being done to young minds by the sight of the ample rump of their mini-skirted mother as she groped for a mouse which had already disappeared under the live rail?

Answer: Home-based education. Yes, dear reader, this is a cautionary tale. Home-based education will change your life. It will call into question your mental health, your sense of responsibility towards your family and yourself, your ability to raise your own offspring, and ultimately may cause you to forsake your wellies and jeans in exchange (albeit temporarily) for a smart cream dress and jacket, and leave you, like me, crawling around the platform of the Underground in pursuit of a mouse.

Rushing headlong into a dangerous situation in an attempt to save a creature smaller, perhaps weaker, always smarter than myself is the story of my life. Inevitably, as with the mouse, the victim of the 'danger' scuttles away unharmed, leaving me hanging from a branch, clinging to a roof, summoned to court or, in this case, dangling over the railway line and in need of being saved. Age and experience have evidently not had any effect. 'Leave it alone' are not words which come easily into my mind. I see something which is causing some distress and act.

So when our children started at the village primary school as 'rising fives' and went quickly from little boys full of enthusiasm for learning to miserable slouching kids who had assumed the demeanour of youths before their time, I had no hesitation in removing them from the place which was the cause of the distress and opting for home education.

The good news is that I have a personal angel. My husband Paul tempers the wild, often impractical ideas which I throw at him with alarming regularity, patiently talking them through, planning, laughing, paying the 'phone bills and living with the piles of paperwork which accompany the latest craze.

'Let's sell up and move to Papa Stour and keep sheep!' I cry as he walks in the front door from a long day in the office; he pretends to believe me.

'Let's get a caravan and live on the edge of a cliff with the five kids and two dogs.'

'Look, I've made us a five foot high indoor scarecrow!'

'If we fit wheels to this Rayburn we'd have a steam locomotive!'

When this kind of life is normal, 'Let's take the boys out of school and educate them ourselves' is not so very radical. Paul sifts through the trail of verbal rubbish which seems to follow me through life and gently, effectively, takes out the gems and discards the rest. The home education idea he recognised to be a gem.*

In fact, our decision was made in the light of a wealth of experience of schools and schooling. We didn't so much believe as *know* that we could do a better job of educating our children than school could. We already had.

Without any formal lessons we had guided them through learning to walk, talk, wash, dress, count and numerous other basic skills, any one of which would daunt the most experienced teacher if it were not for the child's natural ability – and desire – to learn. The fact that our eldest child could read fluently before starting at school was due entirely to his own efforts. He was never pressurised to do so, but he remains an avid reader now.

---

*   See the booklist for details of *Getting Started in Home Education* by Mary Rose and Paul Stanbrook

However, on starting at school, he was given picture books and restricted to a literary diet of *Letterland* and *One, Two Three And Away* when he wanted *The Famous Five*. His younger brother, although unable to read at the same age, was quite capable of supervising and assisting in the making of a lasagne, but school's version of cooking turned out to be putting some icing on a digestive biscuit and decorating it with jelly sweets. He was not unnaturally disappointed in his 'lesson'! Perhaps this was the problem – they both knew too much.

The children had been looking forward to going to school, but their initial enthusiasm quickly turned to dismay and boredom. They became ill, frequently complaining of tummy aches, experiencing nightmares, sleepwalking, bed-wetting, tantrums and asthma attacks. We took the boys to our GP who, after a thorough examination, pronounced them physically well children and suggested stress may be the problem. Could we think what the cause of the stress might be? Well, yes: a school which had openly stated that one child was a problem because at the age of seven he read too much, and that his younger sibling didn't want to come to school because we had made home too interesting. After that, there was really no point in continuing in the exercise of school.

We experienced the euphoria which is familiar to many families the moment the fateful words, 'You don't have to go to school any more' are spoken. A cloud lifted from our whole household. The dogs barked, the cockatiel burst into song. 'Hurrah!' shouted the boys, and skipped off to play (children skip when they are happy – if they don't skip into school there is probably something wrong).

One test of the correctness of educational procedure is the happiness of the child.

Maria Montessori

So we embarked upon a journey into the unknown with the people in the world we know best of all, our own children. We were not aware of how long the journey would be, how difficult to route or where it would lead, but already we could make out a distant light. Was it the end of the tunnel, or something more sinister?

Within a week a letter from the LEA arrived, asking for details of how, where and when we intended to educate our children. The information requested included names and qualifications of all those involved in the education process, plans and a school timetable. We were ignorant of our rights, but not dismayed or fearful. I simply reasoned that I would give them so much information and justification for home educating that they would be sorry they asked.

I set about filling in the form, giving details of the children's names, ages and address, crossing out most of the rest and writing N/A across the timetable. The accompanying notes extended to several thousand words, liberally punctuated with educational jargon and references to philosophy to back it up. We sent it off, had our visit and were not bothered again for twelve months. In fact our LEA visitors were very supportive, pleasant people. They struck up an immediate relationship with the children, playing marbles on the floor, gamely trudging up the garden through the mud and nettles to see the tyre-swing, chickens and goats, and politely munching their way through the biscuits which the children had made in their honour. The latter was the real test, devised by me in case they should ask to return in a hurry – 'Have another of Ned's cakes!'

As it turned out, our visitors are so popular that their return is keenly anticipated for several weeks in advance of the annual visit. I now know the visits are neither necessary nor compulsory, but it is the pressure from the children rather than the LEA which I cannot resist. I trust the children's instincts – they can tell adults who are genuinely interested and interesting at fifty paces. These people from the LEA are not ogres, they are simply people who have the job of making sure that the children are receiving an education. Because they are the only educational professionals to whom I have access, I am not about to make an enemy of them, and I am in any case too busy to look for confrontation where it has no need to exist.

So, that light in the distance turned out to be no more than a couple of railway engineers with a dim torch, following the line but unsure of the route and blissfully unaware of the danger. We see them from time to time, pleasant people, trying to do a difficult job with few, if any, resources at their disposal and no guidelines at all from their management as to how to carry out their task. Their saving grace is that they have a genuine and sincere love for and interest in children, the way they learn and their development.

But what's this? Surely that light in the distance must be the end of the tunnel??

Then it was Christmas. Not being part of school can be sad at Christmas. We've never seen our little ones in the Nativity play, never raided the tea-towels and cut up old sheets to construct shepherd's costumes, or ripped down the front room curtains to provide a King with a cloak. But we do other things, we go to church, take part in the local traditions of Mummers plays, learn carols (which the children enjoy so much they still sing them heartily in flaming June), and put on puppet shows for anyone who will watch. Decorating the house has become a ritual. By not being at school we can avoid much of the commercialism of Christmas, dodge the rush and truly appreciate the religious significance of the festival. Christmas in our house starts on Christmas Eve, and continues until Epiphany.

Christmas brings the usual round of visits to friends and relatives. When news is exchanged, questions inevitably turn to the education of the children. Questions come in profusion. So does advice. 'What about the social side?' 'Is it legal?' 'Do you have to follow the National Curriculum?' 'How will you do games / chemistry / languages…?' An almost predictable set of questions are a regular feature of social gatherings. When our eldest child reached eleven, the message was: 'You've had your fun with the kids, now it's time to be sensible and do the responsible thing – SEND THEM TO SCHOOL!'

The most frequent comment regards a child's need to socialise. The fact that the children have socialised all day long, mixing confidently with all age groups and playing peacefully with everyone is insufficient 'evidence' of their competence in social situations, it seems. Comments are made about their 'exceptional' manners (actually we consider it to be normal to say 'please' and 'thank you', but it is so rare to find good manners in schooled children that it merits remark).

Standing our ground and giving our answers causes some people to become annoyed and frustrated. On one occasion a governor of a large and prestigious school stormed out of the room. We have been called over-protective, arrogant, selfish. When I was accepted for a part time university course I was openly accused of neglecting the children.

Even while they teach, men learn.

Seneca

There is also the subliminal message, 'I don't know what you're doing or why, but I have to answer to my friends when they ask about the children, and home educating them puts us in a very difficult position when people say, 'How's so-and-so getting on at school?' Our friends and neighbours think you're hippies, drop-outs or weirdos, and your decision and life-style is a source of great embarrassment to us. Until you tell us the children are going back to school we'd rather not discuss it, thank you.'

Of course different generations see things differently. All normal, respectable children go to school. We fly in the face of this doctrine, and it upsets people.

There are as many, if not more, positive comments, but these usually come from strangers: the Electricity Board man who enquired why the children were not at school when he called and then talked himself into home educating whilst testing the wiring; the lady in the charity shop – an ex-headmistress who fully supports home education, and the local handyman who has a lot of time for home-educated children and takes a pride in protecting them from the aggression of school children in the neighbourhood.

The light this time turns out to be a crowd of people sharing a candle. They are struggling to make sense of what we can see clearly. Their attempts to push towards the little light cause them to bump, trip and fall, angering each other and annoying themselves. Their path is worn and in need of much repair. Some would suggest it is beyond repair. The strongest survive but many fall by the wayside and injure themselves. Some are trampled underfoot. Too many never recover. They know there is another way, they see we have found it, and envy us our light.

We believe that no matter how high or lowly, rich or poor, educated or without a single qualification, the way forward is clear enough if people can only let go of the familiar and look again in a different direction. It is not possible for everyone to see this.

We cannot help these people. They stumble on their way. Perhaps they will meet others like us and, when they do, feel delighted to be able to join in with, 'Oh, I know another family who home educate, and their children…' Because everyone is interested in the education of their children, and everyone is an expert – well, we've all been to school haven't we? We have all seen it done so often, teaching is a job anyone could do. You just stand up and talk, point at something with a stick and the children get their heads down and write. That's teaching isn't it? That's what you do at home? Well actually, no. Perhaps one day they will come back, turn on the light and have a closer look.

The burden of responsibility for opting for home education extends beyond the 'Mummy and Daddy know best' philosophy. Our deliberate choice has had a knock-on effect upon the whole family. Perhaps we have unwittingly hurt people whom we love and to whom we meant no harm. Is this the sacrifice which needs to be made for the continued happiness and well-being of our children?

We wait patiently on our platform for the next arrival, tending the children's needs, listening to their chatter, reflecting upon the events of the journey so far, wondering what is to come, where we will go and what mode of transport will take us there. At first the platform seems deserted, but as our eyes become accustomed to the lighting the ghost-like figures of other families just like ours begin to appear. All races and creeds are represented. Travellers brush shoulders with middle-class, middle England people from the leafy suburbs. For some, the ticket for this journey has been costly. Others have rejected a ride in a taxi to take this train. Why? The more we talk, the clearer they become. The platform is filling up. Some give up and vanish, some decide to take a later train or try a different route, knowing that the option of returning to the station is always available. Most stay, and suddenly the place is filled with light and sound as a new train rushes into the station.

The passengers are laughing, talking to each other, animated in discourse. Children point and wave at us through the windows. As we move towards it I glance at the electronic sign above the platform: *'Home Education – non stop all the way, calling at everywhere.'*

The doors hiss open and we are welcomed aboard. This compartment is already crowded, but the train is long, surprisingly long, and there is plenty of room. I still have no idea where we are going, but the children are happy and learning, our family is secure and I have a sneaking feeling that, although I only caught a glimpse of the driver, I've seen his face somewhere before...

What really happened next...
'Get up' ordered a stern voice behind me. I know that voice of old, and obeyed without question. 'The mouse will be all right. It lives down there. There must be lots for it to eat, and it's happy!'

'But we could release it on to some grass, in the sunshine,' I protested, racking my brain to think of where I might find 'some grass' in central London suitable for a mouse.

'No. This is where it lives. It wouldn't survive. Leave it alone.'
Perhaps I should turn my energies to mouse rehabilitation programmes. I could become the Dr. Barnardo of the Underground railway mice...

Our train arrived, we boarded and joined the other commuters, sitting in near silence. The silence on Underground trains has reached epidemic proportions. Even the children fell silent, daring only to whisper questions about the map of the Underground, which way are

we going, what are the flashes of blue light outside, will we see fish when
we go under the river Thames... Only home-educated children, I
thought, could be fascinated by the view from the window of an
Underground train.

And us?
Paul had found a few books in Ancient Greek, the children now had
some concept of Big City, Bright Lights, learnt not from picture books
or CD-Roms but from sore feet and tired eyes, and I had made my
debut as a researcher at a conference on home education and found out
about microphones which don't work very well.

Learning at home extends all of us, pushes us to our limits, and then
teaches us that those limits don't really exist after all. We take up
university courses in subjects we ditched thirty years ago and do well in
examinations. People like me who failed the 11+ study for doctorates,
and children who have attended a school for no more than two terms
as infants are offered a place at the local Grammar school.

Then we went home.

Postscript
Joe visited the Grammar school. His verdict? 'Looks like a prison.' He
decided to stay at home and learn something.

An eternal question about children is, how should we educate them?
Politicians and educators consider more school days in a year, more
science and math, the use of computers and other technology in the
classroom, more exams and tests, more certification for teachers,
and less money for art. All of these responses come from the place
where we want to make the child into the best adult possible, not in
the ancient Greek sense of virtuous and wise, but in the sense of one
who is an efficient part of the machinery of society. But on all these
counts, soul is neglected.

Thomas Moore: *Care of the Soul*

A little bit country, a little bit rock'n'roll

Tabitha Knight and Callum Church

My first encounter with home education had me running for cover, swearing I would never become like 'one of those people'. I was at a Green Fair, listening to a parent happily prattling away about allowing the children to stay up and play Lego while he went to bed. Having spent three-and-a-half years trying to get Dominic to sleep in his own bed, this could only be seen as a nightmare!

Cut from a messy relationship breakdown to a few years later with a new partner and a new baby. Dominic had started school, adjusted and seemed relatively happy, until he had an awful teacher who told him off in front of the whole class for telling tales on children who were talking when he was trying to do his work. He was also wrongly accused of misbehaving in the playground and subsequently punished. For such a righteous-minded child, he felt incredibly indignant about all of this.

When he reached the Juniors, although he had a really nice teacher, he wanted to do more work than he was given, but couldn't. He felt victimised at times for having longish hair, being a strict vegetarian and not conforming to the trainers and football shirt brigade. To top it all, he was always tired and always had headaches.

Jasper started school a few months after his fourth birthday: much, much too soon, but I was at college and it suited me. I had forgotten about home education and did not realise that I did not have to send him to school until he was five, if at all. Jasper was tired, tired and more tired and, like Dominic, he started picking up horrible schoolboy habits. He was just way too young to be stuck in a classroom for six hours every day.

> *School days are, I believe, the unhappiest days in the whole span of human existence. They are full of dull, intelligible tasks, new and unpleasant ordinances, brutal violations of common sense and common decency.*
>
> H.L.Mencken

As the school year was finishing and we knew that we would be moving, we thought about removing them from school. This was partly for the above reasons but also because we did not want them to change their personalities in order to fit in at school. We got all the relevant information from the various home education organisations and informed the headmistress of our intentions. She supported our decision, saying that if any of the parents at the school could do it then we could. We wrote to the LEA to inform them of our decision and the boys left at the end of term. Freedom at last!

I think we gave the children a few weeks' holiday and then started home educating. We did reading and writing, maths and two wonderful projects on the Solar System and the Stone Age. I assumed that our local Education Otherwise co-ordinator would contact us and help us to meet others and organise outings; I even sent out a distress letter which was at first ignored. We began to feel really isolated. Eventually we were sent a list of events in our county but they were all miles away. We did get involved in a tree-planting scheme for a few weeks which the children enjoyed, however personal circumstances meant that this had to stop.

We were put in touch with one local family who were teaching their only child at home. Their child was willing to do a lot more work than our children, very keen to be taught at home, whereas ours did not seem to have such self-motivation for work, being more cerebral than practical (perhaps something they have picked up from us). This made us feel inferior because we assumed that every other home educator would be as successful as this family, whilst we were struggling. To top it all, we had to move (again!) and couldn't find anywhere to live. Time was running out, times tables forgotten about.

The house in which we ended up was the house from hell: no sooner had we moved in than we were informed that we would have to be out within six months. Complete chaos ensued, boxes remained packed, brains stopped working and home educating appeared to be failing us completely. We felt that we were the only home educators in the world who were miserably flailing about in the dark.

I tried writing letters to people on the contact list but no one responded. Although we began to wonder if there was any point continuing in our efforts, we contacted the nearest co-ordinator outside our area and hope was rekindled. We met up once a fortnight with a group of people who were nice and thought along the same lines as us. The children got to play with other children of the same age at last, and we got to talk to grown ups who were doing the same as us.

A few months ago, I had another bash at increasing our home education circle by writing loads of letters to people on the contact list. Again, the response was very disappointing: only one person wrote back. From that, however, we have now met another nice group of people who meet up regularly, and the boys have started their swimming lessons with them once a week.

Two years into home educating, I would say that we still feel quite isolated at times, and worry that we are complete failures. I find that having a toddler to deal with as well as the other two makes things very difficult. It is hard to divide my attention between all three children, and now there is another one on the way to add to the chaos. I think that just having one or two children of similar age must be so much easier; however, one parent I have met has six children and she manages perfectly well, so it must be us!

Our children are not extraordinary geniuses and I doubt very much that they are advanced as far as SAT tests go. I imagine, however, that they are much deeper thinkers than a lot of the children who go to school, often asking profound questions which we struggle to answer, if at all. They do not spend a free afternoon studying anything for fun; generally if left to their own devices, they will sit glued to the computer or fight and bicker non-stop.

Autonomous education simply does not work for us, but it would be suicidal to attempt to enforce a full, strictly regimented timetable. Some days I spend ages persuading them just to do half-an-hour of maths and English, but on other days they do their work without any fuss and seem to get a lot out of it. Our home is brimming with all sorts of books, workbooks, paper, paints, educational things (computer and otherwise), but they never take the initiative to suggest anything.

Apart from all our apparent failings, we still believe that home education is the best way to raise our children. I think school would change their personalities and stifle their creative thinking and confidence in their own opinions and beliefs. I think that the only possible positive benefit of sending them to school would be the social aspect, but even then there is no guarantee that, in a group of thirty people their own age, they would find one person with a similar outlook on life, and school friends can be so fickle.

Sometimes it seems that their education springs out of unexpected places. We recently read *Skellig* by David Almond, which provoked a lot of discussion on subjects from death and angels to what it would be like to be a bird, or how they would feel if our forthcoming baby were to be born prematurely or needed to have an operation. This sort of learning will probably stay with them for longer as it is self-inspired rather than force fed; yet I still find it hard to believe in my convictions that this is sufficient education for them. Only time will tell.

Callum Church

As badly as it seems our home educating is going, the thought of sending the children to school now could only be a last, desperate measure and we try to reassure (or sometimes threaten!) the children that this is the case. My own memories of school are not particularly valuable, I just felt myself steered through year after year of set texts, learning parrot fashion in order to pass exams which are meant to demonstrate an expert knowledge of the subject. I did not question it at the time and certainly never knew of any alternatives: it was just what everybody did. However, knowing there is an alternative gives us every reason to keep the children out of school and I am sure that they are benefiting from it, despite the self-doubt that keeps rising to the surface.

> *Education is what remains after one has forgotten everything learned in school.*
>
> Einstein

It was only when I went to University five years ago that it really hit home how structured and constrictive formal education is. I was fortunate enough to undertake an Independent Study Degree (now defunct) that allowed me to design my own course, set my own essays and learn about what I was interested in. For the first time, I could remember that I actually wanted to learn, and enjoyed the experience. I suddenly realised, at the age of twenty-nine, that this is what learning is really about. I was actively seeking to learn in a way that I never had previously, whilst all around me education was being dished out in great chunks to lecture halls full of passive students, who could basically take it or leave it.

There is little room for such learning in school. Teachers are provided with a curriculum, a tower of educational building blocks that is deemed suitable for all children to learn from. But why should someone else decide what is right for your child to learn? Who can know better than yourself? To have that choice, to have a guiding hand in your children's education is surely a better option if you are willing to sacrifice a good part of your life to it.

The good thing is that you do not have to follow the National Curriculum, which allows the creative freedom to explore subjects in new and interesting ways, and we try to incorporate different subjects when we do project work. For example, we are doing a 'geography' project in which the children have to get around the world in eighty days. They have both planned their journey from a world map and at each country they 'visit' (utilising book and computer resources), they complete a fact sheet about that country. They also 'take photos' of interesting places by printing off pictures from the computer encyclopaedia. In essence, it is a geography project, but by keeping a journal of their travels they are doing English, they use maths skills to calculate distances and travel times and by accessing the computer they are improving IT skills.

This mix seems to work well when it does work (a similar time-travelling history project has yet to take off the ground!) and the children enjoy it. As well as working, they are role playing, too.

However, while it is nice to work away from the curriculum, it is always tempting to look at what children of their Key Stage group are expected to know, to buy books of SAT tests, just to reassure yourself that you are doing something right. Of course, the reality is that the children are probably not up to the same level as others their age and this can be disappointing, but you have to remember that children at school are being geared up solely for these tests and that it shouldn't really matter whether or not they would pass this or that exam at this or that stage.

School is the easy option. Apart from having to get up early to get the children ready and actually taking them to and from school, the rest of the day is yours. I'm sure that most parents in that position treasure this time, but then you have to question your motivations for sending children there in the first place.

The sad part is that neither of the children has a really good friend whom they see and play with regularly. They get social interaction with other children, which is great, but the meetings seem to be just too far apart and quite often involve travelling that little bit further. All this could change, though: we have found other activities in which to involve them, outside of the home educating circle, such as drama, basketball and Warhammer and it may well be that they find a good friend this way.

I think we were expecting a 'handbook to home education', something that would guide us step by step through a successful transition from school to home. No such thing existed, much to our chagrin and in view of our desperation for help. We were only guided to the contact lists and basically left to our own devices.

We have eventually reached the conclusion (after all this time!) that the more you put into home education, the more you get out of it. There is no magical mentor to take you by the hand and lead you along an easy path. You have to make the effort to find other people whom you like, children whom your children will like, in order to get the reassurance that you are not alone in your experience.

We have to keep reminding ourselves that we are doing the best thing for our children, educationally and socially, by keeping them out of school.

Home educating us all

Caroline Spear

I think that I was lucky to have met a home educating family prior to the birth of my second daughter; I was impressed that two young children were happy to ignore the biscuit tin, and that a teenage boy conversed easily with me. An American family loaned me a book called *The Three Rs At Home* which gave me further inspiration: the tone of the book, and its ability to point out the failings of the 'system' spoke to the reluctant rebel in me. All my life, I had been brought up to conform and to believe that the state system existed to benefit me. It took the unnecessarily cruel delivery of my first daughter for me finally to learn that the system expected total compliance.

When we moved away from the city to a very quiet town, Freya started at the only state nursery there. They believed that the way to help children achieve independence was to give them the freedom to choose what to do and the atmosphere there was electric, humming with activity; and with not an adult to be seen, until I looked closely and saw the bigger heads amongst the smaller ones. These were a happy two years for Freya and it was a joy to see the confidence of the children there. I could stay, together with Zsofia, and be as involved as I liked.

At last came the time when Freya would have to go to school. I told her that if she wanted to be educated at home she could be, but she chose school and, at the time, I was relieved. I was pregnant, and with the baby due a month after Freya started school and Zsofia starting at a playgroup, it all seemed to fit in nicely.

I remember the lump in my throat as I watched Freya at her introduction session at school, how eagerly she lined up and went off with the other members of her class to meet their new teacher. My baby was now a little girl, and going off to be influenced by others.

The beginnings of my doubts with school began within a month. Erica was so keen to be born that she arrived before her Papa even got home! Freya had the next day off, only to come home from school the following day with the news that she had missed the number three and it would probably not get covered again until next year. I was baffled. We now had three children and the number would come up regularly. Freya started to come home tired and bad tempered. This became worse with the introduction of reading words, photocopied from their reading scheme on to pieces of paper. We could not understand why she was unable to read these words. They were in her books and we went through them with her, only to find that she could not recognise them two minutes later. This led to much confusion and upset all round. She became despondent as her friends progressed to the next books and she did not, and then started to say she did not like maths. She was just five years old.

Meanwhile Zsofia wanted to go to nursery school. I flinched, because a friend had been taking her to playgroup whereas now I would have to become 'super-taxi'. Well, I tried but Zsofia wanted me to stay with her and now, with a new baby, I was knackered by the time I had got all of us out of the house.

Freya's moods were getting worse and I knew that I was beginning to lose my daughter. Something had to change. Talks at the school did not make any difference, so I started to look at alternative schools. In reality they were all much of a muchness and a car drive away, too. I had to consider what we would do if the car was out of action, or if I was too ill to drive, because there was no one else locally who could help out.

A home educating friend loaned me her collection of John Holt and Education Otherwise books. I was inspired all over again, but vacillating about what to do. It seemed too 'alternative' to home educate; what would others think? As I turned this over in my mind, a friend from London came to stay and announced that they were going to home educate. I immediately turned to Marco and said: 'That's it, if it's what Freya wants, so will we.' Freya said yes without hesitating, and I left Marco to talk with my friend's partner about this decision. Again, it was fortunate that the menfolk were able to cover a lot of ground about their concerns, and be supportive.

During the summer holidays, I wrote the letter asking the school to deregister Freya. We took the letter together and she posted it. Our final walk back from the school was the happiest ever: we both felt as though the shackles had been removed.

We had some negative reactions: it is sad how many children believe that they can only learn at school and say this to Freya, although she cheerfully tells them otherwise. My mother-in-law was convinced that Freya would become stupid and never get a job. I felt insulted, but as she and my father-in-law were immigrants, maybe I could understand this worry a little. My own parents were concerned about exams (Freya was five!) As a teenager, I had worked in local markets where some stall owners could barely read and write, yet most owned big houses and expensive vehicles.

A lot of fellows nowadays have a B.A., M.D. or Ph.D. Unfortunately, they don't have a J.O.B.

Fats Domino

Others asked about socialisation: wouldn't the children miss out? Asking how many of them worked with thirty-two other people of the same age usually ended that particular line of questioning. Did I have to be a teacher? I have been since my children were born, and they teach me too. Sadly, another thing I hear too often is: 'I could never bear to have my children round me all the time.' I feel so sorry for the children of people who say this. In any case, my children often do their own thing and I could not always tell you what that is.

Zsofia went to nursery that September, and I was not too sure how this fitted in with our educational philosophies. We believe that children learn best when left to explore and make sense of their world in their own time, and that teaching to pass exams does not allow a deeper understanding to develop. Further, we do not believe that it is natural or healthy to spend extended amounts of time wholly within your own age group. Fortunately, I now had the confidence to follow an alternative route and to listen to Zsofia's needs, which included being at home with me. Three weeks after she returned to nursery, we took her out permanently. Now that we were a home educating family, I no longer had to try to be super mum with so much taxi-ing around plus a baby to care for. Freedom!

I decided that as we did not have to follow the National Curriculum, we would not do so. I wanted my children to have their childhood back, to be able to play. Freya's school experience of learning to read and do maths had been so damaging that, although a perfectly capable child, she was now frightened of even trying; I felt it was best not even to mention reading or maths to Freya. I also knew that my ignorance about how children learn had contributed to her bad experience, and to the unnecessary pressure she had felt. Rather than structuring our days, I simply let them unfold, although it took a whole term to get used to going out without having to look at the time. Gradually, Freya began to relax and my confident, strong-minded, curious, affectionate daughter returned.

I received an intimidating letter from the LEA requesting time-tables, details of tutors, lesson plans and all kinds of other information. I promptly wrote back saying that none of this was acceptable nor legally required, and requesting details of the qualifications of their Inspector. After a vague apology, I heard nothing more.

Freya spent a lot of time studying the garden and its wildlife. We had said 'no' to any more pets, so she caught woodlice and told me as much about them as could be found in our encyclopaedia. I was a little worried about how to reintroduce maths, especially as it is not my strongest subject. One day, I picked up some cuisenaire rods cheaply in a sale. I simply left them out on the table, and was thrilled when Freya suddenly called me in to show me the balance which she had built from them, and how she used it.

I would catch her engrossed in activities: one vivid memory is of my little girl standing on a chair at the kitchen sink, blowing bubbles through a straw. She would blow quickly, then slowly, hard then soft, looking at the amount of bubbles she had made, lifting them to the light to stare at the colours reflected in them. I crept out of the kitchen, not wanting to distract her. She did not need a bell to push her on to another activity.

> *Education is a private matter between the person and the world of knowledge and experience, and has little to do with school or college.*
> Lilian Smith

Christmas was looming, and my frantic attempts to write the usual million cards were getting nowhere fast. Freya had not done any writing for a few months, but suddenly saw a use for her gold and silver pens. She began by writing her alphabet, then had a go at writing her own cards. Considering that she had not been practising, I was impressed by the standard of her writing: it was as good as that of her school friends. This illustrates the observations from educationalists that children can write when they have achieved the necessary mental and physical development required for such skills. Freya also had a reason to want to write and this spurred her on.

One year later it was Zsofia's turn to choose where to be educated. We talked about the pros and cons of school and home and she was interested in school, until she realised that she could not eat and drink when she wanted to (she grazes all day), and would not be able to spend as long as she wanted on an activity. She immediately opted for home education. I confess to having felt great relief at her choice.

Two years on from beginning home educating, we now have four children. Freya is beginning to read and her handwriting, with no practice at all, has become neater and smaller. Zsofia has taught herself the letters of the alphabet. Unlike Freya, Zsofia has not had any formal handwriting tuition, yet her writing is similar to any other child of her age. She picks up information aimed at Freya very quickly.

Freya is beginning to get her head around numbers, and I am beginning to see and understand some of the ways in which she is learning. Talking about maths, for example, Holt stresses the importance of children actually being able to understand what is going on with numbers, as opposed to learning sums by rote. Freya no longer continually uses her fingers, she is beginning to trust that, for instance, 5 will not 'disappear' when adding 2, and adds 2 straight to 5. Once she had mastered adding up to get ten, she then moved onto higher numbers with confidence. As I write this, I have just realised that she is not fluent in reading numbers – she does not always recognise them, but she is fluent mentally.

Our days are varied and busy. Home educating gives us so many options: from days spent quietly at home with our books, TV, CD Roms and other resources, to meeting up with other children at Education Otherwise activities, or exploring our local area. When the sow at our local open air museum was due to have her babies, we were able to go every day for a week. Although we missed the birth, we saw the day-old foal and calf, watched the herdsmen resolve feeding problems and got answers to all of our questions. The children always have the time to get involved, to handle museum exhibits and to listen to stories of the 'olden days' from the museum volunteers. They speak confidently with adults (something about which people often compliment me) and expect to be treated with the same respect which they show to others.

Any place that anyone young can learn something useful from someone with experience is an educational institution.
Al Capp

Some people ask me if I want to return to my paid career. Yes, I sometimes miss the buzz, but nothing compares to the joy of being the first to hear my children read, of seeing their first writing, their art achievements or their latest acrobatics, of hearing them theorise about 'what would happen if...' Yes, we go without regular holidays and brand new clothes, but the benefits more than outweigh this. All of us are 'learning all the time.' And it is fun!

A recent MORI poll, commissioned by the *Campaign for Learning*, found that 90% of adults were favourably inclined towards further learning for themselves... The bad news is that 75% said they were unhappy and alienated in the school environment and that, therefore, they preferred to learn at home, in the local library, at their workplace – *anywhere* other than a school-type setting.

Roland Meighan: *Education Now*, issue 26

FAQ no.7   How do they do science?

Children never stop 'doing science'. It begins with dropping things from a high-chair and discovering that the greater density of a spoon ensures that it makes a better noise than a sock or a teddy. Later on, it may involve attaching carrier-bag parachutes to dolls before lobbing them over the banisters, and rigging up pulley systems to haul them back again.

Although this sounds very simple, popular images of science as something which can *only* happen in a laboratory owe more to media portrayals than fact, and perhaps go some way towards explaining the frequently-voiced concern that children are 'put off' science because they view it as something difficult and incomprehensible.

Far from being an arcane mystery, science is happening around us all the time – and children are constantly asking questions about it. Well, why *do* toy cars run faster on lino than on carpet? Why *do* you use washing-up liquid? Dab vinegar on wasp stings? Blink? Cough? Dig compost into soil? Put baking powder in cakes or Pyrex in a hot oven? From cooking and gardening to making rockets out of old plastic bottles, every activity will prompt questions or encourage experiments: science can also be creative play at its best.

As these questions become more complex there are plenty of books, dictionaries, websites and computer programmes. There are also TV documentaries and wildlife programmes, and, increasingly, interactive science museums, some of which offer school holiday workshops.

Straightforward tools like thermometers, magnets, scales and stopwatches are easily come by and you probably have at least some simple chemicals in your kitchen; a few more can be readily bought from the chemist. More specialised equipment can be obtained by mail order, as can chemistry sets, electronics project kits or solar-powered models; soil-testing kits, ant-farms and caterpillars; cardboard skeletons and plastic body-parts. Some suppliers are listed on the **Free Range Education Website**, or those of **Choice** and **Education Otherwise.**

The **British Association for the Advancement of Science, Youth Section,** will offer guidance on setting up science clubs locally, and can put you in touch with child-friendly scientists in your area. Some home education groups have managed to arrange access to school laboratories out of hours.

Bear in mind that the average school child has little access to laboratory facilities until GCSE is in prospect. If your child reaches this point, you will have had plenty of time to seek out other help, distance learning programmes and local college courses.

Leaving school at 13

Sue and Mike James

We are Mike, Sue and Sam: an atypical family of three who live in a rural area in the North East of England. I say 'atypical' because, since Sam was born, both of us have worked from home doing the same relatively technical job dealing with computers and, in the recent past, the Internet. Sam had a fairly standard early upbringing, playschool, primary school, hobbies and holidays, but has always been surrounded by hi-tech gadgets, which he saw not just as 'better toys' but also as the everyday tools of his parents' trade.

Withdrawing from school midway through the secondary stage is usually as a result of being deeply unhappy. In Sam's case this wasn't so. His time at school could be described as 'balanced', with a range of experiences both good and not-so-good, and just a few isolated bad events. Bullying by peers is probably the most common reason for parents to remove a teenager from secondary school, with victimisation by teachers being a less common but equally disturbing cause. Again, Sam suffered neither of these problems in extreme measure – although he had encountered both, and been made thoroughly miserable by other children and by adults at several points in his career.

In common with an estimated five percent of the population, Sam is hampered by a set of learning difficulties referred to by the term 'dyslexic'. He was fortunate in that, when he was seven, his problems with reading were recognised as genuine and not the result of a poor attitude or laziness, as some of his earliest teachers had assumed. 'Dyscalculic', a term that has only recently started to gain currency, also applies to Sam. The set of problems it describes is one we instantly recognised: a tendency to form numbers back to front, to miss out numbers when counting and to confuse pairs of numbers (in Sam's case 12 and 20). Even with these problems in arithmetic, Sam was obviously good at algebra, geometry and mathematical reasoning. He also showed enthusiasm and ability for science subjects, but while his mismatch of skills came as no surprise to those who understand dyslexia, his maths and science teachers at secondary school tended to focus on his shortcomings and take the attitude that he should simply 'try harder'. This attitude became a real problem in mathematics because Sam's ability at maths was being discounted due to his difficulty with simple arithmetic.

I remember that I was never able to get along at school. I was always at the foot of the class.

Thomas Edison

With hindsight, it is obvious that the rift with the school system had started almost as soon as Sam started secondary school. Even so, the decision to home educate finally happened suddenly – our attitudes moving from: 'If this situation doesn't improve home education is the option of last resort', to: 'Home education is obviously the best solution' within a matter of days. The reason for such a rapid shift was that not only had we uncovered an attitude we found unacceptable, but we were also up against a bureaucracy that could be used to block possible alternatives.

It is not unusual for teachers and pupils to differ about priorities – usually with teachers demanding greater commitment to the subject which they hold dear. We were all the more perturbed, therefore, that enthusiasm for an academic subject, maths, was met with hostility by the head of the school's maths department. It was his comment of: 'Get a Life!' (rather than study maths beyond the syllabus) at the meeting arranged to discuss the future arrangements which could be made for Sam in school, which turned a difficult situation into an untenable one. If the head of maths thinks that the eager pursuit of his discipline is unnatural, then it is high time to leave him out of the equation.

So, how easy is it to start home education at age 13 and go it alone? Having been covering the entire spectrum of curriculum subjects, one problem is knowing what to focus on and what to discontinue. In our case the situation was simplified in the initial few months because Sam had a well-defined goal: he wanted to take GCSEs in maths, physics and chemistry. The exams were just three months away, so there was a lot of ground to cover. This also overcame any difficulties with motivation, at least as far as these subjects were concerned, because he was keen to chalk up some success.

The immediate priority was making arrangements to sit the exams. The situation with entering private candidates has recently changed but the basic steps remain the same: you need to decide on an exam board and then find a convenient examination centre. Due to mergers there are now only three examination boards in England and Wales and of these, just two accept independent candidates. Normally a centre can offer 'accommodation', i.e. a desk in the exam hall alongside its own pupils, to external candidates in any subject, even if the external candidate is doing a different subject, but it is left to the discretion of a centre's Examinations Officer.

A continuing issue was that of providing suitable tuition. We are doubly lucky in that maths and science are areas in which Sam's interests coincide with those of his father who, being self-employed and working from home, was readily available to answer questions, mark work and provide suitable support for self-study. We did need exam-oriented materials and these fell into two categories: specific information about the syllabus, plus past papers from previous exams. These were available for purchase from the exam board and additional information was free on request; it was just a matter of knowing what to ask for.

A wealth of exam-related material, particularly for GCSE, is readily available. The problem really was making a choice between competing products. We spent a few man-hours browsing the selections in large branches of WH Smiths and Waterstones to try to keep within a reasonable budget. As well as revision books containing questions and model answers (an ideal resource for exam preparation) we found CD-Rom computer software packages for revising both maths and science. As well as providing an alternative method of study, these offered the advantage of immediate feedback. However, the subject matter they contained was insufficient, and for this a school textbook was needed.

Many GCSEs involve coursework in addition to examinations. This might be considered a problem for home-educated students but we found it a very positive experience and were rather disappointed that, in the case of maths, private candidates are steered towards a syllabus which substitutes an extra paper in place of coursework. School candidates have their GCSE coursework marked by their teachers, who submit the marks to the exam boards, which then undertake a standards testing procedure known as moderation, in which they re-mark a small proportion of scripts. In the case of a private candidate, the scripts are marked by the board's moderator and so the coursework itself has to be sent away, together with a declaration that the work has been done by the candidate. The candidate has to nominate a person to 'authenticate' the work – i.e. to oversee its origination and confirm that there has been no cheating. The person best placed to authenticate Sam's work was his father, who could sign in his capacity as tutor, but we were advised that, while this was acceptable within the regulations, it would almost inevitably lead to an interview to establish the authenticity of the work. Finding a teacher to sign the form could have avoided an interview, but in the event Sam really enjoyed his chance to talk to the examiner about his science experiments!

One's mind, once stretched by a new idea, never regains its original dimensions.

Oliver Wendell Holmes

Due to revised regulations which now state: 'A relative may NOT act as your authenticator', we are going to have to find someone else to be involved in Sam's future coursework. This development seems to make life even more difficult for home-educated students.

Doing physics and chemistry as separate subjects entailed devising four items of coursework. Many of the standard examples were precluded on the grounds of lack of equipment, but other types of investigation were possible simply by virtue of having longer continuous periods for observation than at school. One idea Sam suggested was to investigate the solubility of salt in alcohol/water mixtures. This involved heating a solution of sodium chloride (ordinary table salt) and methylated spirits, which is readily available from hardware stores and chemists, although it can only be bought by adults. Heating could be done in many ways, but the most efficient was to do it on the kitchen stove. The downside of this was that our home reeked of meths and salt for a complete week, a situation we put up with in the interests of a good exam result! A slightly more socially acceptable experiment involved copper plating. Again, this didn't need any exceptional equipment – the copper tube was from a builder's merchant and the copper sulphate could be purchased from a local chemist. It did require a power supply and we also needed suitable timing devices. We relied on a clock with a prominent second hand and a watch with a stopwatch capability.

By selecting topics which didn't need specialised laboratory equipment, GCSE coursework was a challenge but not a problem. The more difficult scenario presented itself in connection with preparing for 'A' Level Physics. This includes a practical examination, and while the local centre was prepared to provide examination accommodation, it drew the line at letting Sam participate in mock exams to gain familiarity with lab equipment. The practical paper itself was a pretty gruelling test, consisting of five short experiments, the timings of which were strict, as all candidates move from one set of equipment in the lab to another, plus one of two more elaborate alternatives. In the case of lab work, practice certainly helps, so we obtained past papers plus the notes detailing how to set up the experiments (which list the equipment to use) and tried to see what we could replicate with a minimal set of items purchased from a laboratory supplier. This proved very frustrating and time consuming. Trying to set up optical experiments on a kitchen table rather than on a purpose-designed bench proved almost impossible. However, the experience was at least partially successful. There are certain fundamentals such as taking an appropriate number of readings, using suitable units of measure, recording units as well as measurement, all of which can be reinforced by such do-it-yourself practical work.

Embarking on home education with a student with relatively limited abilities in literacy, we were worried about motivating reading and writing. Coursework filled the requirement for factual writing and, removed from the pressure of school, Sam 'discovered' the notion of reading for pleasure for the first time ever. He also widened his reading abilities as a by-product of developing interests which he wanted to pursue – converting a scrapped VW Beetle into a beach buggy. This involved stripping and rebuilding both engine and body, and required him to develop skills in motor mechanics and welding. Keeping a diary, if somewhat sporadically, of this project was another opportunity for writing, as was exchanging information and opinions with other enthusiasts on Internet news groups.

We were rather surprised at how easy it was to satisfy the Local Education Authority's Advisor that we were providing adequate coverage of the curriculum. The National Curriculum is mandatory in maintained schools in England and Wales and most LEAs use it as the yardstick against which to evaluate home education, but in actuality there is no compulsion for home educators to cover the entire spectrum of subjects. Even so, we considered it important to maintain a balance and have tried to cover what might loosely be considered arts subjects. Initially, and perhaps idealistically, we imagined that without the constraints of the school timetable, we might include more travel and let it count towards geography and modern foreign languages! In practice, watching documentaries and language programmes on TV is, in terms of time, a more cost-effective way of covering such subjects.

The Internet is a great resource for everybody involved in education and gives those at home access to a wider range of resources than might otherwise be possible. Television is another resource which can extend the range of subjects that are covered. History (which, incidentally, seems a good choice for an exam subject because the coursework topics place emphasis on local history) is an area that is particularly well covered by TV and radio, with programmes which not only present factual information but which are also thought-provoking. Discussion and dealing with controversy are aspects of education that could be lacking without the school environment, but there is plenty of stimulus available via TV and newspapers and it is then up to family and friends to join in the debate.

As Sam did not want to go away to University until he can join in its social aspects as well as the academic ones, it looked as though he was going to be studying independently for four years. This didn't sound too bad from either his perspective or ours – but it did hold the prospect of marking time when our original motivation was freedom to follow a faster track. 'If only the Open University accepted under 18s', was a thought that crossed our minds more than once and then transmuted into: 'Let's find out whether the OU ever makes an exception'. This was indeed a question worth asking. At the time of the enquiry, we learnt of an unpublicised pilot scheme for under-age entrants and Sam was allowed to enrol, albeit with a number of restrictions such as not being permitted to attend Summer Schools. The usual comment made by OU students is that the courses are rewarding but hard work and Sam is no exception – although he has to admit that it is not nearly so daunting when you don't have to juggle a full-time job at the same time.

Reflecting on the decision to abandon the school system and go it alone, we are convinced we made the right choice, if somewhat belatedly! School appeared to be about levelling, across pupils and across subjects. Even when teachers recognised the mismatch in Sam's abilities, they were forced by timetabling and other administrative pressures into identifying him as a 'weak' student. The advent of the National Curriculum and Key Stages has made the situation worse and while there was a suggestion voiced by David Blunkett, Education Minister, that able pupils be encouraged to sit GCSEs early, it hasn't been widely repeated, no doubt due to the practical problems of how to cope with providing an onward route for fast-track pupils. In fact the National Curriculum makes it more difficult for schools to deal appropriately and sympathetically with any pupils who differ from the norm.

As we go into the 21st Century, more scientists and mathematicians are needed. To be of the right calibre, they must be encouraged to out-perform school teachers in these subjects from an early age. Home education appears to be one route to do this – and in our case appeared to be the only feasible one. It is proving to be hard work, not just for the student but for both of us in the role of tutors, lab technicians, librarians, exams admissions officers and general education administrators. However, our satisfaction comes from seeing Sam achieve his potential, and in being liberated from the containment factor otherwise known as school.

Often it was not in school, but outside of it – in extracurricular activities or during time spent altogether away from school – that calling appeared. It is as if the image in the heart in so many cases is hampered by the program of tuition and its time bound regularity.

James Hillman:
The Soul's Code – In Search of Character & Calling

What is essential is to realise that children learn independently, not in bunches; that they learn out of interest and curiosity, not to please or appease the adults in power; and that they ought to be in control of their own learning, deciding for themselves what they want to learn and how they want to learn it.
John Holt: *How Children Learn*

Saving Sam

Louise Verran

My name is Louise. I have worked in a factory, an office, a shop and a restaurant, as a nanny and a child-minder; I trained as a nurse and worked as a lecturer at a college of further education. I am now a full time home educator and mother to three sons. My eldest son (Tom) is in school and always has been; my second son (Sam) has been to school, left, returned to try once more and has now come back again to home education; my third son (Joe) went to school for four weeks at the age of seven.

How we came to home educate
We were once very conventional and conservative, with conventional and conservative aspirations. Our ideal school was an affordable prep-school, and I considered boarding school a good arrangement for teenagers. Unlike some people who know from the outset that they intend to home educate, we were rather forced into it by circumstances. Looking back over the last thirteen years, I have to say that it was a gradual disenchantment which brought us to a place where we question everything and do not tolerate having our energy used up by activities which are of no personal benefit.

My eldest son was not an enthusiastic school attender and we had many mornings of tears and occasional hanging onto doorframes as he refused to leave the house. In those days I thought that being a good mother meant kindly-but-firmly insisting that he had to go to school; there wasn't any choice, was there?

School was the unhappiest time of my life and the worst trick it ever played on me was to pretend that it was the world in miniature. For it hindered me from discovering how lovely and delightful and kind the world can be, and how much of it is intelligible.

E.M.Forster

Number one son's reaction to going to school was utterly eclipsed by the reaction of number two son, whose misery was so intense that we were having serious problems by the time he was six. By eight, we could face no more and gave him a simple choice: go to school and learn, or stay at home and learn. He didn't hesitate, and thus began what I have always referred to as our homeschooling adventure. At that point we were living in the USA and, fortunately, in an area well endowed with experienced homeschoolers.

What we did then

Like many people who remove children from school, I initially imitated it: we had a timetable, curriculum, lesson plans and so on. I had loved playing school with my dolls as a child and now I had a real live human being to work with. It was a disaster. Sam was resistant, awkward and evasive, whilst I got cross, feeling that I was losing control of the situation and fearing that: 'He'll never learn anything, get a job, be independent, cope as an adult'. Eventually it dawned on me what a terrible thing I had done: I had taken my school-hating and stressed child out of school and had then brought school home. Now he had nowhere to go, nowhere to hide. Realising this couldn't continue, I 'phoned a friend – a home educator who worked for an American organisation called 'Growing Without Schooling'.

'Just let him be,' she counselled, 'he has to de-school, get the whole schoolish way of doing things out of his system.'

So we stopped doing school and I just let him be. And he played basketball on the driveway hour after hour, day after day. 'This is ridiculous,' I thought as the noise of the ball banging away drove me nuts, so I 'phoned the friend again.

'Just leave him alone, he'll stop when he's ready and eventually move on to something else.'

A short time later, as we were sitting at the computer, looking something up in Encarta together, I realised that he had indeed stopped playing basketball and we were indeed doing something else – something that was in fact quite 'schoolish'.

The best example I can give of the approach we developed is by describing what followed a few weeks later. I read a book called: The Secret in the Barrel to the boys, simply because I thought it would be interesting. It is the story of a boy who travels with his uncle to the gold fields of Colorado. It was a great read and mingled in with the fiction were a lot of facts. We drew some maps of the USA marking out the various places and rivers mentioned in the story and, as we read, we plotted the journey of uncle and boy. We looked up the States mentioned in the story to find out the State capital, the State bird, flower and anthem. Uncle and boy had a dramatic crossing over the Mississippi so we looked briefly at rivers: how they are formed, the names of the biggest rivers in the world, which led in turn to a brief study of the Yangtze River and China. A particular type of wood was used to make the arch for the wagon, so we bought a book to identify trees and, on our daily walk with the dog, we tried to find the trees that they had used. We wrote down the dates given in the story and calculated the length of the journey. We read a list of the food they took and speculated on what provisions we might take on such a journey, how they might be stored and preserved. Various characters mentioned in the book were real people, so we went to the library to find out more about them. All of this generated an interest in American history, particularly the Californian gold rush, and the settlers of the West. We began listening to folk music of the period and tried to learn a few songs. We read more fiction; to this day, we are still working our way through the *Little House on the Prairie* series.

Just as eating against one's will is injurious to health, so study without a liking for it spoils the memory, and it retains nothing it takes in.
Leonardo Da Vinci

Without really trying, we had done some math, history, music, geography, social history, art appreciation and nature studies, all without coaxing, bribing or threatening on my part and reluctance or bored toleration on theirs. Suddenly the 'interconnectedness of all knowledge' that I had read about began to make sense.

Reading
Reading was a key issue for us, firstly in terms of Sam's difficulty in learning to read and secondly in terms of the emotional issues which it raised for him. I decided that whatever reading we did had to be fun,

because if we couldn't imbue the whole experience with pleasure, then we would get nowhere. We took the pressure off and would sit cuddled up under a blanket whilst I read to him.

One of the problems we faced was that, for a number of years, his comprehension of a story and his use and understanding of language far exceeded his ability to read. It was therefore a challenge to find books with a lively, easy-to-read text which were not boring, patronising or repetitive. We began with a great series of books at our local library, initially reading alternate sentences and then working our way up to alternate paragraphs. Gradually Sam built up his knowledge of words and began to feel more confident about attempting to decode them. It wasn't long before he was reading road signs and shop signs confidently, and we knew we had made a breakthrough when he volunteered to read a comic book out loud in the car, in front of his two critical brothers *and* his grandparents.

With my younger son, Joe, I was rather overawed at the prospect of teaching him to read from scratch. I always thought that it would be impossible to teach a child to read unless you first received copious amounts of training and understood all the complicated technical phrases which teachers seem to know. In fact, I feared that doing it the 'wrong' way could do a considerable amount of damage.

Reassured by accounts of late readers from articles in the *Growing without Schooling* magazine, I decided not to panic until Joe was about nine or ten. Increasingly I had come to feel that, more than all the academic success in the world, what matters is emotional health / intelligence and I didn't want Joe to feel under any pressure to perform. I felt that If I could keep my children connected to and excited about books, then I would have achieved something worthwhile. If the reading didn't happen at all, an expert could always be called in at a later stage.

Joe and I started off by playing simple word-card games, progressing to the occasional page from *The Phonics Handbook,* learning to recognise the shape of each letter and its name and sound. When we had enough letters, we began blending them to make simple three-letter words and practised both shape recognition of whole words, and phonetic sounding out of individual letters. There you have the full details of my method of reading tuition! We also had the luxury of doing this when Joe felt like it rather than when he was bored, tired or interested in some-thing else. There was no one to compete against nor struggle to catch up with; there was no one to laugh at mistakes or call him stupid. We could spend as long as we wanted on whatever he wanted. I had no agenda regarding when he learned and, as his mother, I was genuinely thrilled when he accomplished something new.

I have never had to do the big sell with regard to reading, and feel I can say that Joe is mainly self-taught. We never did reach the end of our phonics book, and the card games have long since lost their appeal. Joe now pores over comics for hours, calling out periodically: 'What does E A U R G G H say?'

Every now and then we read through a book together, sharing the reading so that it remains pleasurable, and both Joe and I are surprised at the progress he has made. Not through reading lessons or 'reading practice', but by living and enjoying books. I still read to the two boys every day, and treat myself to a read when I feel like it. Sitting down during the day to read my book or newspaper shows my children what an important part reading plays in my own life. If children never see their parents reading, I think it is hard to convince them of its importance.

I have probably made our start in Home Education sound terribly smooth and easy, but I have to say that the idea terrified me and I was initially totally convinced that it wouldn't work for us. When I talked to people about Sam's unhappiness at school and heard them recommend homeschooling, I felt that no way would I be able to cope with having him at home all day – the beginning and end of each day were quite bad enough. My wiser and more experienced friends told me that he would be a changed child once he stopped going to school. They were right and, so far, everything that they ever told me has turned out to be true.

How things have developed

Our approach has developed over the years into a child-led, diagnostic/ prescriptive, unschooling blend that works well for us all. We assess the usefulness and enjoyment of everything. We change in accordance with the maturing of our children and their shifting interests. Since coming back to the UK, we have started to collect information on the various ways GCSEs might be tackled. Or shall we do them at all? Should we go straight to 'A' levels? Now nothing is taken for granted nor done because 'that's what everybody else does'.

I used to wonder why it was that a child of three with an insatiable appetite to know why, to copy everything, to spend hours each day exploring the world, became an eight or nine-year-old who had to be coaxed, cajoled, bribed or threatened into learning. Is this really a natural progression? I have come to think that the claims made by pioneers in the homeschooling movement, that school actually damages and destroys a love of learning, may not be so wacky after all. It is so nice when the questions start flooding back, when your child *asks* to learn the three-times table or practise spelling.

> *Who does not recall school at least in part as endless dreary hours of boredom punctuated by moments of high anxiety?*
>   Daniel Golema: *Emotional Intelligence*

If we have an educational motto, it is 'excellence in personal development': the freedom of home education enables us to personalise our children's education.

Socialisation

Any discussion of home schooling inevitably includes the 'S' question – socialisation.

I often wonder how on earth school ever came to be considered representative of society at large. When you home educate, you quickly realise that real socialisation is entirely different from the 'school' version. In our time of homeschooling, the boys have mixed with an enormous variety of people of all ages, backgrounds and educational standards, with varying life experiences and in a wide variety of situations. Seeking out this sort of experience and opportunity is something I consider to be a key element of my job as home educator.

Some people fear that the home-educated child will miss out on learning how to cope with unpleasant experiences and unpleasant people. A relative once asked me how the boys would learn to cope with bullies, apparently an essential preparation for adult life. 'When,' I asked, 'have you, as an adult, had your face pushed into the sand?' There was no reply.

I remember that someone once asked: if you were to send someone out to work in a land where everyone was starving, would you starve them in preparation or feed them up well? I think that the traumas of school weaken rather than strengthen, and I prefer my children to start adult life from a position of confidence.

My role as home educator

Over the last four years, I have come to realise that central to what I do is not how much I know or how well informed I am; the crucial factor is my relationship with my children. Do I really listen? Do I take their interests and concerns seriously? Am I mindful of them? How well do I know them? This necessitates my asking the same questions about myself, taking care of myself. I have to acknowledge that I need time away from my children and it is important that I factor this into my life. I cannot be at my best if I am tired or in need of a break. I have to acknowledge my limits and be honest with my children so that we can work towards meeting the needs of everyone in the family.

I see myself not as a teacher but as a facilitator or a kind of librarian. If you go to the library looking for information, the librarian will not know the content of every book but should be able to point you in the right direction to find the information that you want for yourself. This process of finding information may at some point involve going to classes, at school or college. Choosing to home educate does not have to preclude any manifestation of school. The real issue is one of control: the control we have as a family, over how we spend our time and live our lives.

A typical day

A typical day? In our house there is really no such thing.

Today

Sam and Joe both did some chores – loading the washing machine, hoovering. Sam had his saxophone practice and Joe worked a page each of his Math and English books.

One of Sam's friends came round bringing a book about batteries and magnets, so we decided to have a go at making a battery. This involved walking to the local hardware shop to buy various bits and pieces. The woman in the shop was friendly and chatted to the boys for a long time. We had our first attempt at making the battery but it didn't work, so we reviewed procedure, put forward theories as to what the fault might be and had a second try. Eventually, we succeeded. After that, the boys set about making circuits with an electronics kit. After lunch we went to the park to collect conkers and meet up with some old school friends. Later we had to see to our animals: two goats, two geese and a number of chickens which live on a field we rent with other homeschooling families – a place where we've laid hedges, dug ponds and built fences. Later, after dinner, we read about Ancient Egyptians.

One day, different from every other day since the beginning of the academic year.

Outlines/plans
I start in September with a broad outline of what I would like to do over
the year. We set out some goals. In this I follow my children's interests
and there is not much in the world that does not interest them. For
example, this year, as we are new back in the UK, they are keen to try
a variety of English sports and see if there are any they wish to pursue.
So we make a list, take full advantage of holiday courses and tick them
off as we go.

We live in Bath at present so we are having a look at Romans,
particularly Romans in Britain. Tomorrow we are off to Fishbourne Palace
to look at Roman remains.

The boys do Tai Kwon Do and gymnastics every week.

Sam learns the saxophone and Joe the piano.

Sam has had spelling lessons from a Dyslexia unit and Joe has been
learning French.

Sam wants to do photography, particularly bird photography as we
are all keen bird watchers. He is also reading about the First World War.

For four weeks starting soon, we have an art tutor coming to the
house.

We meet twice a week with friends for shared activities and have
developed an impromptu science club.

We do not follow the National Curriculum; we have a math
curriculum for each of the boys and they work through that, time
permitting. They do all the measuring around the house, they work out
their own change and budget their pocket money.

Both boys have English work books – the goal is at least a page a
day, but sometimes we have places to go, people to see. As well as
reading, they write shopping lists, letters to pen friends, thank you
notes. I try to make all that they do truly useful, not just page-filling for
the sake of it. I would like to read about some real heroes this year,
having read a fair number of Greek myths and legends last year, and I
intend to get some biographies to read to the boys.

To keep track of our somewhat eclectic approach to education, I
write down in a desk diary what we have done every day. On the not-
so-good days (and they happen) I am always amazed and reassured by
looking back over it. All the books we read, the things we discuss, lead
us into other areas of study: in home education there is no end to where
you can go, and what you can learn along the way. The greatest problem
our family faces is that there simply are not enough hours in the day or
days in the week.

Education means 'to lead out.' We seem to understand this as leading away from childhood, but maybe we could think of it as eliciting the wisdom and talents of childhood itself. As A.S.Neill, founder of the Summerhill School, taught many years ago, we can trust that the child already has talents and intelligence. We believe that the child intellectually is a tabula rasa, a blank blackboard, but maybe the child knows more than we suspect.

Thomas Moore: *Care of the Soul*

When the buck stops

Peter Tuffnell

Help! We agreed to write this chapter eight months ago, and all I have got are a few scrappy notes and false starts. I am furious and frustrated with myself. Jo would have done it in a couple of days and still managed to cook meals, do laundry and organise friends for the children; but I insisted that this was one for me, so I'm shut in my room looking at an empty page on my computer screen, hiding from the children it's all supposed to be about, feeling useless. Why?

I am back inside my nine-year-old self: Sunday evening, looking at a blank page in my composition book, white with panic. I get top marks in English, I could read long before I went to school, so why is writing an essay so painful and difficult? I can see it's because I'm trying so hard to please the teachers, to give the right answers, to say what they want to hear. With a spelling or maths test, that's no problem – there's just one right answer. I can do that, but an essay? That needs something from my imagination, something from my heart, something from me, and I'm not sure where that is. And if I did, it probably wouldn't be acceptable. So I have to write from the me that they want me to be. I ask Mum for help. She hates these panics as much as I do. Between us, we patch together an idea from pieces of the Famous Five, and I painfully construct a safe, formulaic essay. The relief when it's done. I see my fragile nine-year-old, balancing his entire sense of self and accomplishment on a pinhead of parent and teacher approval.

In walks another nine-year-old. No, sorry, I tell her, I'm going to be on the computer all day. OK Dad. (It's the computer she wants, by the way, not me!) I look round at her. My God, she's so strong. She knows who she is. In my raw state, I am shocked to remember just how close we came to pushing Ava into school. At three-and-a-half years old.

Ava had attended a little local playgroup, but this was just a place with more friends and toys than home, and Mum was always right there. Some of her friends were moving on to the proper 'pre-school' school. We still hadn't found the school of our dreams, so why not let her try it out? Thus, along with most of the other well-meaning parents of the modern age, we found ourselves at that gut-wrenching point – usually a point of no return – where we watch our dearly beloved disappear through that door. The teacher reassured Jo with absolute confidence that: 'By the time you're out of sight, she will have stopped crying.' When Jo came to collect her, the teacher explained that although Ava had cried quite a lot, she had always been able to 'distract her'. Jo was assured that this was all quite normal and Ava would settle down in a day or two. Indeed, when we 'debriefed' her that night, she was clearly quite taken with the whole variety of resources and sensations at the school. It was only many years later that Ava was able to tell us what really happened: whenever she got upset, the teacher would say, 'Stop crying – you're upsetting the other children.' Ava had no prior experience of this kind of emotional ultimatum, and no way to protect herself from it. Unaware of this hidden wound, Jo was more than a little surprised when – on the way for her second day – gentle, mild Ava declared with total conviction, punching the air with her fists to emphasise, 'I am never, ever going back to school again!'

That was how it started for us. Confronted by Ava's remarkable will, we found our own resolution beginning to crack. This is not what was supposed to happen. Ava should have been 'broken in' like all the other good three-year-olds of the modern world. Instead, we found ourselves 'breaking out' with her. All our own doubts and fears and questions about school began to topple out. At that moment, we knew this was more than superficial fear or insecurity. Ava was telling us that her very *self* was in danger – her beautiful, fragile, emerging *self*. With us, she was safe to laugh, to cry, to need, to moan, to cling, to be spontaneous, to be herself, to *be*. In school, she could only do a very few of those things, and then only at the prescribed times and places.

For a child's soul, still fresh from the free flight of pure being, this is a difference like life and death. It doesn't matter if the 'teachers are really nice' or there are 'lots of wonderful toys and books and paints' or even 'lots of new friends'. If her basic freedom to express, create and demand her emotional reality is reduced or taken away, what is left? A pile of blocks, some marks on paper, but it sure ain't childhood.

Years ago, Jo had bought John Holt's *Teach Your Own,* and it was still on the shelf. I remember that first evening as I excitedly read aloud to Jo little bits and pieces of Holt's liberating wisdom. How we were both swept up in a beautiful but terrifying awareness that something had been let loose that could not be dismissed or forgotten. Ava had opened a doorway in our hearts. That is not to say that we became born-again 'Holtians' overnight. It simply meant that, from that moment, we knew there was no easy pre-packaged solution to our child's education anymore than there had been for her birth, her diet, her vaccinations. Once again, we were 'on our own', having to work out for ourselves what was right in the face of the prevailing orthodoxy, having to follow our own hearts in the face of God-knows-how-much opposition from family, friends, neighbours, experts and State.

Another important support was the writing of John Taylor Gatto. He was newly installed as New York State 'Teacher of the Year' when he astounded his fellow professionals by disavowing the whole business of mass education. In *Dumbing Us Down,* he points out that in 1776 – long before mass education spread through America – Thomas Paine's *Common Sense* sold 600,000 copies in a population of three million, one-fifth of whom were slaves and servants. Gatto asks, 'Were the colonists geniuses? No, the truth is that reading, writing and arithmetic only take about one hundred hours to learn as long as the audience is eager and willing to learn. The trick is to wait until someone asks and then move fast while the mood is on.'

Our embryonic educational philosophy was something like this: if Ava is raised in an atmosphere of love, security, patience, mutual respect and questioning, she will probably remain emotionally open and balanced, be able to motivate herself, and learn whatever she wants to learn whenever she wants to learn it. Above all, we believe she will have the spiritual and emotional strength to cope with real life. If the foundation is weak, the cracks will show up, even decades later. If the foundation is strong, anything can be built upon it. Perhaps the only real requirement for pre-teens is to feel loved, listened to, respected and protected, while they play, sing, make friends, splash about and follow their enthusiasms. (If this sounds unscientific, I recommend *Evolution's End,* by Joseph Chilton Pearce, a superb synthesis of contemporary research into the development of intelligence.)

The exams that matter in the 'global market place' (and then only for certain types of vocation) are 'A'-levels and beyond: the ones you take from sixteen years and up. The bottom line is that if she can read and write competently by sixteen, has enthusiasm and self-esteem and can cope with emotional stresses and strains, she will be able to pass any exam she decides to pass. As we now know, this seems to be the norm among home educating children. They need an exam, they go get it. Their enthusiasm has not been sedated, their motivation has not been clipped, they have not been labelled, streamed and tested to distraction.

While we were getting our home education philosophy sorted, and becoming confident enough to expose it to friends and family, something very different was growing in our midst: Iona.

If Ava is the mountain, solid, assured and deep as a copper mine, Iona is the mountain stream. Some days rippling gently between the trees, other days raging across the rocks, and always following the line of least resistance. A teenager at five. If it is exciting, fashionable and forbidden, Iona wants it. Clearly, if Mum and Dad are into 'not going to school' but the rest of the world is, this will not rest easy with Iona. At the very least, she's going to need a uniform. We were certainly not going to impose home education on Iona. We had set out upon home education by attending deeply to Ava's needs. We now had to do the same thing with Iona, and accept that it might lead somewhere very different. Her need to experience school – or, perhaps, her need not to be excluded from it – was so powerful at five, that we arranged for her to attend three mornings a week at a local Waldorf-Steiner Kindergarten. And, sure enough, she was the only one in uniform, brilliantly cobbled together from charity shop bits and pieces.

At least Steiner has a positive spiritual approach, and does not attempt to teach reading, writing or mathematics until 'the change of teeth'. Steiner died in 1925, and – as is usual in a movement with a spiritual teacher at its root – followers are inhibited about moving too far from the founder's guidelines. This certainly hits problems with older children, many of whose issues and priorities were not dreamed of seventy-five years ago. However, for the younger ones, it is a peaceful and gentle setting, with painting, singing and stories. More significantly, Anne, the teacher, and Iona had spontaneously fallen for each other when Iona was about two years old, so it felt very integrated emotionally.

So, in a year or two we had flown to the heights of home educating idealism and immediately had to swoop back to the plains of school-going pragmatism. At least, we thought, this must be the most harmless schooling on the planet, and only three mornings a week. Nevertheless, almost immediately we began to notice the tell-tale effects of the schoolyard – even though this schoolyard was actually an idyllic forest, and the teachers were committed to high spiritual ideals. Through deep listening to Iona, we began to uncover the tribalism, the jealousies, the exclusions, the vicious words that are still stinging at bedtime. We gave her some strategies for dealing with typical schoolyard conflicts and Iona built quite a bit of self-esteem through seeing these work, but in the end the current was too strong and, on bad days, would erupt in actual bullying. In the end it no longer really worked for Iona, and gradually we all mutually and happily agreed that she would not go back after the summer holidays.

We knew this would bring a different dynamic to our home school. Ava needed security, not structure. She might do a couple of hours intensive number work, then she would have to 'run around to release all this energy'. Then off to the piano, or to feed her snails. Often, Ava would play complex and imaginative animal games for whole days at a time, sometimes with, but usually without adult accompaniment. We knew Iona would demand convincing looking desks, schoolbooks, timetables. She would want supervision, and packets of gold stars; sometimes I would have to be headmaster and dish out ferocious punishments.

Imagination is more important than knowledge. Knowledge is limited. Imagination encircles the world.

Albert Einstein

Iona forced us to look at the whole business of teaching more rigorously. For instance, how to teach and what to teach. If there was ever a good case to send the children to school, it would have been to avoid sitting with the pain of our own ignorance. We finally had to face the fact that we knew nothing at all. Of course, we could read a book and do basic maths, but that was about it. Also, apart from music, neither of us has any creative, artistic or manual skills to speak of. This was shocking in more ways than one. Firstly, it meant that neither of us had remembered anything at all from our own schooling – and we were both what would now be called 'high achievers'. More relevantly, it appeared to mean that we were the last people on Earth to be teaching our own children.

Jo has a strong image of the perfect home educator – who is everything she feels she is not. Someone who would be wholly at ease to be asked 'What is a Volcano?' and would immediately set about making a perfect model that would explode and spew lava everywhere, then choreograph a volcano dance, and generally be able to make 'volcano' a beautiful and unforgettable experience. Jo recently met such a parent, complete with abundant vegetable garden, tree-houses and dens everywhere, arts and crafts on the walls and shelves, children studiously engaged in every room. Jo says she is on a journey to accepting that she is a 'good enough' home educator. We are both coming to accept that learning with a child is primarily to do with mutual discovery – and that the discovery can actually be more mutual and exciting if both parties are equally ignorant.

We can also encourage our children to question everything. Not to accept the fickle truths of the age, however powerfully or expensively they are presented. We can help them understand the trickery with which ideas and products are sold, so they can deconstruct them and not be fooled, seduced and hypnotised.

On bad days, our doubts and fears coalesce into a black panic that, because of our inability to teach, our children will never learn. So far, just before the panic defeats us entirely, some little miracle occurs. We had not been able to teach Ava to read – which, in conventional education, is the key to learning everything else. She might allow us to play at reading lessons once or twice a year, but that was about it. Four years, five, six (oh dear, will she ever...), seven (whisperings among friends), eight (oh help), nine... she quietly picks up the Radio Times and starts reading it. She has rightly suspected that we haven't told her about all the programmes she might want to watch. Then she reads a book about rabbits. Then just about everything in the house that looks interesting to her. It really works! The black cloud of doubt lifts for a day or two. Jo asks her why she hadn't been interested in the Non-Stop Reader and other reading aids we had offered her. 'There was nothing in them I wanted to learn. I wanted to know what was in the rabbit book, so I read it.' Of course.

Spoon feeding in the long run teaches us nothing but the shape of the spoon.

E. M. Forster

Britain and America lead the world in early literacy. In much of Europe, it is regarded as pretty inhumane and certainly counter-productive. Having watched Ava playing so fully and imaginatively through her 'illiterate' years, I have come to accept that it can be a wonderful thing for a young mind to remain free of 'symbol knowledge' – for as long as it naturally wants to. Oral traditions and cultures ensure that knowledge is never separated from a person, from a heart. When the head and the heart come apart, all sorts of problems arise. Like Western civilisation.

Ava actually learned to read music several years before words, which feels quite a healthy way in to symbol knowledge. As part of her own de-schooling, Jo consciously chose to avoid the soul-stifling method by which she had been taught, and which had put her off written music for twenty years. Once, when she lapsed, she instantly hit Ava's uncompromising buffers. 'How will I learn if you tell me I'm doing wrong?' In the end, Ava taught herself to read music; Jo's role was to listen, praise occasionally, play duets, answer if asked, and get hold of more piano music. We also learnt not to get attached to Ava becoming a great musician, or to use her achievement to bolster our ratings as home educating parents to the unbelievers! Her musical phases come and go. Nevertheless, we were inspired by her motivation and commitment.

Yes. Motivation. That is certainly one I have had to struggle with. My motivation has always seemed rather shallow. First it was: keep Mum happy. Then: keep the teachers happy. Then: make girls happy. Finally: make the gods happy. I am still on a pilgrimage to the real source of my motivation, and I hope I find it soon. I am sure it is related to the development of the will, the thing that is so much feared by parents as the 'terrible twos'. Parents and teachers routinely crush the emerging will, in much the same way that factory farmers cut the beaks off chickens. It makes them much easier to manage. It also makes them unhappy and dysfunctional chickens. I remember Iona at two or three, locking horns with me on some issue or other, building into a mighty torrent of willpower. I suddenly felt I was in the presence of something absolutely sacred. I knew I was witnessing my child's will, the engine that must power her right through her life, breaking out. At that moment, instead of wanting it to shut up or go away, I felt proud of it. Let it roar. Roar like a Harley-Davidson taking off! Of course, it helped that at the time she wasn't lying on the floor of the supermarket humiliating me in front of tut-tutting grannies, or embarrassing everyone on the train. This experience convinced me that the will needs to be positively encouraged and is the source of healthy self-motivation. We need to react to a child's will like a martial artist, not like the factory farmer. It is a force to reckon with – creatively.

A key support on our journey has been the Parent Network, which grew out of the brilliant work of Ivan Solokov and Jaqui Pearson. They had painstakingly collected together all the key books and papers in the fields of parenting, psychology and child development, and had brilliantly synthesised the best bits into a simple, practical course. It is the Swiss Army Knife of parenting. A few simple tools to solve a thousand difficult situations.

We learnt to describe a child's work rather than blandly praise; to avoid all labels, good, bad or funny; to acknowledge and embrace all feelings, however difficult; to listen 'reflectively' so a child can move deeper and be really understood. And a lot more. 'Now', I hear you say, 'I'm reading this book to find out about home education, not parenting.' Of course, but the basic difference in our lives as home educating parents is that we spend a much greater amount of time with our children, and therefore do masses of parenting. If we don't learn to do it consciously, we find ourselves doing a thinly disguised version of what our parents did to us. If yours did a great job – and you turned out perfectly – then you don't need it.

We conclude that the basic difference between good and bad parenting is simply to do with fear and trust. Trust suggests that a healthy child comes equipped with everything it needs to live a long and fulfilled life. It learns to walk and to talk without expert help, and – given the chance – will learn everything else too. Fear suggests that if the lad hits his little sister at seven, he will be locked up for GBH at twenty, therefore I must threaten him so much he will never do it again. Or if she writes her '4's backwards today, she will do it at her GCSEs, so I must keep correcting her. Or if he uses a four-letter word in front of Granny at ten, he will be a social leper at thirty, so I must ground him for a week. And so on. All these fears are irrational unless, of course, we make them true by over-reacting, by withdrawing our love, or falling back on bribes and threats to control behaviour. A child invariably knows she has done wrong long before the adults start piling on the guilt and blame. Almost all punishment arrives after the child has already realised and regretted whatever it was, so it's a bit like kicking a man when he's down.

> *Most of us are tactful enough with other adults not to point out*
> *their errors, but not many of us are ready to extend this courtesy (or*
> *any other courtesy, for that matter) to children.*
> John Holt: *How Children Learn*

Last year, the local Education Welfare Officer contacted us to say that one of our neighbours had reported that our children didn't go to school. We wrote a detailed, confident but non-confrontational letter about our educational approach. I figured that they would just want to hear that we knew what we were doing, and sounded capable of doing it. We haven't been bothered since. No doubt their hands are full elsewhere with the real casualties of education.

It is not just the neighbour – or the 'man in the street' – who fears for our children. Friends and family are naturally concerned too. Ideally, this prompts them to give us a hand, but the message, usually unspoken, is: 'You are taking a huge risk with your children!' True. All we can say is: 'Everyone is taking a huge risk with their children. Only difference is, you lucky sods can blame the school. If *we* fail, or think we have failed, or if our children think we have failed them, there will be no one to blame but ourselves'.

One lovely family we know are so doubtful about our ability to educate our children, and so suspicious of all those newspaper reports of home educating success, that they searched the entire World Wide Web to look for stories of home educating failure. They couldn't find one anywhere, so they concluded that home educators just never talk about their failures – especially to journalists.

I can understand their cynicism. Logically, home educators should be miles behind in everything, and on the road to disaster. After all, the average school child is provided with a whole range of specialised 'learning environments', a team of trained teachers and a vast array of material learning resources. The methods applied have been developed over many decades by legions of educational experts and child psychologists. The reading, writing and mathematical programmes have been refined and developed through use with millions of children world-wide. There is a budget of billions.

The average home-educated child has none of these things. No space – just a corner of the sitting room or the kitchen table between meals. No trained teachers – just a busy, overstretched, untrained parent. No method – just bits and pieces picked up from friends or books. The home-educated child simply doesn't stand a chance. No space, no teachers, no resources, no experts, no billions. No chance. And yet...

Our friends will not be persuaded. They will still believe in the conspiracy of silence, and be reassured that because their children go off to school with such enthusiasm, it must be right.

We are shut up in schools and college recitation rooms for ten or fifteen years, and come out at last with a bellyful of words and do not know a thing.

Ralph Waldo Emerson

I went to school very enthusiastically too. My mum had taught me reeding, riting and rithmatic before I went, so I was a star pupil. In infant school I was usually some teacher's pet; in primary school I even rose to be headmaster's pet. A few panic attacks were a small price to pay. It only began to unravel for me when my high achieving took me to a school for high achievers, and I found myself sitting in a whole class of ex-head boys. Trouble was, most of them were natural rugby players or boffins or concert pianists as well. My only real skill was being nice to teachers. This didn't seem to work any more. At thirteen, I fell off the pinhead. Luckily, it was 1968, the music was brilliant and I wasn't the only student in the world feeling unhappy, so I was able to leap aboard the passing rocket ship of revolution and set off to change the world.

I go into the kitchen. Ava is showing Helena her candle-making experiments. She has been known to make candles for two or three days, with barely a break to eat and sleep. She has carved a hole in a stale loaf of bread, and Helena is fascinated by the way the candles go out when she pops them in the hole. Ava is trying to explain why.

Ah yes, I didn't introduce Helena. We were only going to have two children... it was perfectly safe. Nevertheless, I found myself saying: 'I hope you're right, 'cos I can sense a whole queue up there! Looking at four-year-old Helena sitting here fearlessly amidst the hot wax and flames, it is easy to see that she had all the necessary skills to busk her way to the front of that queue, distract everyone, grab the last ticket and leap in.

Iona comes in with a huge pile of books. Maths, science, drawing books, anything that looks a bit schooly. Some are for real, some are props. She has drawn two shimmering pictures, a house and a flower. She is happy with them, but doesn't want to admit that someone else drew the outlines. She so wants it to look professional. Her inner critic is so strong. Luckily, so is her will and her concentration, so it's only a matter of time.

What a privilege. Three vast and beautiful beings. I wouldn't have missed this for the world. According to the prevailing orthodoxy, Jo and I should probably be working as computer programmer and counsellor, buying a house in the South East and letting child-minders and the State take care of the children. What madness.

Thank you, Ava, for turning our lives upside down.

Thank you, Iona, for forcing us to be a bit organised about it.

Thank you, Helena, for making it fun.

Thank you, Jo, for letting me write this.

I feel almost healed. But I wouldn't mind that gold star.

Earth and sky, woods and fields, lakes and rivers, the mountain and the sea, are excellent schoolmasters, and teach some of us more than we can ever learn from books.

John Lubbock

I do not pine for a different place and time. I only point out what we have traded off. I think certain good things are recoverable, though without the life that once surrounded them they must inevitably take on different meanings. One of these is the tradition of parental and communal responsibility for the daily instruction of the young. Today this is denied us because teaching has been institutionalised, a convenience in a time of industry and profit when citizen-labourers perform economic functions more efficiently without children present. But for whom is such a state of affairs indeed convenient?

David Guterson:
Family Matters – Why Homeschooling Makes Sense

FAQ no.8   How do they do exams?

As you have probably deduced from individual articles in the book, there are three principal ways of taking public examinations:

1. By attendance at a local college
2. Through a distance learning programme/correspondence course
3. As an independent candidate

If you are sixteen or over and interested in the first option, it is as simple as making a few 'phone calls to find out where the subjects in which you are interested are offered. If you are under sixteen the situation is not so clear-cut. Some colleges are happy to accept U-16s, but this is entirely at their discretion and you may well have to pay for the course.

The second option is probably the one most often chosen by U-16 home educators. There are a large number of distance learning programmes available and further information/addresses can be obtained from home education organisations, or the **Free Range Education Website.** You will have to pay for these courses. It is worth getting recommendations from other home educators and also making your own enquiries because the standards of tuition/cost can vary widely.

The third option is perfectly feasible, particularly if a friend or family member can help with course work, and will probably be the cheapest for U-16s, unless it is necessary to use a private tutor. Syllabuses and past exam papers can be obtained from the relevant Exam Boards (addresses of these are obtainable as above) but you will have to make your own arrangements for accreditation of course work.

Home education gives you the freedom to choose which qualifications, if any, are relevant, and to opt for vocational qualifications instead of the traditional GCSEs/'A' Levels. Often, such qualifications are more highly regarded by potential employers

It is important to say that the 'school' path of GCSEs at 16 followed by 'A' Levels at 18 is only one of many possible approaches to exams. There is no particular magic about it. It is not necessary to take several GCSEs simultaneously, nor do you have to pass GCSEs before taking 'A' Levels. There is no lower age limit for sitting any of these exams. In practice, this means that home-educated children can spread GCSEs over several years, or miss them out altogether and go straight to 'A' Levels.

You do not automatically need any of these exams in order to get a degree – some people have left school without qualifications but later entered University via an Access Course. The Open University has no entrance requirements and, as you will see from Sue and Mike James's piece, it is not always necessary to be 18 or over.

EDUCATING ARCHIE By SEG

We hear a lot about the advantages of home education – but SURELY there are one or two snags??

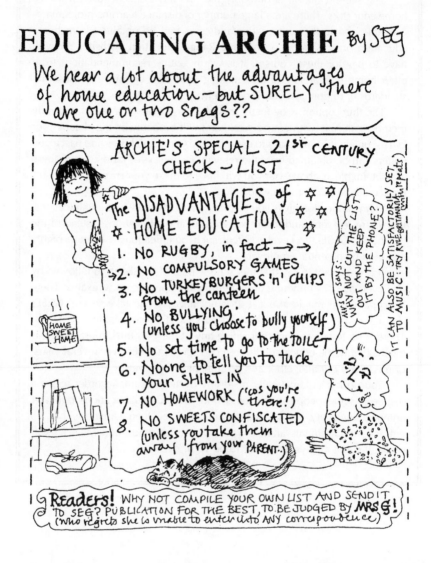

ARCHIE'S SPECIAL 21st CENTURY CHECK – LIST

The DISADVANTAGES of HOME EDUCATION

1. NO RUGBY, in fact → →
2. NO COMPULSORY GAMES
3. NO TURKEYBURGERS 'n' CHIPS from the canteen
4. NO BULLYING (unless you choose to bully yourself)
5. No set time to go to the TOILET
6. Noone to tell you to tuck your SHIRT IN
7. NO HOMEWORK ('cos you're there!)
8. NO SWEETS CONFISCATED (unless you take them away from your PARENT..)

MRS G SAYS: WHY NOT CUT THE LIST OUT AND KEEP IT BY THE PHONE?

IT CAN ALSO BE SATISFACTORILY SET TO MUSIC: TRY RVE BRITANNIA HAT RACE (WITH ALL THE PARTS)

HOME SWEET HOME

Readers! WHY NOT COMPILE YOUR OWN LIST AND SEND IT TO SEG? PUBLICATION FOR THE BEST, TO BE JUDGED BY **MRS G!** (who regrets she is unable to enter into ANY correspondence)

Flexible people for the new millennium

Kate Oliver

We've flexed!
Some days, Felix is fired up with all the exciting learning opportunities at the secondary school which he now attends full time; other days he is tired and disaffected and would prefer to read for most of the day at home. He's relatively lucky – the school does not have a uniform and the teachers are all known by their first names; the school is divided spatially into two distinct units, which halves the size of the effective community; the only four lessons a day are 70 minutes long and he can choose to go by bus or cycle to school.

We were all somewhat anxious about how he would adapt to full-time school after an entire primary career of flexi-time education. It would be very misleading to say that it has been trouble free – it has not; but it would also be unfair to blame all of the trouble on the adjustment needed. More of it lies in the cultural disjuncture between our values at home and those of many (or is it only several?) boys in his tutor group, and in the confidence which he has gained from learning at home for the greater part of his eleven years: confidence to recognise and articulate his feelings; to learn in his own way for his own interest; to connect with global issues; to know quite a lot about how the economy operates from day to day.

Meanwhile, for three days a week Beatrix attends the local, very pleasant primary school. She is mostly not actively unhappy there, although increasingly so since 'The Hours' kicked in. On the first day at home after Felix had started at full time school, I was thinking how delighted Beatrix would be to have quiet time at her own pace with much more of my attention for her. She started the day with a lament on how boring and quiet it would be without him – his continuous lusty singing or chatting, his high burn energy and enthusiasm, and his furies, of course. But she has adapted the two days without him to suit her own interests, and I am glad she has had this chance on her own.

She has time to read in bed in the mornings if we do not have an outing planned; enjoy long, relaxed music lessons in the middle of the day when she is not tired; bake wonderful cakes, buns and biscuits much better than those her parents make; practise and get more confident at riding her bike around town. Some days she wants to fiddle around in her bedroom on her own – writing stories and diaries and schemes and schedules, sketching in her tiny sketch book. Other days she wants to DO something – so we go down into the cellar and practise our very elementary carpentry, or revitalise her garden patch, or play badminton, or construct an exhibition board for the local regeneration scheme. Now she wants to make a wrap around skirt just like the one her friend's older sister sported in the summer. At school she is in the 'top set' for those lessons where they are 'setted', and all despite having been to school for only three days a week and enjoyed what amounts to a four day weekend.

Flexi-time schooling is choosing when to be educated, using schools just as they are. Time arrangements can take the form of so many days or part-days per week, or a block of weeks in school and then a block of weeks out of school.

Initially, flexi-schooling was taken to mean, *The part-time arrangement whereby school and family share responsibility for the child's education in an agreed contract and partnership* (Meighan, 1988). This is now more accurately seen as flexi-time schooling.

School becomes one of many resources, such as libraries, computers or television, to be used when the child and the parents choose, according to an agreement between them and the local school. The parents are as involved as the teachers in their children's education, and the children are encouraged to learn for themselves as well as being taught.

Flexi-schooling is choosing how, when, where, with whom. It amounts to the democratisation of learning, the demise of coercive teaching, and would require the complete redesign of the existing educational system. For this to happen, a school has to adopt a policy of reform towards more flexibility in several or all of its teaching methods, learner roles, curriculum specifications and parental roles.

Ultimately, flexi-schooling can lead to flexi-education, a more flexible approach to all aspects of education, and can be applied to aims, power, curriculum and organisation as well as to location and time. This can lead to schools becoming open centres for learning, more like adult education colleges and the Open University, in which both 'lococentric' and distance learning methods are available. The curriculum is negotiated to suit the individual child and the teacher can adopt further roles – amongst others already existing – such as one more like that of a tutor. Flexi-education has been described as:

...alternatives for everybody, all the time.

Education Now Ltd

Flexi-time schooling, therefore, is the temporary expedient for those who cannot wait for the above, but who, for various reasons, do not want solely to home educate – perhaps because they also want to put some energy into pushing for flexi-schooling and on to flexi-education!

Our flexible ethos, or 'Flexos'
I believe that if we are busy and happy, we are probably either learning something new or interesting, or consolidating our learning, or benefiting from the fruits of it. It seems that, give or take the odd 'bad hair' day, we all do this – independently of each other for at least part of each day and with support or company for the other part – without even trying. So that is our neat, simple, clear philosophy. Not that I had worked that out when we started on flexi-time schooling: the philosophy has evolved along with the rest of us.

So, why did we start? It was just a feeling really; a feeling that Felix had too much energy, too many very pressing – to him – needs, too much interest and enthusiasm to be enclosed in one room with one adult and lots of other needy children for blocks of five days a week. Beatrix was still breastfeeding and sleeping a lot and it seemed cruel to lever her into an artificial, externally imposed regime in order to get Felix in and out of school each day. What is rewarding is that the seed of an idea bore such voluptuous fruit.

We started a small pre-school group two mornings a week, meeting in our house or on the common or wherever. The parents and carers met once a month to discuss the notion of carrying on with this through the primary years as an alternative to school. I was very disappointed when, during the summer of the year a majority of the children in the group turned five, all but one of the parents pulled away from the idea. They needed or wanted to work, and using the full-time childcare offered by school was the only way they could afford to do that. I sympathised. I too have always enjoyed my paid work and I did not want to give it up, not even for my children! Since they were born, I had always worked in a job-share and their father has worked from home for most of that time. Why shouldn't they be able to go to school part time? They could have the best of both worlds, even if it did mean taking on board some of the worst of one world! So that is what we have done.

Three days a week the children have gone to school, and four days a week we have had a fantastic time to grow and learn and love together. Each half term, both children have re-made the decision to flex or attend school full time. One year, Beatrix adored one of her teachers and loved the work so she chose full time for half a term. The three days away from each other without much control over our lives, hurrying for trains to work and struggling to hear each other's needs while cooking a too-late supper, have meant that we have relished, revelled in and celebrated our four days' freedom on a weekly basis.

It wasn't quite as simple as that – but I knew what we wanted and I assumed I would get it. Now, having tried to inform and support others who have wanted the same, I realise that it was much simpler than it might have been. So how have we arrived where we are, and how did we get what we wanted?

Flexing the system

As well as participating in our own pre-school group, both children attended the local primary school's nursery for two hours a day from the age of 3+. During this year I explored the dynamics in the school and developed a dialogue with the head teacher. By the end of the nursery year, she had agreed that Felix, and any other children who were not yet five years old, need not attend the reception class full time. Several other parents, mostly of boys, joined us in attending part-time. Felix chose to go for three full days because he fancied the school lunches – his first experience of regular junk food opportunities! So I organised my job share around this.

I spent the Reception Year researching the possibility of flexi-time schooling. The head teacher was curious, but said she would agree if the LEA was comfortable with the idea. Her own inquiries to the school's advisors were not positive.

I decided to approach the Director of Education myself before the idea drowned in too much water under the bridge. I wrote a briefing note to the Director and asked for an interview with her. I was still optimistic as I knew that she had been an enlightened governor of a free school in London and head of a large London comprehensive school. We had a good talk and she let on that she was an admirer of John Holt. She wanted to agree to my request for my children to enjoy part-time schooling if they chose that option, but she had no information which countered the assumption that it was illegal. The meeting concluded with her saying that if I could prove that it was legal and had the support of the head, then she would agree to the arrangement. Yippee! There was still a chance!

A rapid letter to Roland Meighan and, hey presto, he sent back a copy of the legal explanation of the Education Act that actually said in so many words that:

It IS legal
In *Home Education and the Law* (Oxford, 1991), David Deutsch and Kolya Wolf clarify the legality of part-time or flexi-time schooling:

> *For some parents the ideal is to educate their children at home for part of the time, and have them attend school for the remainder. This is sometimes called 'flexi-schooling'. Combining schooling and non-schooling education in any proportions is perfectly legal, provided that the net effect is to provide proper education for the child (and the LEA must satisfy itself that this is so). However, the school in question must agree to the arrangement. In a flexi-schooling arrangement the child is a registered pupil at the school and is deemed to be 'absent with leave' under sections 39(2) and 39(5) of the Education Act 1944 during periods when he is being educated away from the school.*

With the coming into force of the Education Act 1996 these provisions are now to be found in its section 444 (3) which makes it an offence for a parent to fail to ensure that a child of compulsory school age attends regularly at the school at which she is registered. Section 444 (3) states

> *The child shall not be taken to have failed to attend regularly at the school by reason of his absence from the school (a) with leave*

and section 444(9) further defines

> *In this section 'leave', in relation to a school, means leave granted by any person authorised to do so by the governing body or proprietor of the school.*

Another provision enacted now in s19(1) of the Education Act 1996 places a duty upon LEAs to make exceptional provision for education.

> *Each local education authority shall make arrangements for the provision of suitable full-time or part-time education at school or otherwise than at school for those children of compulsory school age who, by reason of illness, exclusion from school or otherwise, may not for any period receive suitable education unless such arrangements are made for them.*

Any school, maintained or independent, may accommodate flexi-time schooling if it wishes to, but no school is under any obligation to do so. Thus one might say that whereas full-time home education is an absolute right (in the sense that any parent who can provide proper education at home must be allowed to do so), and full-time school education is an absolute right (in the sense that the LEA must find a place for any school-age child whose parent wants him to go to school, nor can an LEA refuse such a child admission to a particular school where there is a vacancy), flexi-time schooling is not an absolute right, because the school is entitled to refuse on arbitrary grounds.

When asked in 1994 to respond as to the legality of flexi-time schooling, the Minister of State for Education, Eric Forth, although obfuscating, confirmed the legality of a flexi-time arrangement with the school's permission.

The situation, therefore, with the Local Management of Schools, is that the LEA can advise governors and the head teacher, but it cannot impose its view. It is legal for the governors and head teacher to agree to a flexi-time arrangement within a particular school.

Another form of flexi-time other than at school is also perfectly legal. Universities or further education colleges can admit children of compulsory school age whom they consider have reached the necessary academic standard to attend their normal courses as part- or full-time students; or where courses are provided for children who are excluded from or failing at school.

And no, it won't affect the school's funding

At the three schools where my own children have attended on an agreed flexi-time basis, the children are recorded as 'educated off-site', which is classified as an 'absence with leave' or an 'authorised absence'. This means that the funding is exactly as for a full-time student and the school returns are not affected. In this country the funding is not split between school and home as it is in the USA's 'Independent Study Programme'.

Practical arrangements with the school

Permission has to be granted by the head teacher and governing body for flexi-time to be an option at a particular school. Without this, the leave would not be authorised and action would be taken against parents by the LEA in cases where a child was absent without leave on a systematic basis.

A learning contract or personal learning plan can be agreed – but does not have to be – to formalise the practical arrangements. This could state, for example:

- The times the child attends school;

- That the child will be encouraged and allowed to attend special events that take place at agreed 'non-school' times in consultation with the child's class teacher;

- Parents/carers have the same access to records, reports and opportunities to meet with teachers as children who attend school on a full-time basis;

- The school has access to all LEA reports regarding the child's education on non-school days;

- Parents/carers have the same statutory rights as those of children who attend school on a full-time basis;

- Arrangement to flexi-time may be terminated by the parent during the academic year, but full attendance must begin at the start of a new half term only;

• The head teacher retains the right to inform parents/carers if he/she believes that the arrangement is detrimental to the progress of the child.

When we embarked on flexi-time, the head teacher asked me not to proselytise until the arrangement had been seen to work. She did have some concerns about whether other parents would stampede for flexi-time, or whether it would unsettle other children in the class who might then lobby their parents for the same arrangement. For this reason, I discussed these concerns with Felix and Beatrix and explained that flexi-time was a privilege, not a right. If they wanted it to continue they should behave discreetly and never use it as an excuse. Knowing how much it was in their own interest, they have succeeded in this without any complaint from either teachers or parents in the fourteen years' flexi-time that, between them, they have notched up.

It is also worth recording that I was right when I suggested to the head teacher that all too few parents could or would want to spend more time with their children: only three other families in the three schools which my own children have attended have undertaken flexi-time. Two of the arrangements lasted a year, and the third, two years.

The other theme to this part of our story is that I was sure that our arrangement would be more likely to last if I was to demonstrate an unequivocal commitment to state education, equality of access to education for all children, support for teachers doing a near impossible job, and support for parents and children who choose to go to school or who feel they have no real choice. So I became a parent governor. A few whole school policies later, a successful campaign to save the school from infant rather than primary status, an OFSTED inspection and a needs-led budget revolt meant that I was gradually trusted by the teachers as well as some of the parents! After I had served a four-year term, Felix and Beatrix warned me that if I stood again they just might ask me to leave home!

The inspection
While a child is registered at a state school, which he/she is if they are flexi-timing, they must satisfy the requirements of the National Curriculum. They may be able to achieve this in the school hours alone, which leaves greater flexibility at home.

As with home schooling, the inspector may request to visit at home. The difference is that while for home schooling the inspector must be satisfied that the children are learning and progressing generally, with flexi-timers this is evaluated in terms of the requirements of the National Curriculum. This need not be very arduous if the children are working well while at school, or if they are at Key Stages 1 and 2. In practice at Key Stages 1 and 2 most of what a child may be busy with at home will reach one target or another!

Structure or not?

This is essentially the same debate as is held in home schooling circles. Some children may enjoy a structured day, others may feel stifled, and their optimum learning times, places and modes may vary from day to day. The difference is that it will depend to some extent on what agreement children and parents have made with the teacher as to what is expected at home. Our experience is that as long as the children are progressing and learning, the schools are not concerned what it is that they are doing or how it is done at home. Other schools or teachers may expect certain work to be done which ties into school topic work and the output returned to school. Age may play a large part in determining this too: at Key Stage 2 there may be much more 'homework' to complete.

If your reasons for flexi-time schooling are because you feel you want your child to progress academically faster than he/she would at school, then what goes on at home may need to be an extension of what goes on at school, and the National Curriculum and close contact with the teacher is what you will need. However, if it is because you feel that there are aspects to education which cannot be offered by schools, then the world is your oyster, although this Big Wide World approach to learning is necessarily limited by the demands of running a household, as well as by the child's own enthusiasms.

The Big Wide World approach is characterised by more first-hand experience than schools, books or TV can offer, by more outdoors time, more time in a greater variety of places, more surprises and unplanned learning, perhaps as much 'wasted' time (though in different ways) but more intense learning time.

We do many of the things that full-time schoolers can, but with more time and out of peak hours. Flexi-time activities that we have enjoyed include renovating a doll's house, dissecting a large fish head, demonstrations of both types of bell-ringing, soap making, bread making, glass painting and calligraphy. We have visited a clock mender, a boat builder's yard and the local bus station maintenance pit, the local water treatment plant, a coal-fired power station and a developing methane-generated plant at the local landfill site. We have done projects on milk (including doing a milk round at 4am), on microscopes and molecules, and on wood and timber and tools, with a visit to a timber yard and sculptures in wood and glue. We produced a dramatic play, 'Boudicca's Battle'. 'Equal Opportunities' and global politics are discussed almost daily.

Our inspector went away happy with the range of outside visits and at-home activities which happen with a bit of discussion and planning round the edges, and those others which are offered but declined by the children! When we started out I did have inconsistent urges to 'do' projects, but if one child was busy measuring tree girths, the other was swearing never to look at a tree again. While one child was delighted by workbooks, the other was eloquently sneering. We soon ended up discussing what we really wanted to do, and doing that – just like at the weekend. When I lost my cool, I would throw 'flexi' at them but that, too, passed quickly.

Flexi-time has worked so well for us. We have experienced twice as much fun time together as most families are able to, with absolutely no drawbacks except those we would have found anyway – those odd days when one of us feels grim and dumps it on the others. I notice it is usually me, and that gets the children down. If I am being rational or if it is the children who feel blue or bad, we can usually retrieve the day pretty quickly.

Flexi-time defunct
Once flexi-schooling becomes a real option, flexi-time need no longer be a separate option in itself. It is arguable that a less rigid approach to learning and education is more appropriate in an era of electronic communications and more casualised, flexible working, and there is considerable evidence to suggest that the loosening of the school structure is already underway. The advent of small schools, the Open School, community education, electronic mail and interactive distance learning, mini-schooling, the emphasis on lifelong learning that the structural changes to the economy and the nature of work are demanding, and the broad remit for the 'deregulated' Further Education Colleges, which allows them to educate people from 4 years upwards should the colleges so choose, all denote choice and flexibility. Combine these institutional responses with the increasing numbers of school refusers, school phobics and excluded children, the ballooning recognition that

so many children have 'special' educational needs and the greater parental awareness and control afforded by Local Management of Schools, and the stage is set.

Many children are voting with their feet. It is my hope that all children and young people, as the main clients of our school services, will soon be afforded the dignity of having a real say in their learning: what is delivered, how, where and when. It is an anachronism, when young people are asked how they want their care to be improved by social services, how they want their out of school care to be improved by leisure services, and how they want their neighbourhood improved by planning, that the National Curriculum is foisted upon them regardless: the diktat of an older generation.

Indeed, distance learning and 'telelearning' on a large scale are impending events. Those education authorities which have embraced aspects of flexi-schooling such as flexi-time, consultation and real partnership with children, parents and carers will be better placed to take advantage of the revolution from schools to learning centres. However, the choice and pluralism advocated across the political spectrum and illustrated in part by these examples can be delivered only if the state extends the subsidy to more various learning contexts and access is freely available.

In 1997, the Birmingham St Paul's Free School for young people, many of whom have been excluded from mainstream school, was awarded grant-maintained status by Government after its LEA funding was withdrawn; and something similar happened four years ago at a small rural school in Warwickshire which was threatened with closure when the LEA was purging 'surplus places'. They are now 'foundation' schools. The University of the First Age and the proposed mentoring between that and the University of the Third Age hint at a more imaginative approach to education in the maintained sector.

The State has yet to rejoice in the possibilities afforded by flexi-schooling and democratic learning in mainstream education. We look forward to a time when the opportunity which our family has enjoyed is readily available at both primary and secondary levels. In the meantime, I encourage you to set out in hope and get what you want.

References:

Roland Meighan: *Flexi-schooling,* Education Now Books, 1988

D.Deutsch, and K.Wolf: *Home Education and the Law,* second edition
   1991 Deutsch and Wolf, 19 New Cross Road, Oxford, OX3 8LP

Kate Oliver
kate@waverider.co.uk

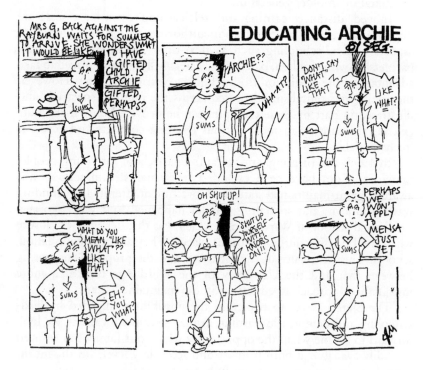

An outline of the law and practice of home-based education

Ian Dowty

By the time you reach here, you will have been able to see for yourself how several different families experience home-based education and you might think it odd that, in a book like this, you come to a chapter dealing with the law. A book about school probably wouldn't tell you that you have to make sure that you send your child to school or you commit an offence, as it's a fair assumption to make that most parents already realise that. However, hard on the heels of 'How do you do that?' asked of the home educating parent, is the question, 'Is it legal?'

So I am here to say what in all probability is completely clear to you by now, 'Yes, it is'. And, if that were that, it would be a short chapter. It is a shame, to put it mildly, that it cannot be. For many parents choosing to home educate in many areas of the country, they need have no greater knowledge of the law. For others it becomes absolutely essential.

This book relates the experiences of home educators living in England and Wales whose courts all operate within the same system. The legal provisions I set out below only apply within that jurisdiction, and reflect the law as at April 2000. Parents are able to home educate in Scotland and Northern Ireland where different legal systems operate, and in many countries abroad, but their arrangements are beyond the scope of this chapter.

Before I get going, I need to make it clear that this is only intended as an introduction to home education law and I have been asked not to include too many source references. The general guidance I give is not designed to answer questions posed by a specific case. Law is not static and changes all the time, whether by will of Parliament or of the courts.

As I cannot know the circumstances of any particular case, I cannot assume responsibility for the application to it of what I say here. If anyone gets into the position of having to argue chapter and verse, I would encourage them to take legal advice. I hope they will be able more easily to understand the advice they receive after having read this chapter.

To understand the legal position of the home educator, it helps to have a complete overview. This will include, for example, what happens if a prosecution is mounted against a home educating parent. The chances of this actually happening are very slim, and if I give the contrary impression it is probably because I deal with those for whom things have gone awry. Nobody goes to see a lawyer unless they really need to! There are those who encounter difficulties from officialdom, in the shape of their Local Education Authority (LEA), and others who have a blissful relationship with theirs. I hope that anyone who unfortunately finds themselves in the 'having difficulty' group will find the information in this chapter some help in coping with their LEA.

My own experience, observations and assessment of the evidence of those who write about home-based education, inform me that mainstream school, if it could rid itself of the assumptions it makes about how to educate, could learn a great deal by understanding how home education works. Studies in the USA and this country have shown that on average home-educated children are two years in advance of their peers in school academically and relate more successfully to a broad age band of adults and children.

This makes it all the more inexplicable to me that there is any hostility to home-based education. I know this is a controversial area, but it seems fair to say that some LEAs do not appear to take kindly to the idea that supposedly 'unqualified' parents are able in law and in fact to home educate. Even down the telephone line I have been able to feel the steam rising from some LEA representatives who find it incomprehensible that parents 'can just do it without our permission'. Too often have I heard representatives of LEAs claim for their authority 'local arrangements' arrived at with the Department of Employment and Education (DfEE), which they appear to believe negate the law of the land. We no longer face the position of the early 'pioneers' who were forced to move home repeatedly to keep one step ahead of the applications for care orders. I really do not know how they managed to persevere, but all those who home educate today are deeply indebted to them. Through their efforts, and in many cases their suffering, it has become accepted that parents are perfectly able in law and in deed to educate their own children. Nowadays, many LEAs are happy to support home-based education and I only mean any criticism to apply to those in other LEAs who are responsible for placing what I consider to be unreasonable and, on occasion, unlawful obstacles in the way of parents exercising their lawful freedom of choice.

SOURCES OF LAW

It might help, for those who have never had to consider it, if I outline where we get our law from. In England and Wales the law of education (as with every other area) derives from legislation passed by Parliament and from decisions of the Courts.

Legislation is primarily made up of Acts of Parliament. Acts are divided into sections, abbreviated to an 's', and subsections which are shown in brackets. Thus section 437, subsection 3 is written: s437(3). There are several Acts which deal with education as a whole, but home educators need only be concerned with the Education Act 1996, and then with only a small part of that. As with other Acts, the Education Act 1996 allows the Secretary of State, a Government minister, to make rules, called statutory instruments, which, after they have been approved in Parliament, form part of the legislation consisting of regulations, abbreviated as 'reg'.

The legislation sets out how education is to be organised and who, or what bodies, have a duty, responsibility or power to act in certain ways or make certain decisions. Such actions or decisions (or failures to act or decide) are generally reviewable by the courts. This would be done either by using procedures set out in the legislation itself, or under general principles which have established that those in authority who make decisions have to make them lawfully, reasonably and rationally. They must take into account all matters they are required to consider and they must ignore matters that should not affect their decision.

The Department of Education and Employment (DfEE), headed by the Secretary of State, is the arm of government which oversees, amongst other things, the school and education system in England and Wales. The DfEE also issues Circulars which set out its guidance on matters of policy and interpretation of the law. These can be very useful in gaining an understanding of the viewpoint of the DfEE but they do not have the force of law, and indeed can be challenged if the advice or instruction contained in them is contrary to the provisions laid down in the legislation.

Beneath the DfEE in the hierarchy are the many LEAs and schools whose officials and representatives carry out the duties imposed by the legislation and the policy decisions made by the Government and the LEA itself.

Whether they come from the DfEE or an LEA, those who carry out any function ordained as a result of policy or legislation can only do what they are in law empowered to do. If they overstep their legal powers, even if they act in accordance with 'policy', any person affected can apply to a court to ensure the law is complied with. Similarly, if there is a dispute over what an Act or statutory instrument means, those affected can apply to a court to resolve the problem and the court will, if necessary, decide what Parliament meant when it passed the legislation in question. In doing so, the court effectively decides what the law is and on occasion can be said to make law.

Legislation always refers to people in the masculine and I repeat that where necessary. However, if I cannot elegantly use a non-specific gender term elsewhere, I have referred to a child in the feminine and anybody else in the masculine. This has the added benefit of aiding clarity of meaning.

THE RESPONSIBILITY FOR EDUCATING CHILDREN

If you ask most people who it is that has the responsibility for educating their children, they will probably answer 'Their school.' It comes as a bit of a surprise to them to find out that is not the case. The law fairly and squarely places the responsibility for the education of their children on parents and they are not absolved from that duty by sending their child to school. For the purposes of the Education Act 1996, the term 'parent' embraces not only a natural parent but also anyone with parental responsibility for a child or 'who has care of him'.

The cornerstone of educational provision is set out in section 7 (s7 from now on) of the Education Act 1996 which states (with my emphasis):

The parent of every child of compulsory school age shall cause him to receive efficient full-time education suitable;
a)   to his age, ability, and aptitude, and
b)   to any special educational needs he may have,
either by regular attendance at school **or otherwise.**

It's the 'or otherwise' bit that makes it all possible. Although the somewhat confusing term 'compulsory school age' is used, it is *education* which is compulsory and *not* school. The draftsman needed a phrase which could cover children of a defined age and lighted upon 'compulsory school age' when it would have been more accurate to have said 'compulsory education age'. What that demonstrates quite well is that there is, without doubt, a bias towards school education; a bias which perhaps results from an assumption never challenged in the minds of those responsible for drafting the legislation, and which regrettably pervades officialdom.

The section states quite clearly that, in discharging the responsibility placed on them to educate their children, parents are faced with an equal choice: 'school', 'or otherwise'. Not all LEAs, or at least not all of their representatives, appear to see it this way. Too many seem to see their task as 'getting home-educated children back to school'.

If the rights of parents needed any reinforcement, it is provided in the European Convention on Human Rights which was adopted in 1950. The Convention will be given effect in law in this country when the Human Rights Act 1998 comes fully into force on 2nd October 2000. The right of parents with regard to the education of their children is affirmed in Article 2 of the First Protocol to the Convention, which states:

> No person shall be denied the right to education. In the exercise of any functions which it assumes in relation to education and to teaching, the State shall respect the right of parents to ensure such education and teaching in conformity with their own religious and philosophical convictions.

The UK has entered a reservation, that it accepts the principle set out in the second sentence:

> ... only so far as it is compatible with the provision of efficient instruction and training, and the avoidance of unreasonable public expenditure ...

This limitation is expressly stated to have been imposed to take account of existing education law, and accordingly the phrase 'efficient instruction and training' needs to be read in that light.

Much is rightly made of the responsibility of the family in bringing up children to be valuable and contributing members of society and it is in my view important that, with that aim in mind, the family unit be not only free, but encouraged, to take hold of that fundamental responsibility and ensure that their children are educated in accordance with their reasonable principles, convictions and philosophy.

Indeed, who is better equipped than a parent to know what will best suit their child and what will best fit in with the arrangements that each family wishes to, and can, make? As a parent it is likely nowadays that, whether you are mother or father, you will have been present at your children's births, watched them develop into independent individuals and seen what they struggle with and what they find easier. Your knowledge and assessment of their abilities will be inherent in your appreciation of your children without any necessity to operate a system of 'tests'. Parents are in the best position to protect and give effect to their children's rights until they can speak (and be heard by society) for themselves.

Home-based education allows parents to provide the education that their child needs, wherever this may be on a spectrum between the formally structured approach, resembling school, to the fully autonomous, where the child is supported in her own quest for knowledge. What each home educating family may come to realise is that they have found a place on this sliding scale of possibilities which suits them and is comfortable, even though that place may vary from time to time depending on changing needs as their children develop.

The law not only makes allowance for this diversity of approach, I would suggest that it is the natural consequence of the proper exercise of the responsibility placed upon parents by s7 to ensure that their children are educated according to their individual attributes and needs. The section provides the only criteria that have to be met by parents who choose to home educate, none other applies.

You do not have to obtain anyone's permission or consent to home educate your children, except if your child is already registered at a special school, at any school as a result of a school attendance order, or at both a pupil referral unit and at a school. You do not have to have any formal teaching or other qualifications. You do not have to follow any particular curriculum, or indeed any curriculum at all. The National Curriculum only applies to state schools, as does the requirement that any curriculum be 'balanced and broadly based'. You do not have to keep school hours or terms. In short, unless that is what you want, you do not have to reproduce a school at home. Provided you satisfy the requirements of s7 you can, in fact, do exactly as you choose.

THE INGREDIENTS OF s7 EDUCATION ACT 1996

So what exactly does s7 mean and how can you be sure that you will be able to meet its requirements?

The education that has to be provided is qualified by the words 'efficient' and 'full-time' but its linchpin is that it has to be suitable to the individual child. Those are the only qualifications imposed by the legislation on the word 'education'; it is a definition wide enough to encompass many different theories and practices of learning.

Apart from the phrases 'compulsory school age' and 'special educational needs', none of the terms used in the section is further defined. When words in a statute are not defined, they are meant to have their meaning in ordinary usage, but that may still leave room for interpretation.

The duty placed upon parents by s7 applies only in respect of their children of 'compulsory school age'. Broadly speaking, that is those aged between five and sixteen years, however there are provisions which establish exactly when the phrase applies to a child. The law defines when a child reaches 'compulsory school age' by relation to 'prescribed dates' in the year, which are 31st March, 31st August and 31st December. Your child reaches 'compulsory school age' on the next prescribed date after her fifth birthday or the prescribed date itself, if her birthday actually falls on it. She ceases to be of 'compulsory school age' at the end of a day called the 'school leaving date', which has been fixed as the last Friday of June each year. If a child attains sixteen before, or on, that date, or will be sixteen after that date but before the beginning of the next school year, she ceases to be of 'compulsory school age' on that date. If her sixteenth birthday is after the start of the new school year, she is still of 'compulsory school age' until the end of the last Friday in June of the following year.

The word 'efficient' needs closer consideration, not only for its definition but for how it needs to be approached by the home educator. It is a word with a commonly known and accepted meaning, but it is helpful to bear in mind that a definition found useful by at least one court, is that an education is '"efficient" if it achieves that which it sets out to achieve'.

This is important because it allows a subjective view of what is efficient, providing always it meets the full criteria of s7. For this reason, I think it is essential that parents establish clearly what they seek to achieve by home educating and how they are going to go about it. If you find this difficult, perhaps it might help to imagine how your child will be at eighteen if her education has succeeded. What of your principles and beliefs do you hope she will value? How will she absorb them and how will she be equipped to make her way in life? What, for you, makes a good education? By what method is your child to learn? Having thus clarified your aims and approach, you should be able to compose a written statement setting them out, which, for want of a better expression, I shall refer to as your philosophy of education. It need not be cast in stone and I would expect you will want to revise it from time to time as you and your children grow and change.

It is in my view vital to have such a document because, when the efficiency of the education you are providing is under consideration, your philosophy is the yardstick against which it will be measured. If you do not define 'efficient' for yourself in this way, then by default you run the risk of being judged according to the precepts of your LEA, whose chief interest lies in the supply of school education.

Before leaving 'efficient', I need to mention that some LEAs, and indeed some legal textbooks, seem to suggest that its meaning is qualified by reference to the National Curriculum and that an education can only be efficient if it incorporates the requirements of the National Curriculum. I am at a loss to understand this because it is made abundantly clear in the Education Act 1996 that the National Curriculum applies only to state-run schools. Neither independent schools nor home educators have to use it, so how then could they possibly be judged against it?

'Full-time' at least should not provide any problem; home-based education is just that, in a way that school cannot be and is not designed to be, so any comparison with its days, weeks or terms is not a relevant one. Home-based education starts when your child awakes and ends when she goes to sleep. Even if you choose to adopt a school-like approach, you may find that 'stopping' at the end of 'term' is not possible, and 'relentless' is perhaps more apt a description!

You would think that 'age' might be an easy word to define, and it is when purely a description of calendar achievement. However, what does 'age' mean in educational terms? Many home educators see an advantage in freeing themselves from learning based upon age banding. Perhaps this is not a problem if 'age' is coupled with the words that follow it, 'ability and aptitude' – yet they might seem to highlight the redundancy of 'age'. It may be unlikely that a child of eleven years would want to have a grasp of astro-physics, but if that child demonstrated an ability and/or an aptitude for that, or some other equally esoteric subject, would an education which failed to meet such a need be suitable for that child simply because it would have met the needs of the majority of eleven-year-olds? I venture to suggest that most home educators would not regard it as doing so.

Finally, in terms of definitions, there is the phrase 'special educational needs' (SEN). This topic on its own is worthy of a much more detailed analysis than is possible here. SEN in respect of a child, is a phrase defined further by the Education Act 1996 as a 'learning difficulty which calls for special educational provision to be made for him.' A child has a 'learning difficulty' if he has a 'significantly greater difficulty in learning than the majority of children of his age' or 'a disability which either prevents or hinders him from making use of educational facilities of a kind generally provided for children of his age in schools'.

There is a considerable amount of legislation which applies specifically to SEN including a statutory Code of Practice. There is provision for an LEA, in consultation with parents, to assess a child if it considers she has, or probably has, SEN. This procedure can be instigated by the parents. A statement of SEN setting out the provision to be made for the child must be maintained by an LEA if special educational provision has to be made for a child, but not every child with SEN has to be 'statemented', only those for whom it is necessary for the LEA to make some additional provision.

Whilst there is no doubt that a child with SEN can be home-educated, as there is reference to it in s7 itself, a parent has to take any SEN into account as it qualifies the suitability of the education to be provided. Whether parents of a home-educated child with SEN feel that their child should be statemented or not may depend on whether it would make any difference to them or to the child or whether it might simply impose further constraints upon them. They might be swayed if it would result in the provision of some assistance by a local authority, and they would need to make their own enquiries about this.

If the statementing procedure is started whilst the parents are home educating, and they do not want it to be completed, they can argue that, as they are making full provision for their child's SEN, and the LEA is not required to provide anything, it is not necessary for there to be a formal assessment or statement. Once made, the statement has to be reviewed annually, although it can be reviewed at any time if the LEA wishes to do so. It may need to be amended if a statemented child is withdrawn from school to be home-educated (which does not require permission unless the child is a registered pupil at a special school, or a pupil referral unit and another school, or is the subject of a school attendance order). Provided that the parent has made 'suitable arrangements' the LEA is not required to make any arrangements for special educational provision for the child.

Whilst it is important to have an understanding of what the constituent parts of s7 mean, it is important also not to lose sight of the whole definition and the way in which the parts link together: an 'efficient full-time education' has also to be 'suitable' to the child's age, abilities and special educational needs. Courts have concluded that this is established if the education provided equips a child to live in a modern civilised society or a particular community within it, of which she is a member, as long as it enables the child to adopt a different way of life if she wished to do so later on.

This might be seen to contradict a matter for which some home educators are taken to task when they are accused of not providing a 'balanced and broadly based' education, which anyway is a requirement of a curriculum that by statute applies only to schools. My illustration of the eleven-year-old astrophysicist might appear to be somewhat tongue in cheek, but some thought does need to be given to this. Parents know their children well and are able to appreciate their interests. They do not need, as schools may, to cast their net wide to catch the interest of a child. Children who are autonomously educated follow, and are supported in, their own interests in any event. If they have a particular and consuming interest which well suits their abilities and aptitudes, would that not justify concentrating on this, even at the expense of some topics in which the child has no interest? Is this not in accordance with the requirements of s7 itself? More often than not, it is inevitable, in order to develop a deep interest, that a child will master what might in school terms be described as core subjects. These will be mastered not as abstracts, but as tools to be used to unlock what the child is really interested in. In this way a child will receive the education that really is best suited to her.

These, then, are the criteria you will need to have in mind when deciding to home educate. Once you have made your decision, how you put it into practice depends first on whether or not your child is a registered pupil at a school.

WHAT DO YOU DO IF YOUR CHILD HAS NEVER BEEN TO SCHOOL?

If your child has never been to school you need do nothing: nothing more, that is, than you have been doing already. Most children, unless there are recognised causes, are pre-programmed to seek out and absorb knowledge. With your help they have learnt a host of abilities as the need or curiosity arose. Home-based education is, for many, simply a continuation of this voyage of discovery. The only difference is that once they reach 'compulsory school age', you have to provide an education which meets your obligation under s7 Education Act 1996.

When your child reaches 'compulsory school age', you can, if you wish, contact your LEA and inform it that you are home educating. LEAs will generally either say that you have to do this, or that they prefer it if you would do so. What you do is entirely up to you: you do not have to inform the LEA and there is no legal provision requiring you to do so. How you exercise that choice may well depend on where you live and how other home educators in your area experience contact with the LEA. I suspect that, for many, it boils down to this: parents may be more likely to contact their LEA if it is known to be sympathetic to home educators. What I say later may help you to understand this more easily and enable you to reach your own decision.

WHAT MUST YOU DO IF YOUR CHILD HAS BEEN TO SCHOOL?

Children nowadays can be registered at school prior to 'compulsory school age'. If you decide to home educate before they reach that age, you can simply remove them from school and your only constraint is one of courtesy. However, it is important that their name is not on a school register after they have reached 'compulsory school age' and for that reason you might feel that it is wise to follow the steps I set out below.

When children of 'compulsory school age' attend at school, their names have to be entered into a register. The parents of a child who is a registered pupil at a school must ensure that she attends at the school regularly. If the parents do not ensure that she does, they can be prosecuted by the LEA in the magistrates' court. Even a short absence can be treated as failure to attend regularly. When you decide to home educate a child who is a registered pupil at a school, whether it be at a state or public (private) school, it is therefore of the utmost importance that you ensure that her name is removed from the school's register. Even if everybody accepts that you are home educating satisfactorily, if your child is still on a school register you are committing an offence.

If your child has been registered as a pupil at a school but for some reason is not actually registered at the time you start home educating, perhaps because you have moved to a different area, you do not have to do anything. You are in the same position, effectively, as if your child had never been to school.

In some schools it is possible to combine an element of home education with going to school. This is called flexi-schooling. The child is a registered pupil at the school but is given agreed leave of absence. Kate Oliver explains how this works in her chapter earlier in this book.

De-registering your child is straightforward in the vast majority of cases. A statutory instrument, the Education (Pupil Registration) Regulations 1995, sets out the grounds upon which a registered pupil has to be de-registered. Unless your child attends at a special school (for those with SEN), a pupil referral unit or at any school in accordance with a school attendance order, all you need to do is write a letter to the 'proprietor' of the school requiring him to take your child off the register, on the basis that she is no longer attending at school as she is receiving education otherwise than at school. The 'proprietor' is required by reg. 9(1)(c) of the 1995 Regulations to remove your child's name from the register upon receipt of your letter. He does not have any discretion, he *has* to do it.

Regrettably, it would seem that some schools and LEAs still believe that they have some say in whether a child is removed from the register in order to be home-educated. This was the position before the 1995 Regulations came into effect. The fact that some LEAs have missed this change in the law is not so surprising when yet others still refer to the 1944 Education Act, which was replaced *completely* by the 1996 Act.

So, when they get the de-registration letter, some schools or LEAs may say that they will not remove the child's name from the register until the LEA has approved the arrangements that the parent is making for her education. Just write again telling them why they are wrong in law, and, when doing so, you might like to point out that the 1995 Regulations are made in accordance with s434 Education Act 1996 which makes it a criminal offence not to comply with them. An intransigent proprietor can face a £200 fine if he continues to demur.

Once you have written to the school notifying it of the position, you need no longer send your child there and you cannot commit the offence of failing to ensure that she attends regularly. The letter you send is an important one and you would be wise to keep a copy of it, obtain and keep confirmation that it was sent and, if you can get it, that it was received. You may, at a later stage need to prove that you notified the 'proprietor' if the LEA does not accept that the letter was sent. So, if you hand-deliver it, make a note of when, where and to whom you handed it over, and get them to sign and date a receipt if you can. If you post it, send it recorded delivery and get the Post Office to confirm it was received. In the letter, ask for confirmation to be sent to you in writing that it has been received and that your child has been removed from the register. If you do not get a reply, pester the school for confirmation in follow-up letters which again say what you are doing. Do not stop until you have an acknowledgement; this is your protection against prosecution.

The letter has by law to be sent to the 'proprietor' of the school – the person or body of people who are responsible for the management of the school. If you do not know who this is, send the letter to the Head and ask for it to be forwarded to the proprietor. Again seek confirmation that this has been done.

The proprietor must tell the LEA that you have withdrawn your child from school to home educate within ten days of removing her name from the register. You yourself do not have to take any further steps and do not, for example, have to tell anybody else that you are home educating, not even your LEA, unless you want to do so. I cannot emphasise this point too much. Anyone seeking to criticise you for failing to do so is, plain and simply, wrong.

Now you have embarked upon home-based education, you need to have some idea of what will happen next. You may not hear from your LEA at all, and this should not worry you. Unless you decide to tell them, your LEA may remain unaware that you are home educating; there are certainly numerous home educating families not known to their LEAs. As I have said, if you have taken your child out of school, the school must tell the LEA that you are now home educating, and there are other ways it might find out. Most commonly, someone might contact the LEA just to let it know; doctors, midwives, health visitors and next door neighbours have all been known to do this.

WHO DO YOU HAVE TO SHOW THAT YOU COMPLY WITH s7?

Although home educators do not have to notify their LEA, or be 'registered' with it, the 1996 Act makes provision for LEAs to require parents of a child of compulsory school age 'to satisfy' them that their child is educated in accordance with their duty under s7 of the Act.

This is the last bit of the Education Act that you will need to know about. The Act makes no direct provision for LEAs to supervise home-based education and what provision there is, is phrased in the negative. Section 437(1) of the Act provides that:

> If it appears to a local education authority that a child of compulsory school age in their area is not receiving suitable education either by regular attendance at school or otherwise, they shall serve a notice in writing on the parent requiring him to satisfy them within the period specified in the notice [which must be not less than 15 days including the day of service] that the child is receiving such education.

This provision applies equally to all parents, whether they home educate or their children attend at school. It might be argued that if a school fails its OFSTED inspection, the LEA should contact every parent with a child at the school with the enquiry envisaged by s437. Of course that does not happen; well not, at least, if it is a school which is the responsibility of the LEA. (LEAs ought, perhaps, also to consider serving such notices upon their own local authority following the findings of the House of Commons Select Committee on Health which reported in July 1998 that 26% of children in local authority care were receiving no education and 75% of sixteen-year-olds in care left school without any formal qualifications.)

But to return to reality, s437 is commonly used only in respect of those who home educate and it is used by LEAs when they come across anyone who is home educating, to check on the educational provision that is being made. This is a task that some LEAs acknowledge is not an easy one. It is not surprising if they find it difficult. The Education Act provides little help and the DfEE gives no guidelines whatsoever to an LEA as to how it should reach any decisions.

The LEA will take action under s437 if it is not satisfied that your child is receiving a 'suitable education'. This does not mean that it is left to the LEA to decide what are 'suitable' methods of education, as the phrase 'suitable education' is defined by the Act as an 'efficient full-time education suitable to [the child's] age, ability and aptitude and to any special educational needs he may have'; in other words, in terms identical to s7. Effectively, therefore, the LEA will want to satisfy itself that you are fulfilling your s7 duty when educating your child at home and the definitions I have already discussed apply. If it is not satisfied, the LEA must consider whether it should make a school attendance order which effectively requires that parents send their child to the school named in the order. The order remains in force while the child is of compulsory school age, unless it is revoked by the LEA or directed by a court to cease to be in force.

HOW DOES AN LEA SATISFY ITSELF?

What, then, is likely to happen once an LEA learns that a child of compulsory school age is being home-educated in its area? Effectively, it is up to the LEA to decide, but if it contacts a parent, what does that parent have to do? The only power the LEA has is derived from s437 of the Act. It is only if the LEA can bring that section into operation that it has any function at all with regard to home-based education.

Where difficulty arises it is in respect to what 'if it appears' actually means, as that is the trigger which brings s437 into operation. Some parents contend, with apparent reasonableness, that this means that the LEA must be possessed of some piece of knowledge or evidence from which the appearance of lack of provision can be suspected or deduced. However, the matter has been tested in court in 1980 in the case of Phillips v Brown, where the parents declined to supply to the LEA any evidence of the educational provision they were making. The LEA made a school attendance order (SAO) and eventually prosecuted the parents, as they failed to comply with it (I have described the procedure in more detail below). In the magistrates' court, the parents still declined to give any evidence that they were providing suitable education as they said that the SAO should not have been made. There was, they contended, nothing known to the LEA from which it could conclude that there was an 'appearance' that no suitable education was being provided. The LEA said that was indeed the appearance, precisely because it did not know anything about the child's education and whether it was suitable for him. The magistrate convicted the parents and they appealed to the Divisional Court (Lord Justice Donaldson) which decided that, while it sympathised with the parents' approach, the LEA had acted perfectly properly and in accordance with a duty, which the court said LEAs had, 'to be alert in order to detect the possibility' that there was the appearance of no suitable education.

When the LEA came across a child about whom it knew nothing, the Divisional Court suggested that the LEA should ask the parents about the provision being made. It would then be up to the parents to decide whether they responded to any request for information. The court made it clear that they were under no obligation to reply but if they did not tell the LEA anything, the LEA might reasonably feel it had no option but to believe that there was no appearance of a suitable education. If the LEA were then to come to this view, it would have to start the procedure set out in s437 and send a formal notice requiring a parent to supply evidence which satisfied the LEA that a suitable education was being provided.

LEAs frequently refer to this decision if they are called upon to justify making immediate contact with the parents of a child when they learn that she is being home-educated.

HOW WILL YOUR LEA CONTACT YOU?

Many LEAs make their first contact by sending you a letter but, for some reason, quite a number of LEA officers think that there is nothing wrong with turning up unannounced on your doorstep, even, it appears, at bank holiday weekends. I often wonder how many would like it, if, when you had a question you turned up on theirs? Is it any wonder that parents approached in this way doubt that their LEA sees them as equals? Perhaps parents also object to being made to feel as if they are doing something wrong, to prevent which the LEA needs to mount a surprise visit to catch them out. Too many LEAs see home-based education as a potential welfare problem and need to see how insulting that is.

If the invasion comes, it will most likely be carried out by an Education Welfare Officer (EWO), an officer of the LEA whose function, according to the DfEE, is to help parents and LEAs meet their respective statutory obligations in relation to school attendance. In some LEAs, EWOs are known as Education Social Workers. The practice is growing of describing the LEA officers who deal specifically with home educating families as 'advisers', although they are not the ones who usually make these initial calls on families.

You might find it helpful to have thought out in advance what to do if someone does turn up out of the blue like this. You will already be armed with your philosophy but will you choose to talk on the doorstep, let them in or bid them goodbye?

At the risk of stating the obvious, you first need to find out who they are and check their identification. Sometimes, they come not from the education department but from social services; some of those who might 'report' you are apt on occasion to exaggerate. Annoyed and upset though you may be, you might feel that it is wise to let social workers see your children, so that any 'welfare' issue is dispensed with immediately. If social workers are denied access, however innocently by you, their department can become very concerned and may feel the necessity to take further action. This, you may feel, is common sense and applies whether or not you home educate.

Once you have ascertained that the door-stepper is only interested in your children's education, it is up to you how you proceed. One thing you do need to bear in mind is that, whilst it could be an enlightening visit, if it is not, it could be a disastrous start that will haunt your first years' home education. Too often, it would seem, initial contacts with home educators by an LEA are heavy-handed, aimed at finding out 'why your child is not at school' and with the agenda of getting her into, or back into, school.

I am left to wonder if some LEAs intentionally make home educators run the gauntlet to earn the 'right' to home educate. Some parents seem to have to face an onslaught designed to break their resolve, rather than meeting understanding and support of their decision. These LEAs point out how difficult they believe it is to home educate and , and sometimes demand to see curricula, timetables, lesson plans, yearly plans and the like. Many give the impression that it is necessary to have a separate room or area of the house dedicated to the learning experience, much like a classroom, and some even ask about fire escapes and first aid provisions! None of these is necessary, let alone a legal requirement.

Regrettably, some LEA representatives are not beyond distorting the law to support contentions about 'needing permission' or 'having to follow the National Curriculum' or 'having to be inspected or visited'. And when a parent who knows the law stands their ground and points out that this is not correct in law, their assertions are sometimes countered by 'well, I think it's just been changed recently' although they are a little fuzzy, when pressed, as to when and by what provision.

As a result of this bombardment, many parents find themselves forced to believe that they have to adopt the model envisaged by their LEA, or they will not be 'allowed' to home educate. This manipulative behaviour should, on the contrary, lead to the conclusion that the LEA has little or no understanding of the practice of home education. Rather, it believes that there is only one way to educate a child: she must be taught and the home educator must be a 'teacher'. Hopefully, if you did not appreciate it before, you will gather from the contributions to this book that nothing is further from the truth. LEAs that cling to such notions have simply not taken the trouble to acquaint themselves with any of the literature on the subject. Perhaps they will read this book? If they do, it might cause them to reflect and appreciate that they are visiting your family home, not a place of work nor a school.

All this may perhaps convince you that the best course of action is to turn away the intruder, telling them to write to you if they have any concerns or questions about your child's education and saying you will reply in writing. This will allow you the time to compose yourself, as well as your letter, and enable you to present a complete picture to the LEA that cannot suffer from any misunderstandings of what exactly you were saying.

From October 2000, a further matter that LEAs will need to take account of is the impact of the Human Rights Act 1998. Article 8 of the European Convention on Human Rights affirms the 'right to respect for private and family life'. The European Court has observed that 'the object of the Article [8] is 'essentially' that of protecting the individual against arbitrary interference by the public authorities' and stated that this 'does not merely compel the State to abstain from such interference ...there may be positive obligations inherent in an effective 'respect' for family life'.

This would seem to apply not only to unannounced visits but also to those where parents are told that they will be visited, rather than asked if they would agree to accept a visit at a convenient time. Some LEAs fail to understand, or actively ignore the fact, that they cannot insist upon visits even as the law stands at the moment. If parents choose to invite them into their house, that is an entirely different matter as long as the parents have done so in the knowledge that they are under no compulsion.

It is worth reminding ourselves here that LEAs can only act in accordance with s437 and their only task, in the final analysis, is to decide whether or not parents have satisfied it that they are providing suitable education. All an LEA can do is say that it is not satisfied. It cannot stop parents home educating; the worst it can do is to issue an SAO and then prosecute if it is not complied with. Only a court can make an adverse finding about whether a parent is providing suitable education.

I am not advocating that parents adopt a confrontational attitude when dealing with their LEA, but hoping to redress the imbalance that too often appears when LEA representatives and others say to home educators that they *have* to do *this,* or that they *have* to do *that.* It is simply not true. What parents do at all times is up to them, as long as they know the consequences that might follow. Parents may end up doing what their LEA has asked, or demanded, but only as a result of their own choice, as their LEA should be told.

There is no provision which allows LEAs to specify the way in which they are to be satisfied, or what sort of evidence is acceptable to it and what is not. Parents can choose what evidence they wish to supply in accordance with their philosophy. In assessing such evidence LEAs must act reasonably. In particular, the Divisional Court has held that LEAs cannot as a matter of policy insist on a home visit as the only method of being satisfied. If formal assessment of children's learning is contrary to the parents' philosophy, LEAs should not attempt to carry it out. Indeed if you decide, as many home educators do, that you are happy to have the LEA visit, there is no need for a formal assessment, as much more can be gleaned from playing and chatting with children. Some home educators enjoy visits such as these.

When your LEA does write, you may find that you receive a request to complete a questionnaire which asks questions of the sort I have outlined above and others such as: At what times will education take place? How long will the lunch break be? What is your weekly timetable? – often ending with one along the lines of: When will your child return to school? If you choose to answer this letter, do not feel under any obligation to complete the questionnaire. Whilst you do not have to answer this sort of general enquiry, you might consider it wise to supply the LEA with a copy of your philosophy and a report in general terms setting out how you go about home-based education on a day to day basis, what resources are available to you, how you make use of them and anything that would show that you are providing a suitable education. If you wanted, you could also complete and return the questionnaire, filling out answers to those questions that apply and marking those that do not accordingly. Alternatively, you could use the questions to raise matters to which you can refer in your report.

A note of caution is needed here as some LEAs refer to their department which deals with home-based education as 'Education Otherwise', and letters to you may bear that description. You should not confuse that with the support organisation of the same name, commonly abbreviated to EO. EO has copyrighted the phrase 'Education Otherwise' to prevent the possibility of misunderstandings as to who is writing to you. If your LEA uses this phrase, I know that EO would appreciate you letting them know so that they can contact the LEA. EO's address can be found under 'Support Organisations' at the back of this book.

If you have just started to home educate, whether that be because your child has just reached compulsory school age or you have just taken her out of school, the courts have made it clear that your LEA should not ask you for any information until a sufficient time has passed to enable you to establish your own arrangements. How long that is may well depend on your circumstances, but it needs to be a reasonable time. If, for example, your child has had the misfortune to be bullied at school and has had her confidence badly dented, it may take a while for her to relax before settling down to any kind of pattern. If you are contacted by your LEA during such a period of re-adjustment explain the position and be prepared to negotiate. You may find that there is no real difficulty; it is only if LEAs find that their enquiries are ignored that they can become understandably concerned.

Much may depend on being able confidently and in sufficient detail to say how your child is learning at home. Some parents find this difficult to quantify for themselves, as the beauty of home education is that knowledge can be gained almost imperceptibly. Often, if you sit and analyse what your child is doing, you will see that she has gained various skills, simply as an adjunct to finding out what she was actually interested in, that might at school be divided into different 'subjects'. For instance, an interest in something like volcanoes might involve, science (which itself might be general or more detailed and involving geology, seismology etc), history, social studies, anthropology, language, geography, and would utilise various skills like reading, writing, drawing, painting, using reference books, atlases, the Internet and asking others for information and discussing conclusions. This analysis can be carried out with any interest your child has and you may find that she naturally covers all the 'subjects' she would cover if she were at school, but not in the abstract nor for their own sake.

Those parents who have a more formal approach to their child's learning may find it easier to describe what they do and also to convey it to the representatives of the LEA, than parents who adopt a more autonomous approach. Because of their grounding in school education, LEA representatives might find it more easy to understand the effectiveness of an education which resembles something they recognise. The younger your child, the easier it ought to be to satisfy the LEA, particularly when you consider that in many European countries formal education, even in state-run schools, does not commence until children reach seven years of age. Indeed, our apparent obsession with lowering the age at which formal education begins is regarded on the Continent as at best counter-productive.

On receiving your report, your LEA may write to say that everything is OK, or that you will be contacted at some time in the future, or indeed both. However, you may be told that an LEA representative, an adviser, will call to see you, perhaps to discuss how you intend to educate your child. At the risk of sounding like a broken record (which probably dates me, anyway!), what you do is your choice. I do feel I need to warn you that sometimes such a discussion is not the friendly chat about the ups and downs of home education that it appeared to be at the time. Too many parents have found out later that some innocent aside, or a question about some difficulty they experience, is blown out of all proportion and appears as an adversely critical reference in the adviser's report. Wait until you know and trust your adviser before confiding your fears, worries and difficulties; until then reinforce the positives. I appreciate this may well offend some LEA officers, but they have only their professional colleagues to blame. It may be that disarming frankness causes no problems most of the time, but when it does, you might in retrospect wish that you had been cautious.

So, for those who are about to have trouble, I need to set out the position clearly. There are still LEAs who believe that you need their permission to home educate and their letter to you will state exactly that. Other LEAs, if they do not actually state it, seem to hint that they will allow you to home educate if they can be satisfied that the arrangements you have made are approved by them. Both are wrong. What it does mean, however, is that you will have to be very careful in all your dealings with the LEA. Whilst your decision to remove your child and take full responsibility for her education causes no difficulty with many schools and LEAs, some find this hard to accept.

You would be best advised when dealing with such LEAs to keep a diary of your contact with their representatives. How you maintain this contact is for you to decide and, if you prefer it always to be by letter, tell the LEA this and do not feel obliged to give them your telephone number, or to use this method of communication, if you do not want to. If you do speak to anyone from the LEA in person or on the telephone, make a note straightaway or as quickly as you reasonably can of what was said. If you can, follow up each such contact with a letter to the LEA setting out the discussion and any important points. Keep a copy of all letters you send as well as any that are sent to you. This will minimise the opportunity for any misunderstandings about what was said or agreed and will hopefully prevent confrontation, as both you and the LEA will know exactly where you stand and there will be no room for dispute.

It is always a good idea, essential in fact, to have a friend (or two) with you if you decide to meet any representative of the LEA. This is not only for moral support, although that may very well be needed, but also so that the friend can make a note of the conversation and make sure that you do not get pressured into agreeing to something that you do not want to do. By making notes, you will always know the exact sequence of events and, if it came to it, you would be able to use these notes to jog your memory if you had to give evidence in court. To be able to use them in this way, they have to be what lawyers call 'contemporaneous notes', that is notes of meetings and events made either at the time of the meeting or event, or at your first opportunity afterwards when everything was fresh in your mind.

Visits do not have to be at your home: you can choose to meet your LEA representative at any convenient place, for example, the LEA's premises, the local library or playground, or a friend's house. You may choose to have your children present for all, part or none of the time. I understand that one parent and LEA representative used to meet regularly in a local pub. Now there's a good idea!

If you decide that you do not want to meet an LEA representative, you will need to consider whether you should take some other action instead. If you do nothing, your LEA may move towards making an SAO. You might feel it best to write to set out your reasons for not wanting to have a meeting and consider supplying a more detailed report. Have in mind that you need to supply sufficient evidence to satisfy a reasonable authority that it is more likely than not that your child is receiving a suitable education. You may not want the LEA to meet or assess your children but you may have friends who are well aware of the educational provision you are making and the abilities of your children. A very useful way of bolstering a report in these circumstances, if not generally, is to include references from such friends, particularly if they have qualifications which the LEA might appreciate. Some parents keep a diary of their children's activities and, if it accords with your philosophy, you could supply copies of entries to your LEA.

You might have more of a struggle with your LEA if you adopt this course, but many do successfully negotiate with their LEA to achieve a formula acceptable to both.

WHAT HAPPENS AFTER YOU HAVE SATISFIED YOUR LEA?

After you have satisfied your LEA that your children are receiving suitable education, you may not hear further for a long while. If you do hear, it may be with the same sort of enquiry that you received when you were first contacted. Even if you encountered difficulty on that occasion, you will be in a much better position this time as you will be more experienced, your child will be more able to say for herself what she does and, most importantly, the LEA knows about you and has already satisfied itself once about the educational provision you are making.

Your philosophy may by this time be a more detailed document, if you have chosen to update it as you go, and answering questionnaires and preparing reports should present less of a problem than before. If you invited your LEA to visit you previously, you are perfectly free to consider whether you want this to happen again should your LEA suggest it. If you did not want another visit, you might reasonably say that, as the LEA was happy with the arrangements seen before, a report on this occasion should be sufficient to satisfy it. Again, what you do is a matter of your choice, informed as it is of the consequences of the LEA saying that it is not satisfied.

If it has been a sufficiently long time since your LEA last contacted you, you may feel that it is reasonable if you are contacted again. Some LEAs ask for periodic reports and you need to consider whether this is acceptable to you. It might depend on the frequency and, perhaps, the purpose. You might feel it is unreasonable to have to make arrangements in advance effectively booking a next visit. You might feel that a request for an annual report is reasonable but that any more onerous suggestion is unreasonable. I have heard that some LEAs try to insist upon quarterly reports or visits, which would seem to me without any justification. I would doubt whether a court would say such frequency was reasonable or indeed necessary unless there was some good reason.

There is no provision, as I have already remarked, in the legislation which explicitly requires or indeed empowers LEAs to supervise or monitor the provision of home-based education. The duty that is placed upon the LEA by s437 Education Act 1996 is a continuing one and it might be that it justifies regular attention by an LEA. When Donaldson LJ approved (in Phillips v Brown) the actions of the LEA in making enquiries to ascertain the position with regard to a home-educated child, it was against the background that the LEA knew nothing what-soever about the child. Once, however, the LEA has satisfied itself that the child is receiving suitable education, it knows a considerable amount about the parents, the child and the educational provision. Consequently, it might be argued that it cannot again 'appear' to the LEA that she is not receiving a suitable education unless there is some specific piece of evidence which indicates to the contrary.

Some LEAs rely upon s443(3) Education Act 1996 as justification for regular contact with home educating families. However, in my view the wording of this provision is, on the contrary, capable of strengthening the argument I have just advanced, as it contemplates an LEA only being able 'to take further action under s437 if at any time [the LEA is] of the opinion that, *having regard to any change of circumstances*, it is expedient to do so' (my emphasis added).

There does not seem to have been a case in which the issue of ongoing 'monitoring' by an LEA has been raised. This may be because no parent has ever decided to challenge the legality of it, or because LEAs have always reached an acceptable compromise with any parent who objected to it.

WHAT HAPPENS IF A SCHOOL ATTENDANCE ORDER IS MADE?

Unless parents have been unwise enough to bury their heads in the sand when contacted by their LEA, it is unlikely that they would reach this stage without the exchange of a considerable amount of correspondence and discussion between them and their LEA. Some LEAs might tend to act precipitately but generally they seek to avoid confrontation in court, unless they believe there is no other option. If parents maintain a supply of information to their LEA, this ongoing communication can often lead to a resolution of any problems.

However, if all else fails and an SAO is made, it requires parents to register their child at the school named in the order. It is an offence contrary to s443 Education Act 1996, heard before the magistrates' court, not to comply with an SAO unless the parents can prove to the court that they are providing suitable education. If the parents wish to continue to home educate they should consider how they would go about proving this to a court, should it come to that, and they should not register their child. This is important because, if they do register their child, they will lose the opportunity of relying on this defence.

This is because, as soon as the parents register their child at a school, they then have the duty to ensure that she attends regularly. If the child does not, the parents can be prosecuted for her failure to attend under the provisions of s444 Education Act 1996. This is what might be referred to as the 'truanting' offence and it is not a defence to this charge to show that the child was receiving suitable education at home. Some LEAs, on making an SAO, take the step of registering the child, too. This cannot have legal effect and, if the child does not attend at the school, can lead an LEA into the error of prosecuting the parents for failing to ensure that the child attends regularly contrary to s444. This charge can only be correctly laid if the *parents* have registered their child at a school, otherwise, the parents are entitled to be acquitted.

If parents fail to comply with an SAO, the LEA must consider what it is to do next. It has a limited number of options, and if it still considers that it is not satisfied that the child is receiving a suitable education, at the head of the list is a prosecution of the parents for the offence of failing to comply with the SAO contrary to s443 Education Act 1996.

To commence proceedings, the LEA has to apply to the magistrates' court for a summons, which the parents will receive from the court, most likely by post. The summons will state the date upon which the parents have to attend at court. It is important that, if they have not seen a solicitor already, at this stage parents go to see one so that they are fully aware of their position and choices and what preparation is necessary to present any defence. This is, in effect, a criminal prosecution and the LEA has to comply with various matters, including disclosing certain material that it is not using as part of its case. Legal aid is available on application to the magistrates' court but the parents may have to inform the court in some detail of the complexity of the matter and stress the importance to them of the outcome.

The LEA has to prove that the SAO was made and that the parents failed to register their child at the school named in the order. The parents can challenge the making of the order itself, but that inevitably will mean that they have to show that they were providing their child with suitable education, which will in any event entitle them to be acquitted. It is a statutory defence set out in s443(1) Education Act 1996 for the parents to prove on a balance of probabilities that they are 'causing the child to receive suitable education otherwise than at school'. Another way of putting the 'balance of probabilities' test is that the parents must show that it is more likely than not that they are educating suitably. To succeed, the parents need to prove that the required education is being provided at the date of the hearing, whether or not it was being provided at any other time, including when the SAO was made.

In order to establish this to the necessary standard of proof, the parents should consider calling evidence from experts as to the efficacy of home-based education and as to the provision being made for their child. How much that might resemble an assessment of their child's education will depend on the philosophy of the parents. If reports from experts are to be relied on, some consideration can be given to whether they should be disclosed in advance to the LEA. The fact that an SAO has been made does not mean you should stop supplying your LEA with information about your child's education. The LEA should take account of anything with which it is provided, and if it becomes satisfied about the suitability of your child's education, the prosecution should be discontinued and the SAO revoked.

If the matter goes to trial and the parents do succeed in proving their case, they will be acquitted and that is the end of the prosecution, and it would be logical to think that it was also the end of the SAO but, somewhat curiously, s443(2) provides that if a parent is acquitted, the court *may* direct that the SAO cease to be in force. The effect of this is that, when acquitted, parents must apply to the court for such a direction. They may also be able to apply for a defence costs order to meet any expenses they have incurred in preparing their defence or attending at court.

If the parents do not succeed in proving to the court that they are providing a suitable education, they will be convicted. The most likely sentence, certainly on a first conviction, is a fine and an order made that the parent pay some or all of the LEA costs in bringing the prosecution. The maximum fine that can be imposed is a 'level 3' fine which at the moment is a maximum of £1,000. If, as is usual, both parents have been summoned for the offence, on conviction both can face the maximum fine. I need to stress that maximum fines are rarely, if ever, imposed and the court will weigh the seriousness of the circumstances of the offence with the means of each parent before reaching a decision, which in most cases will be very much less than the maximum. Other sentences are available to a court including a parenting order, however, space does not allow me to expand further and I can in any event only reiterate that anyone facing this situation would be best advised to consult a solicitor, as they should if they wished to appeal against any decision.

One further provision needs to be mentioned: before mounting a prosecution, an LEA must consider whether it should, instead of, or as well as, a prosecution, apply to a family proceedings court for an educational supervision order (ESO) under the Children Act 1989. The court might sit in a magistrates' court but it is not constituted in the same way as the court which would hear any prosecution under the Education Act, and the two cannot be heard at the same time.

An ESO can be made by the court if it is satisfied that a child of compulsory school age is not being educated properly. This has the same meaning as 'suitable education' in s437 Education Act 1996 and is in the same terms as the requirements of s7 of that Act. It would help if the same phrase were used in all statutes, but then who would need lawyers? An ESO places the child under the supervision of the LEA, which appoints a supervisor, usually an EWO, whose duty it is 'to advise, assist and befriend, and give directions to' the child and his parents 'in such a way as will, in the opinion of the supervisor, secure that he is properly educated'. The supervisor has to 'ascertain [their] wishes and feelings ... including, in particular their wishes as to the place at which the child shall be educated' before making any direction, but there is no requirement even to take them into account. If parents persistently fail to comply with a direction, they commit an offence unless they show that they have taken all reasonable steps or that the direction was unreasonable. If the child persistently fails to comply, social services will become involved.

In order to get an ESO, the LEA has to produce evidence to prove a negative, namely that the child is not receiving proper education. This might be a difficult task to accomplish were it not for the fact that if an SAO has been made, and it is not being complied with, there is a statutory assumption that the child is not being properly educated, unless the parents prove to the contrary. If it applies, this effectively removes from the LEA the burden of proving its case and places the parents in the same position and with the same considerations as when they contest a prosecution for failing to comply with an SAO.

If parents are convicted of failing to comply with an SAO, the court may direct that the LEA commence proceedings for an ESO unless, in consultation with social services, the conclusion is reached that 'the child's welfare will be satisfactorily safeguarded' without one being made.

Before the enactment of the Children Act 1989, courts could make care orders in the same circumstances as they can now make ESOs. The law was changed, as it was not felt that this drastic step was appropriate simply if a child was not receiving a suitable education. However, if a parent repeatedly failed to educate suitably or was repeatedly convicted of failing to comply with SAOs or ESOs, this might well result in a care order being made on the application of the local authority's social services department, if it was believed that this was causing 'significant harm' to the child. It would seem likely, if this situation developed, that social services would have other concerns about the child's parenting and it would not be purely an education matter.

If the parents of a child registered at a school as a result of the making of an SAO wish to withdraw her from the school to home educate, they will first have to apply to their LEA for the order to be revoked 'on the ground that arrangements have been made for the child to receive suitable education otherwise than at school'. The LEA has to revoke the order 'unless it is of the opinion that no satisfactory arrangements have been made for the education of the child otherwise than at school'. It is only when the SAO is revoked that the child can be removed from the register. This effectively places the parents in the position of having to ask the LEA for permission to home educate, and the LEA will need to be shown in advance how it is planned that the child is to be home-educated. This puts the parents at a disadvantage and they may have to revise their arrangements to satisfy their LEA.

Parents in this position should remember that it is likely that, no matter with what intentions they set out, almost every family that starts home-based education finds that, over time, they change the way they go about it, as it evolves into a pattern that suits them. Many LEAs have no difficulty in understanding this.

'TRUANCY SWEEPS' UNDER s16 CRIME AND DISORDER ACT 1998

A few words need to be said about the provisions of s16 Crime and Disorder Act 1998 which provides a power for the police to take truants back to school or to another place designated by the LEA. The power can only be used after the LEA has first notified the police that it has provided designated premises in which to detain children believed to be truanting. Then an officer of at least the rank of superintendent has to specify the location in which, and period of time for which, the powers can be exercised. Guidance on the power to remove truants issued by the Home Office states that truants should not be taken to police stations as they do not commit an offence by failing to attend at school.

It perhaps speaks volumes about schools that truanting has become such a problem. It is the Home Office view that 'Truancy is closely associated with crime', and statistics used by it show that, on a conservative estimate, a million children a year are regarded as truanting to some extent. One study showed that 10% of fifteen-year-olds truant at least once a week. It is quite clear that home-based education is not seen as posing this particular problem and the Home Office Guidance, with which all police officers engaged in the sweeps should be familiar, makes it clear that it is not directed at home-educated children.

The power to remove is a novel one, bearing in mind that the child removed has not committed an offence. A home-educated child out in public at a time when school children should be at school breaks no law and is not liable to 'removal' under s16, or indeed any other enactment. The Home Office Guidance states: 'No further action should be taken where children indicate that they are home-educated – unless the constable has reason to doubt that this is the case.'

Thus the simple statement 'I am home-educated' should suffice to dispense with any police interest. However, police officers will usually be accompanied by representatives of the LEA who might be keen to discover the identity and address of the child so that they can carry out checks later. A child should not have to give her name or address, as neither can establish whether they should be at school or not. The power granted is an instant one, to remove or not to remove, and there is no power to request details for supply to the LEA for their subsequent investigation.

If you are already in contact with your LEA, any request for further details is no more than an imposition. However, difficulty arises where a family is not known to their LEA and wishes to keep it that way. I cannot pretend that there is an easy answer to this, it is a position that remains despite heavy lobbying by home educators who foresaw the difficulties this legislation would present to them. It must be up to you and your child to decide how to cope if the assertion of home education does not prove sufficient to satisfy the police. As a fall-back, you might like to give your child a letter or a contact telephone number to hand to the police. Choice in Education, whose address is in the Contacts List at the back of this book, produces a credit card sized 'Truancy Information Card' designed to be used by children in this situation. It sets out s7, affirms that the holder is not a registered pupil and therefore not a truant and requires that they be allowed to go. If police detain anyone wrongfully, they may be liable to damages if sued and they will, or should be, aware of this.

Children will still be stopped in truancy sweeps even if they are with their parents. A home educating parent can make the decision as to whether to walk on or not. If police officers attempt to use force to prevent this, they may act unlawfully and a parent who resists might not be held to commit an offence, but few would want to put this to the test. It is a very difficult area both for parents and for the police; if you do not want to give your name and address but prefer to stand your ground, you present the police with a considerable problem and it might well be that no one would move to prevent you from simply walking off.

The uncertainties which this particular piece of legislation has produced have, to my knowledge, made some home educators reluctant to venture out during school hours, which is a quite intolerable curtailment of their liberty.

The police power to remove can only be used if the conditions of s16 are satisfied and it is a sweep authorised by a senior police officer. If anyone is stopped by the police at a time other than when an authorised truancy sweep is in operation, they do not have to stop or give the police any details unless the officer states that he believes that they have committed an offence.

IN CONCLUSION

I hope that this chapter has been informative and will be useful to those contemplating home-based education, without making it seem that they have a frightening task. Many officers in many LEAs do understand and support home educating families, and those families and those officers have no need to consider the matters I have dealt with. I have not intended to offend officers such as these. However, other families are not in such a fortunate position and I see the suffering that can be caused by an insensitive and sometimes bullying approach. Even that approach can be mollified by discussion and explanation, and I hope I may have been able to give some structure and material for that task. Home educators all too often have to take on the education of those around them to defeat an unthinking response and gain acceptance. It can be galling in the extreme to have gained the understanding of one LEA representative, only to find that the 'convert' moves on and is replaced by another for whom the process has to start again.

Home educators ought to be able to expect that LEA officers, who are appointed to deal with them, are alive to the practice of home-based education, appreciate its effectiveness and acknowledge and respect the rights of parents and their children to find a way of learning that uniquely suits them. LEAs need to be open to the advantages that home-based education can offer, advantages that are increasingly understood by parents. The number of families home educating in this country is growing in line with the expansion in other countries, such as the United States, where its contribution to the richness of national life was recognised by the Senate in the Resolution it passed designating a week in September 1999 as National Home Education Week. The Resolution, in its acknowledgement of the value of home education, contained the following statements:

> ... training in the home strengthens the family and guides children in setting the highest standards for their lives which are essential elements to the continuity of morality in our culture;

> ... home schooling families contribute significantly to the cultural diversity important to a healthy society;

> ... home school students exhibit self-confidence and good citizenship and are fully prepared academically to meet the challenges of today's society;

The number of home educators is increasing in North America, and recent research (Spring 2000) in Canada has shown that the number of children being home-educated there is growing at the rate of 10% per annum and currently stands at 1.5% of all children of school age.

Nobody knows just how many home-educated children there are in this country at the moment, but all the available evidence points to it being a very significant and rapidly growing number. As political and economic entities grow ever larger, it is of vital importance that variety and diversity are acknowledged as the healthy signs of a successful and tolerant society. There is seldom one 'right' way to do anything, and in the field of education it is especially important to recognise that there are many different ways of learning. Home-based education originates within the family – on which children's well-being and healthy development so depend, and which richly deserves every encouragement and support. The fact that home-education is flourishing, therefore, should be seen as a very hopeful sign for the future.

Ian Dowty, BA (Oxon)
Solicitor

Finding support and information

The Free Range Education Website is at:
http://www.free-range-education.co.uk

Come and visit us here! Use our 'Ask FREd' e-mail service to get in touch with an experienced home educator who can answer practical questions, help you decide whether home education is for you, offer you personal support and point you towards other sources of information and help. Our experienced legal team can answer your queries about the law. You can also find addresses for suppliers, URLs for websites, reading suggestions and much more besides.

There are several support organisations and services for home educators and those interested in alternative forms of education. Their details follow, together with a brief description, in their own words, of what they offer. Further information can be obtained by contacting them direct.

Choice in Education is not an organisation, but a publication produced by a co-operative group of home educators who seek to promote and publicise the alternative to mainstream schooling in our society. Choice in Education produce Truancy Information Cards to help give children confidence when out and about during school hours. They also organise the Home Educators Seaside Festival (HesFes) every May, which is the biggest gathering of home educators in Europe. It is a week of camping, workshops for adults and children, HE discussion groups, lots of fun, games and entertainment.

For more information on any of the above, subscriptions or sample copies of the Choice in Education newsletter, please contact:
Choice in Education, PO Box 20284, London. NW1 3WY
Website: http://www.choiceineducation.co.uk

Education Otherwise is a membership organisation which provides support for families whose children are being educated outside school, and for those who wish to uphold the freedom of families to take proper responsibility for the education of their children. EO is not committed to any 'correct' system of education, and it does not undertake to provide syllabuses or materials. Rather it tries to help families establish what is suited to the needs of their own children, in accordance with their own beliefs.
For further information, visit the EO website at:
http://www.education-otherwise.org
or send an A5 SAE to:
Education Otherwise, PO Box 7420, London N9 9SG

Home Education Advisory Service (HEAS) is a registered charity which supports and advises families who wish to educate their children at home instead of sending them to school. HEAS produces information leaflets, the *Big Book of Resource Ideas* and the *Home Education Handbook*. Subscribers receive the quarterly Bulletin, access to the Advice Line and the Dyslexia Helpline, a concession card and list of local contacts. The organisation offers information about educational resources, GCSE, special educational needs, information technology, legal matters and curriculum design.
HEAS, PO Box 98, Welwyn Garden City, Herts AL8 6AN.
Tel/fax: 01707 371854
E-mail: enquiries@heas.org.uk
Website: http://www.heas.org.uk

The **Islamic Home Schooling Advisory network** is for Muslims who are home educating their children. For more details, write to:
Islamic Home Schooling Advisory Network
PO Box 30671
London
E1 OTG

Schoolhouse is a national Scottish charity which offers information and support to home educators and those with an interest in home education. It has an enquiry line, young people's newspaper project and home educators' newsletter (both published quarterly), and a teenage peer support network. Individual/family membership by voluntary donation; membership also available to organisations.

Schoolhouse Home Education Association
PO Box 28946
Edinburgh
EH4 4YU
Tel: 0870 7450967
E-mail: info@schoolhouse.org.uk
http://www.schoolhouse.org.uk

Internet Resources and Support

The Home Education Website is a significant and growing independent website bringing together many different home education resources including homepages for the 'UK-Home-Ed mailing list', the 'Home-Education UK webring' and the 'TCS-Autonomous-Ed mailing list'. It is also an Amazon associate bookshop where many educational books are reviewed.

http://www.home-education.org.uk

The UK Home Education Support List is an Internet List which exists to provide mutual support for UK based home educators and those interested in home education, to allow the sharing of knowledge and experience between established and prospective home educators and to establish a forum for the free discussion of issues surrounding any and every aspect of home education. Further details can be found on the Home Education Website (above).

Or send an E-mail to:
UK-HOME-ED-REQUEST@AOL.COM

The HE-Special UK website is for those who are home educating children with special needs. For more information, and details of how to join the HE-Special e-mail list, visit their website:

http://www.he-special.org.uk

The Jewish Homeschoolers e-mail discussion list is US-based but has a worldwide membership. For further details, send an e-mail to:
Zimra@aol.com

Muslim Home Educators List: for more details visit:
http://groups.yahoo.com/group/homeeducatorsandukmuslims

Other organisations of particular interest to home educators

Education Now seeks to foster new initiatives and developments in educational practice which actively involve learners in developing and defining their own curriculum in partnership with others. The present style of curriculum followed in the education system of this country, and in most of the world, does not recognise the crucial importance of democratic participative learning. The current persistence with a predominately authoritarian approach is consigning our children to the obsolescence of a rigid mind-set, wasting the talents of many people, damaging the self-confidence of many young people and creating a dangerous cohort of frustrated and alienated youth.
Education Now, 113 Arundel Drive, Bramcote Hills,
Nottingham NG9 3FQ   Tel/fax: 0115 925 7261
http://www.gn.apc.org/edheretics/ednowabout.htm

Human Scale Education is a national charity which believes that children's needs are best met and their potential most fully realised in human scale settings. The organisation is encouraging new educational initiatives in this country such as the restructuring of large schools into smaller units and the setting up of new small schools and learning centres in which children can be treated as individuals. For more information contact:
Human Scale Education, 96 Carlingcott, Bath, BA2 8AW.
Tel: 01972 510709

Travellers' School Charity Helping travellers with the successful education of children. If you wish to subscribe to TSC you will receive the quarterly newsletter and help us with funding, fuel and communications. Please send £5 cheques/POs payable to 'TSC' to:
TSC, PO Box 36, Grantham, NG31 6EW

Useful Addresses for all those places mentioned in the FAQs

A website containing links to many youth organisations can be found at: http://www.youth.org.uk/directory/youth.htm

Amateur Theatre Network
PO Box 536, Norwich MLO,.Norwich, NR6 7JZ
http://www.amdram.org.uk/sitindex.htm

Amnesty International United Kingdom
99-119 Rosebery Avenue, London EC1R 4RE
Tel: 020 7814 6200
http://www.amnesty.org.uk

British Association for the Advancement of Science – Youth Section
23 Savile Row; London W1X 2NB
Tel: 0207 973 3060
http://www.britassoc.org.uk/info/intro.html

BBC Information
PO Box 1116 , Belfast BT2 7AJ
Tel: 08700 100 222 (24 hours)
http://www.bbc.co.uk/education/schools

Central Council of Physical Recreation
Tel: 020 7828 3163

Channel 4 Customer Services
Tel: 01926 436 444
http://www.4learning.co.uk

Duke of Edinburgh's Award Office
Gulliver House, Madeira Walk, Windsor, Berks SL4 1EU
Tel: 01753 810753
http://www.sonnet.co.uk/dea/

English Heritage Education
23 Savile Row, London W1X 1AB
Tel: 020 7973 3442
http://www.english-heritage.org.uk

Film Education (National Schools Film Week)
21-22 Poland Street, London W1V 3DD
Tel: 020 7851 9450 Fax: 020 7439 3218
E-mail: postbox@filmeducation.org
http://www.filmeducation.org

The Guide Association
17-19 Buckingham Palace Road, London SW1 0PT
Tel: 020 7592 1818
http://www.guides.org.uk

National Arts Collections Fund
Millais House, 7 Cromwell Place, London SW7 2JN
Tel: 020 7225 4800

National Association for Gifted Children
Elder House, Milton Keynes, MK9 1LR
http://www.rmplc.co.uk/orgs/nagc/index.html

National Association of Volunteer Bureaux
Tel: 0121 633 4555
http://wavespace.waverider.co.uk/~navbteam/

Parent Network National Office
2 Winchester House, 11 Cranmer Road, London SW9 6EJ
Administration: 020 7735 4596
Parent enquiry line: 020 7735 1214
E-mail: info@parentnetwork.demon.co.uk
http://npin.org

St John Ambulance
1 Grosvenor Crescent, London SW1X 7EF
Tel: 020 7235 5231
http://www.ambulance.net.au

Scouts
Baden Powell House, 52 Cromwell Road, London SW7 5JS
Secretaries Dept: 020 7584 7030
E-mail: ukbphscout@aol.com
http://www.scoutbase.org.uk/

Woodcraft Folk
Head Office: 13 Ritherdon Road, London SW17 8QE
Tel: 020 8672 6031
http://www.poptel.org.uk/woodcraft/index.html

Young Archaeologists Club
Bowes Morrell House, 111 Walmgate, York, YO1 9WA
Tel: 01904 671417
http://www.britarch.ac.uk/yac

Young Ornithologists Club
The Lodge, Sandy, Beds. SG19 2DL
Tel: 01767 680551
http://www.rspb.org.uk/youth

Youth Hostels Association (England & Wales)
Trevelyan House, 8 St Stephens Hill, St Albans, Herts AL1 2DY
Tel: 0870 870 8808 Fax: 01727 844126
E-mail: customerservices@yha.org.uk
http://www.yha.org.uk

Suggestions for further reading

John Holt: *How Children Learn,* Penguin, 1991, ISBN 0140136002; *How Children Fail,* Penguin, 1990, ISBN 0140135561; *Teach Your Own,* Lighthouse, 1997, ISBN 0907637094; *Learning All the Time,* Addison Wesley, 1990, ISBN 0201550911

Roland Meighan: *The Next Learning System,* Educational Heretics Press, 1997, ISBN 1900219042; *Learning from Home-Based Education,* Education Now, 1992, ISBN 187152606X

Alan Thomas: *Educating Children At Home,* Continuum, 2000, ISBN 0304701807

Jan Fortune-Wood: *Doing It Their Way,* Educational Heretics Press, 2000, ISBN 1900219166

Mary Ann Rose and Paul Stanbrook: *Getting Started in Home Education,* Education Now, 2000, ISBN 1871526426

Jean Bendell: *School's Out,* (out of print but your library may have a copy)

Postman & Weingartner: *Teaching as a Subversive Activity,* (now out of print, but worth tracking down)

Carl Rogers: *On Becoming a Person,* Constable, 1974, ISBN 0094604401

Mary Sheedy Kurcinka: *Raising Your Spirited Child,* Harper Perennial, 1992, ISBN 0060923288

Thomas Moore: *Care of the Soul,* Piatkus, 1992, ISBN 0749911689

James Hillman: *The Soul's Code,* Bantam, 1997, ISBN 055350634X

John Taylor Gatto: *Dumbing Us Down,* Anthroposophical Press, 1991, ISBN 086571231X

Matt Hearn (Ed): *Deschooling Our Lives,* New Society, 1995, ISBN 0865713421

Linda Dobson: *The Homeschooling Book of Answers,* Prima, 1998, ISBN 0761513779

David Guterson: *Family Matters – Why Homeschooling Makes Sense,* Harcourt, 1993, ISBN 0156300001

Nancy Lande: *A Patchwork of Days,* Windycreek, 1996, ISBN 0965130304

Anna Kealoha: *Trust the Children,* Celestial Arts, 1995, ISBN 0890877483

Mary Griffith: *The Unschooling Handbook,* Prima, 1998, ISBN 0761512764

Grace Llewellyn: *Real Lives – 11 Teenagers Who Don't Go To School,* Lowry House, 1993, ISBN 0962959138; *The Teenage Liberation Handbook,* Element Books, 1997, ISBN 1862041040

Raymond & Dorothy Moore: *School Can Wait,* Brigham Young University Press, 1989, ISBN 0842513140

Home Educating Our Autistic Spectrum Children
Paths are Made by Walking
Edited by Terri Dowty and Kitt Cowlishaw

Published by Jessica Kingsley: www.jkp.com
JKP paperback 300 pages (December 2001)
ISBN 1843100371

In this book, parents who home educate their children with autism or Asperger's syndrome tell their personal stories: how they reached the decision to educate at home, how they set about the task, and how it has transformed their children's lives.

Twelve families contributed to the book, from England, Scotland, the United States, and Australia. Their children range in ability from Kevin, who at age five had the vocabulary of a 16-year-old, to Greg, who doctors predicted would never learn to talk. Some have embraced home education as a way of life; others have used it as a temporary measure to prepare their children to return to school.

Following the personal stories, the final chapters offer practical suggestions for getting started with home education, legal advice from an expert in education law, and contact details of support organisations on three continents.

More information about this book is at:
http://www.cary.demon.co.uk/paths/

Other books from Hawthorn Press

If you have difficulties ordering Hawthorn Press books from a book-shop, you can order direct from:
Booksource, 32 Finlas Street, Glasgow, G22 5DU
Tel: (08702) 402182 Fax: (0141) 557 0189

Muddles, Puddles and Sunshine
Your activity book to help when someone has died
Winston's Wish

Muddles, Puddles and Sunshine offers practical and sensitive support for bereaved children. Beautifully illustrated in colour, it suggests a helpful series of activities and exercises accompanied by the friendly characters of Bee and Bear.

32pp; 297 x 210mm landscape; paperback; 1 869 890 58 2

240

Helping Children to Overcome Fear
The healing power of play
Russell Evans

Critical illness can cause overwhelming feelings of abandonment and loss. Difficult for adults to face alone, for children the experience is magnified. They have to leave home for an alien hospital world, without the comfort of familiar daily rhythms. Jean Evans was a play leader who recognised ahead of her time the importance of enabling children to give voice to their feelings, providing opportunities for play and working in partnership with parents. These requirements are now core principles in the training and working practice in the fields of nursery nursing, play therapy, childcare and Paediatrics.

128pp; 216 x 138mm; paperback; 1 903458 02 1

Set Free Childhood
Parents' survival guide to coping with computers and TV
Martin Large

Children watch TV and use computers for five hours daily on average. The result? Record levels of learning difficulties, obesity, eating disorders, sleep problems, language delay, aggressive behaviour, anxiety – and children on fast forward. However, *Set Free Childhood* shows you how to counter screen culture and create a calmer, more enjoyable family life.

'TV programming is geared to hold children's attention, so that they find it hard to walk away. Children, therefore, need adults' help with switching off.'   (The Independent)

240pp; 216 x 138mm; paperback; 1 903458 43 9

Storytelling with Children
Nancy Mellon

Telling stories awakens wonder and creates special occasions with children, whether it is bedtime, around the fire or on rainy days. Encouraging you to spin golden tales, Nancy Mellon shows how you can become a confident storyteller and enrich your family with the power of story. Children love family storytelling and parents can learn this practical, magical art.

192pp; 216 x 138mm; illustrations; paperback; 1 903458 08 0

Free to Learn
Introducing Steiner Waldorf early childhood education
Lynne Oldfield

Free to Learn is a comprehensive introduction to Steiner Waldorf kindergartens for parents, educators and early years' students. Lynne Oldfield illustrates the theory and practice of kindergarten education with stories, helpful insights and lively observations.

'Children are allowed freedom to be active within acceptable boundaries; who are in touch with their senses and the environment; who are self assured but not over confident; who are developing their readiness to receive a formal education – in short, children who are free to be children and 'free to learn.'
(Kate Adams, International Journal of Children's Spirituality)

256pp; 216 x 138mm; paperback; 1 903458 06 4

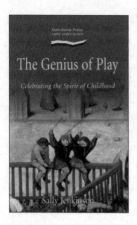

The Genius of Play
Celebrating the spirit of childhood
Sally Jenkinson

The Genius of Play addresses what play is, why it matters, and how modern life endangers children's play. Sally Jenkinson's amusing, vivid observations will delight parents and teachers wanting to explore the never-ending secrets of children's play.

'Enchanting photos and vignettes of young children at play.'
(Marian Whitehead, Nursery World)

224pp; 216 x 138mm; paperback; 1 903458 04 8

Games Children Play
How games and sport help children develop
Kim John Payne
Illustrated by Marije Rowling

Games Children Play offers an accessible guide to games with children of age 3 upwards. These games are all tried and tested, and are the basis for the author's extensive teacher training work. The book explores children's personal development and how this is expressed in movement, play, songs and games.

Each game is clearly and simply described, with diagrams or drawings, and accompanied by an explanation of why this game is helpful at a particular age. The equipment that may be needed is basic, cheap and easily available.

192pp; 297 x 210mm; paperback; 1 869 890 78 7

Pull the Other One!
String Games and Stories Book 1
Michael Taylor

This well-travelled and entertaining series of tales is accompanied by clear instructions and explanatory diagrams – guaranteed not to tie you in knots and will teach you tricks with which to dazzle your friends! With something for everyone, these ingenious tricks and tales are developed and taught with utter simplicity, making them suitable from age 5 upwards.

'When we go wrong playing Cat's Cradle, we call it Dog's Cradle!'
(Megan Gain, aged 6, London)

128pp; 216 x 148mm; drawings; paperback; 1 869 890 49 3

Kinder Dolls
A Waldorf doll-making handbook
Maricristin Sealey

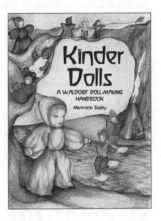

Kinder Dolls shows how to create hand-crafted dolls from natural materials. A range of simple, colourful designs will inspire both beginners and experienced doll makers alike. These dolls are old favourites, originating in Waldorf Steiner kindergartens where parents make dolls together for their children, and for the school.

'Maricristin's book is a fine source for the beginner doll maker. It is a valuable primer, full of practical tips, simple designs and clear, easy to follow instructions.'
(Sara McDonald, Magic Cabin Dolls)

160pp; 246 x 189mm; paperback; 1 903458 03 X

All Year Round
Christian calendar of celebrations
Ann Druitt, Christine Fynes-Clinton, Marije Rowling

All Year Round is brimming with things to make; activities, stories, poems and songs to share with your family. It is full of well illustrated ideas for fun and celebration: from Candlemas to Christmas and Midsummer's day to the Winter solstice. Observing the round of festivals is an enjoyable way to bring rhythm into children's lives and provide a series of meaningful landmarks to look forward to. Each festival has a special character of its own: participation can deepen our understanding and love of nature and bring a gift to the whole family.

320pp; 250 x 200mm; paperback; 1 869 890 47 7

Festivals Together
Guide to multicultural celebration
Sue Fitzjohn, Minda Weston, Judy Large

This special book for families and teachers helps you celebrate festivals from cultures from all over the world. This resource guide for celebration introduces a selection of 26 Buddhist, Christian, Hindu, Jewish, Muslim and Sikh festivals. It offers a lively introduction to the wealth of different ways of life. There are stories, things to make, recipes, songs, customs and activities for each festival, comprehensively illustrated.

'The ideal book for anyone who wants to tackle multicultural festivals'
(Nursery World)
224pp; 250 x 200mm; paperback; 1 869 890 46 9

Festivals, Family and Food
Guide to seasonal celebration
Diana Carey and Judy Large

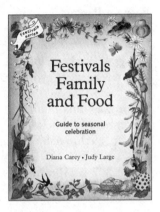

A source of stories, recipes, things to make, activities, poems, songs and festivals. Each festival such as Christmas, Candlemas and Martinmas has its own, well illustrated chapter. There are also sections on Birthdays, Rainy Days, Convalescence and a birthday Calendar. The perfect present for a family, it explores the numerous festivals that children love celebrating.

'It's an invaluable resource book' (The Observer)
'Every family should have one' (Daily Mail)

224pp; 250 x 200mm; illustrations; paperback; 0 950 706 23 X

The Children's Year
Seasonal crafts and clothes
Stephanie Cooper, Christine Fynes-Clinton, Marije Rowling

You needn't be an experienced craftsperson to create beautiful things! This step by step, well illustrated book with clear instructions shows you how to get started. Children and parents are encouraged to try all sorts of handwork, with different projects relating to the seasons of the year.

Here are soft toys, wooden toys, moving toys such as balancing birds or climbing gnomes, horses, woolly hats, mobiles and dolls. There are over 100 treasures to make in seasonal groupings around the children's year.

192pp; 250 x 200mm; paperback; 1 869 890 00 0

Being a Parent
Parentline Plus

Being a Parent helps you think about what support you and your children need. It gives ideas on how to make family life a little easier.

'I consider this book and other Parentline Plus courses to have great value, because I believe that parents deserve all the help they can get...'
  (Alan Titchmarsh, TV and Radio Broadcaster, Author and Gardener)

96pp; 297 x 210mm; paperback; 1 869 890 81 7

Parenting Matters
Ways to bring up your children using heart and head
Parentline Plus

Parenting Matters helps you bring up loving and happy children. Here is the heart to becoming the more confident, sensitive relaxed, firm and caring parent that you truly are – enjoying your children and family.

'... a chance to sort out your thinking and raise your kids in the way you really want to, instead of in a series of knee-jerk reactions.'
            (Steve Biddulph, family therapist and parenting author)

240pp; 297 x 210mm; paperback; 1 869 890 16 7

Naming
Choosing a meaningful name
Caroline Sherwood

'Caroline Sherwood's *Naming* is a completely new and far more useful approach in which the meanings of names are the prime focus. With a deep respect for language, she offers a fresh way for parents to set about finding the right name for their child.'
            (Rosie Styles, The Baby Naming Society)

304pp; 246 x 189mm; paperback; 1 869 890 56 6

Free Range Education: Order form

Dear Reader
If you want to order additional copies of *Free Range Education*,
please fill in your name and address on the order form and send it to:
Booksource, 32 Finlas Street, Glasgow, G22 5DU
or Fax: (0141) 557 0189

Name _____

Address _____

_____ Postcode _____

Tel. no. _____

Please send me _____ copy/ies at £12.99 (plus p&p £1.95 per
order + 45p per book).

Please debit my credit card

Number _____

expiry date _____

or

Enclose a cheque for £ _____

made payable to Booksource